Y0-BSE-889

RENEWALS 458-4574

DATE DUE

DEC 1 5			
NOV 2 9			
MAR 1	WITHDRAWN		
APR 0 1	UTSA Libraries		
MAR 1 0			
MAY 0 9 2008			
FEB 2 4 2009			
PR 2 4 2009			
GAYLORD			PRINTED IN U.S.A.

The Holocaust and the Text

The Holocaust and the Text

Speaking the Unspeakable

Edited by
Andrew Leak
and
George Paizis

in association with
THE INSTITUTE FOR ROMANCE STUDIES AND
THE INSTITUTE FOR ENGLISH STUDIES, SCHOOL OF ADVANCED STUDY
THE UNIVERSITY OF LONDON, AND THE WIENER LIBRARY

First published in Great Britain 2000 by
MACMILLAN PRESS LTD
Houndmills, Basingstoke, Hampshire RG21 6XS and London
Companies and representatives throughout the world

A catalogue record for this book is available from the British Library.

ISBN 0–333–73886–1 hardcover
ISBN 0–333–73887–X paperback

 First published in the United States of America 2000 by
ST. MARTIN'S PRESS, INC.,
Scholarly and Reference Division,
175 Fifth Avenue, New York, N.Y. 10010

ISBN 0–312–22866–X

Library of Congress Cataloging-in-Publication Data
The Holocaust and the text : speaking the unspeakable / edited by
Andrew Leak and George Paizis.
p.   cm.
Includes bibliographical references and index.
ISBN 0–312–22866–X (cloth)
1. Holocaust, Jewish (1939–1945), in literature.   I. Leak, Andrew
N., 1956–   .   II. Paizis, George.
PN56.H55H65   1999
809'.93358 — dc21   99–43178
                                                          CIP

Selection and editorial matter © Andrew Leak and George Paizis 2000
Text © the various contributors 2000

All rights reserved. No reproduction, copy or transmission of this publication may be made
without written permission.

No paragraph of this publication may be reproduced, copied or transmitted save with written
permission or in accordance with the provisions of the Copyright, Designs and Patents Act
1988, or under the terms of any licence permitting limited copying issued by the Copyright
Licensing Agency, 90 Tottenham Court Road, London W1P 0LP.

Any person who does any unauthorised act in relation to this publication may be liable to
criminal prosecution and civil claims for damages.

The authors have asserted their rights to be identified as the authors of this work in accordance
with the Copyright, Designs and Patents Act 1988.

This book is printed on paper suitable for recycling and made from fully managed and sustained
forest sources.

10   9   8   7   6   5   4   3   2   1
09   08   07   06   05   04   03   02   01   00

Printed and bound in Great Britain by
Antony Rowe Ltd, Chippenham, Wiltshire

**Library
University of Texas**
at San Antonio

Contents

Notes on the Contributors

Bryan Cheyette is Professor of Twentieth-Century Literature in the Department of English, University of Southampton. He has recently edited *Contemporary Jewish Writing in Britain and Ireland: an Anthology* (1998) and co-edited *Modernity, Culture and 'the Jew'* (1998). His next book is a critical history of British-Jewish literature to be published by Yale University Press.

Martin Crowley teaches in the French Department at the University of Manchester. He is the author of articles on literary theory and Marguerite Duras, and is currently working on a book on ethical questions in Duras's work.

Robert Eaglestone teaches literary theory and contemporary European philosophy in the English Department at Royal Holloway, University of London. His publications include *Ethical Criticisms: Reading Levinas* and articles on theory, ethics, European philosophy and historiography.

Robert Gordon teaches in the Italian Department at Cambridge University. He has published *Pasolini: Forms of Subjectivity* and is currently working on a book on Primo Levi.

Anna Hardman is currently completing her PhD research in the school of historical studies at Birmingham University. Her principal research concerns women's Holocaust literature.

Samuel Khalifa lives in Paris and is completing a research degree on memory and the representation of urban space in the works of Patrick Modiano and Georges Perec. He is active in the arts and has adapted literary works for the cinema.

Berel Lang is Professor of Humanities at Trinity College (Hartford). He has degrees from Yale and Columbia, and has taught at the University of Colorado, State University of New York at Albany, the Hebrew University and Wesleyan University. He is author or editor of 16 books, including *The Concept of Style*; *Act and the Idea of Nazi Genocide*; *Writing and the Holocaust*; *Mind's Bodies: Thought in the Act*; *Heidegger's Silence*, and (forthcoming) *The Future of the Holocaust: between History and Memory*.

Andrew Leak is Senior Lecturer in French at University College London. He has published books on Sartre (1989) and Barthes (1994) and is currently writing a book on Georges Perec, whose work he has also translated.

George Paizis is Lecturer in French at University College London. His main research is in the field of literature and ideology.

Ann Parry teaches at Staffordshire University, where she is Associate Dean in the School of Humanities and Social Sciences. She has written a book on the popular poetry of Rudyard Kipling and articles on the Victorian press. Her current research and most recent articles are focused upon the representation of the Holocaust and Jews in contemporary European literature.

Andrea Reiter is Senior Research Fellow at the school of Research and Graduate Studies at the University of Southampton. In 1995 her book *'Auf dass sie entsteigen der Dunkelheit ...' Die Literarische Bewaeltigung von KZ-Erfahrung* was published in Vienna. She is currently working on exile literature (Hans Sahl) and on the literature of the children of survivors.

Sue Vice is a Lecturer in English Literature at the University of Sheffield. Her recent publications include *Introducing Bakhtin* (1997). She is working on a book about contemporary Holocaust fiction.

Leon I. Yudkin teaches in the Department of Hebrew and Jewish studies at University College London. He has published eight books of literary criticism on modern Hebrew and Jewish writing and has edited a further five. His most recent book is *A Home within: Varieties of Jewish Expression in Modern Fiction* (1996).

Acknowledgements

Chapter 7, 'Idioms for the Unrepresentable: Postwar Fiction and the Shoah' appeared in the *Journal of European Studies*, Vol. 27, No. 108, December 1997, and is reprinted here by kind permission of the editors.

We would also like to thank the staff of the Institute of Romance Studies (University of London) and the Wiener Library and Institute for Contemporary History for their administrative and financial support. Special thanks go to Professor David Cesarani for giving time, advice and encouragement.

Introduction

Andrew Leak and George Paizis

> Today, I am not sure that what I wrote is true. I am certain it
> is truthful.
>
> Charlotte Delbo

It is a striking feature of human ageing that recent events seem to fall
victim to oblivion most readily – as if they were of only marginal
importance to the fading organism – whereas events that occurred 50
or 60 years previously return vividly, as though they had happened
just yesterday. But this phenomenon appears to operate also at the
level of collective memory: whereas today's news – our actuality –
normally fades gracefully from individual and collective consciousness, until it acquires the dignified if somehow slightly impotent
status of 'history', the events of the Holocaust seem perversely to
become ever more present, as though refusing to become 'history'.

To say that the term Holocaust refers to events which took place in
Europe between 1933 and 1945 may be literally true but it misses the
point.[1] Like the locating in space of Auschwitz (where *is* Auschwitz?),
the locating in time of the Holocaust is also problematic: just as
'Auschwitz' (turned into a different kind of 'place', or trope) overflows
its 40-or-so hectares of Southern Poland, so the Holocaust refuses to be
bounded by two dates. It is scarcely possible, today, to open a newspaper or watch the television news without being reminded of the
continuing presence of the Holocaust. For example: Swiss, French and
British banks – and doubtless others – stashed 'Nazi' gold, some of it
extracted from the mouths of camp inmates, then, on the defeat of
the Axis, simply 'purloined' it; the British government confiscated
assets of foreign 'enemy nationals' – even when those 'enemy nationals' turned out to be murdered German or Hungarian Jews – and only
now is a commission being established to determine compensation;
the Swedes laundered Nazi capital and oiled the German war machine;
the Catholic Church acted as a conduit for Nazis fleeing to South
America ... the list seems endless. Every week brings fresh revelations.

1

In France, a series of high-profile arrests and trials – Barbie, Touvier, Papon – has forced the French political establishment (and, indeed, 'ordinary' French citizens) to re-examine their own role in that inglorious episode of French history. More importantly, such trials have raised questions in the minds of a younger generation who were not directly involved in the events of the Occupation, but who have been raised on heroic myths of the Free French and the Maquis.[2]

In all of this, that which 'should have remained hidden' has 'come to light', and continues to do so, but the return of this particular repressed is more predictable than uncanny. If the Holocaust has the persistence that we have ascribed to it, if it is capable – of its own accord, as it were – of protecting itself from oblivion, then what possible need could there be for books such as this one? In reality, of course, if banks, corporations and even national governments are being forced to acknowledge past misdeeds, it is due more to the labours of historians and survivor pressure groups than to some mysterious capacity of the events themselves to resurface autonomously. But the reconstruction of the Holocaust is by no means only the preserve of historians: at no other time since the war has so much 'discourse' been produced about the Holocaust: historical studies, of course, but also memoirs, oral testimony, documentary films, fictional films, novels, poems, plays, monuments ... Since the present volume is a further contribution to this accumulation, we should pause to address the question: why?

This question never arose for the first generation of survivors. Primo Levi wrote in his afterword to *If This is a Man*: 'those memories burned so intensely inside me that I felt compelled to write as soon as I returned to Italy.'[3] A similar compulsion is expressed by Robert Antelme in *The Human Race* and by countless other survivors. To talk about their experiences in the camps was at one and the same time a psychological necessity and a way of bearing witness for others. The early testimonies each added to the sum of knowledge we now have about the events referred to as the Holocaust. But all those who had a story to tell have, by now, told it: even if, more than 50 years on, an aged survivor chose to break his or her silence, their testimony would probably add relatively little to the sum of 'hard' knowledge we possess about the Holocaust. Which is to suggest that 'bearing witness' means something different today to what it meant in the years immediately following the end of the conflict. In the postwar years, bearing witness had a judicial and political function, as well as a psychological function: it was part of a legal process which demanded that the facts be established. It was all the more important to establish 'who did what to whom, and where', as the physical evidence of the genocide was being destroyed – by bulldozer, by dynamite or by fire – almost as fast as it was being discovered. Even today, it is true, a pathetic old figure – a shadow of his former terrible self – will occasionally be hauled out of his obscurity in the anonymous suburbs of London or Chicago to face trial for crimes against humanity. Witnesses are found and their testimony is heard. But soon there will remain neither perpetrators nor survivors. There will be no one left to point the finger, and no one left to deny. The memory of those events will no longer be embodied in a real human presence, whether that of the perpetrator or the victim: we will have preserved the knowledge, the facts, but meaning floats dangerously when it is no longer incarnate. In his introduction to a recent volume of essays on 'shapes of memory', Geoffrey Hartmann makes a similar point: 'for, while no recent event has elicited so much documentation and analysis, knowledge has not become understanding'.[4]

None of the authors in the present volume is writing from the point of view of a survivor; the volume is not concerned, directly, either with historiographic modes of representation, or with first-hand testimony; but it works precisely in this gap between knowledge and understanding. Recounting his liberation from Dachau, Robert Antelme makes it clear, that if he writes, it is to counter the incomprehension with which the outside world will greet the news of what happened in the camps. Words, Antelme realizes, are not just for telling, but also for the hearers to hide behind: 'Frightful, yes, frightful ... when a soldier says something like that out aloud, a few guys try to tell him what it was like. The soldier listens at first, but then the guys go on and on, they talk and talk, and pretty soon the soldier isn't listening any more.'[5] It is, then, not enough to 'tell [him] what it was like'; the more you speak the less people listen. This reaction (now known in mediaspeak as 'compassion fatigue') elicits a further effort on the part of the survivors: 'All the stories the guys are telling are true. But *it requires considerable artfulness to get even a smidgen of truth accepted*' (p. 289; emphasis added). One must assume that 'acceptance', here, implies a far more active attitude than mere 'suspension of disbelief': something akin to 'taking on board'. In this uncannily prescient passage (written in 1947), Antelme sketches a certain history of Holocaust writing. This history is reflected by the writers represented in the present volume who exploit the whole gamut of 'artful' strategies, from the falsely naïve 'telling it like it was' to what could be described as 'telling it like it was *not*' – that, is, counterfactual narratives such as George Steiner's *The Portage to San Cristobal of A.H.* or Robert Harris's controversial dystopian novel, *Fatherland.*

But before discussing these matters – which bear directly on complex questions of representation and meaning – it is worth specifying the question 'Why this book?' a little more closely, and asking: 'Why this book *now?*' If only because the question, with its emphasis on a shared actuality, should be easier to answer than most.

Back in 1957, the French theorist Roland Barthes remarked that any proposed demystification of the ideological sleight-of-hand he baptized 'myth' would have to contend with two possible negative reactions on the part of his readership: 'prove it!' and 'so what?'[6] These two reactions could be characterized as, respectively, denial and complacency. The danger is that the more we are confronted with revelations concerning the Holocaust (that is, the more 'present' it becomes), the less effect each new revelation will have: 'pretty soon the soldier isn't listening any more ...'

Denial is the more specialized of the two reactions. Holocaust denial is an historiographic 'genre' than can involve a whole range of claims,[7] stretching from the outright denial that the camps, the gas chambers and the crematoria ever existed, through a downward 'revision' of the numbers who perished in these camps (in the case of those who admitted their existence, of course), to a relativizing comparision between the Nazi death camps and the camps of – typically – Stalin's Soviet Union: the point of this latter strategy is not, needless to say, to bring the horrors of the Soviet camps to the attention of the public, but – by tossing one horror into one pan of the scales, and a supposedly *equal but opposite* one into the other – to nullify both, leaving the Nazi genocide as, in Jean-Marie Le Pen's words, a 'mere detail' of the history of the Second World War.[8] The key figures amongst the negationists are the French self-styled 'historians' Robert Faurisson and Paul Rassinier and their English colleague David Irving. Nadine Fresco has memorably described the negationists as 'born demystifyers on the edge of mental pathology, textual obsessives, and antisemitic shock troops recruited from within the extreme right'.[9] It is true that such individuals will not be given cause for thought by one jot or tittle of the present volume, but then this volume is not for them.

Nauseating as it is, negationism is arguably less dangerous and corrosive than complacency. As Fresco goes on to point out, the theses – if they merit this term – of this rag-tag assortment of 'pathological cases' actually find an echo amongst considerable numbers of people right across Europe, and beyond. It seems incredible that with the Holocaust still so present in public consciousness, politicians of the far right can legally employ a diffusely racist, xenophobic – in some cases explicitly antisemitic – discourse on public platforms. But such is the case. In Austria, support for the Freedom Movement accounted for more than 20 per cent of the popular vote in the last parliamentary elections; the Italian National Alliance and Social Movement for more than 15 per cent between them. In France one in six voters over the last five years – at every level from local to national – has voted for Le Pen's avowedly racist *Front National*. In Vitrolles, in southern France, the fascists are in the town hall: they have not started to burn books yet, but they have removed them from the shelves of the municipal library and replaced them by more 'politically acceptable' ones. A similar – if slightly less extreme – picture emerges in Belgium, Denmark, the Czech Republic and the Netherlands. In reunited Germany itself, the neo-fascist Deutsche Volks Union (DVU) recently took 25 per cent of the popular vote in the former East German province of Saxony-Anhalt; and this was a party with no offices and no recognizable candidates, running on the crudest of xenophobic platforms.

It has become something of a truism – some would say, a meaningless platitude – to warn that those who ignore the past are condemned to relive it. The neo-fascists do not ignore the past, far from it: the past serves as their ever-present justification, whether it be in the form of the Nazi insignia worn by their thugs, or their onomastic commemoration of the birth date of Hitler, or the proud continuation of the lineage of Mussolini in Italy, or – more insidiously – by a discourse which constantly harks back to a mythical golden age of the racially pure nation state.

The very existence of influential far-right parties poisons the body politic, even in so-called mature democracies; even where a far-right party does not have an absolute majority, it often holds the balance of power. Politicians of all persuasions find themselves adopting right-wing policies on such matters as immigration, naturalization, the right to work and asylum, ostensibly to appease perceived public opinion and forestall, were the far right to be elected, much more extreme measures, but often, in reality, purely to stay in power themselves. The contaminating effect of the far right was amply demonstrated in France in the wake of the recent elections to the regional assemblies where mainstream politicians of the RPR and the UDF cut shameful deals with the *Front National* in order to retain their personal grip on some vestige of power.

But what does any of this have to do with a volume of academic essays on the representation of the Holocaust? Clearly, there is no single explanation for the resurgence of the extreme right at this moment, just as there is no single determinant behind the growth of nationalisms across Europe. Everything points to a highly complex bundle of factors which it is certainly beyond our competence to discuss. We seek, in a sense, to set the scene: the present historical moment is one in which racism and xenophobia are back on the agenda not only of the lunatic fringe, but also of mainstream political parties. If one assumes that not all of the 15 per cent of French who regularly vote FN are unreconstructed racists, and that many of them remain open to persuasion, then it is clear that a battle for hearts and minds needs urgently to be waged, and, we reiterate, the battleground is that gap between (historical) knowledge and understanding. But until very recently the dominant attitude in the face of the resurgent far right has been complacency. The editors of this volume feel that to continue to represent (re-present) the Holocaust, and to debate and theorize the modes of its representation(s), is and will continue to be, for a long time, urgent. Each new attack on a migrant worker hostel in Germany, every insidious advance of the far right on the chequerboard of electoral politics underlines this urgency.

We argue, then, that one justification for this book's existence is 'historical'; that is, as a tiny event in itself it constitutes an intervention in a given historical reality and, just perhaps, brings about a subtle modification in that reality.

This is not a work of history, but the essays here all take history, to a greater or lesser degree, as their subject. Robert Gordon examines the birth of Holocaust writing in Italy in the immediate postwar years and he shows how the great majority of survivor-narratives in Italian from this period were marked and imprinted – in their very formal characteristics – by a particular historical conjuncture. Gordon also suggests that 'the tools of literary criticism find their most appropriate contribution to Holocaust understanding when used historiographically, to excavate these layers of our historical imaginings'. But what does it mean to use literary criticism 'historiographically'? And what, precisely, are 'historical imaginings'? Are we not dealing here with something akin to an oxymoron? For, if an event is in any real sense 'historical' it has not been 'imagined'; by the same token, an entirely imagined event may well be historically accurate, that is, it may coincide with what actually happened, but it could be so only fortuitously. Yet the world of hard, historical fact and that of the imagination are not separated by an impermeable boundary. A relationship of *mutual implication* might best describe the imbrication of these two domains in the context that concerns us here. There is, perhaps, a useful parallel in Jean-Paul Sartre's account of the relation between the real and the imaginary. The real – the correlate of an act of perception – and the imaginary – the correlate of an act of imagination – are, says Sartre, radically disparate: as different modes of consciousness, they cannot co-exist in a single act of consciousness. And yet they imply each other: without the imagination, the world of seen things would remain precisely that: a flat and meaningless aggregate of percepts. Without the imagination, the world – here understood as a synthetic totality – would not exist. Conversely, the imagination is logically dependent on the real, since it is itself, by its very essence, the negation of a given reality from a certain point of view.[10]

Imaginative accounts are frequently compared – unfavourably – to an historical mode where facts 'speak for themselves'. But facts never speak for themselves, not even in the meticulous historical narratives of Raul Hilberg or the terrible, flat testimonies, punctuated by pregnant silences, of Lanzmann's *Shoah*. Or, at least, they may speak for themselves, but we cannot necessarily guarantee that they will be heard correctly ... Hayden White has demonstrated that all historical narratives deploy the devices of literature, and that 'emplotment' is required in order to enable facts to 'speak themselves'[11] and Lawrence Langer has analysed the more surprising, but no less powerful impulsion towards 'literary' narrativization in the oral testimony of survivors.[12] We need not recapitulate these points here. The simple point we would like to underline is this: between the experience itself and its transmission to others (listeners, readers, viewers, etc.) a great many layers of mediation may intervene; the very notion of immediate (here in the sense of 'without mediation') experience is illusory: even direct experiences of the most appalling and traumatic kind are always necessarily mediated: to experience a death camp as a Jewish inmate was not the same thing as experiencing it as a political detainee, as a Kapo, as a common law criminal or – as Anna Hardman shows – as a woman. In other words, the specificity of a subject-position conditions the experience itself – even before it is represented to others or to oneself. This same factor comes into play *a fortiori* at the level of the reception of representations. But is it legitimate, or even decent, to speak of a 'subject-position' when evoking the world of Auschwitz? Certainly, Primo Levi suggests in *If This is a Man* that survival in Auschwitz depended, precisely, on setting aside everything that one knew, everything that one was upon entering that particular inferno, in a ghastly parody of rebirth into an alien universe: those who perished most surely were those who clung to their life 'before', and those who – supreme folly in that world of anti-reason – tried to *understand* what was happening to them: *Ne cherchez pas à comprendre!* The paradox is that Levi himself, who never foresook his 'civilized Cartesian phantoms', nevertheless survived.

But a further paradox hangs on Levi's representation of his experiences in works such as *If This is a Man*. Levi's account is clearly 'authentic' in the sense that he, the narrator, of the events, actually experienced them first hand. But there is perhaps a way in which Levi's account fails the authenticity test: if Auschwitz was the world-turned-upside-down, if the reality of Auschwitz was anti-reason itself (*Hier ist kein warum!*), then how can Levi's representation of that reality – a representation which attempts to arrive at a *rational understanding* of the experience and to communicate that understanding – be 'authentic'? To take this a little further, how can any narrative do anything but betray its subject, when its subject is the Holocaust? The most basic emplotment – of the kind, for example, famously described by E.M. Forster in *Aspects of the Novel*[13] – establishes causal links between events rather than simply situating those events in time, and it thereby adds a first level of interpretation of the events, a first 'gloss' on/over them. But what if the events themselves quite simply lacked meaning? Any narrativization of them would then constitute a falsification. And what criteria do we have at our disposal for legitimating one 'falsification' over another, for stating that – while all representations are somehow 'inauthentic' – some are more/less inauthentic than others?

All of this raises particular theoretical and practical questions in the realm of historiographic representations, which make special claims for the truthfulness of their narratives. However, we are concerned here not with historiographic but with fictional representations – acts of imaginative reconstruction – where the implicit pact between text and reader does not involve the same claims with regard to historical accuracy. As we have seen, it is impossible not to adopt a point of view when recounting an event – whether it be the point of view of participant in the event, that of uninvolved by-stander, that of God, or any number of positions in between. And to adopt a point of view – that is, to *choose* to adopt this point of view rather than any other – is to give shape to, and therefore interpret the event. One sometimes has the impression that the moment of interpretation is the one that historians most dread: the facts have been established in as objective a way as possible, now comes the point where the historian must let go of the handrail of fact and take the plunge: what does it all mean? No such concerns normally constrain the writer of fictions, who must take responsibility for the world he has created, but not for the conformity of that world to the one we actually inhabit. Historians are typically caught in a cleft stick: they recognize that interpretation of the world they are re-creating is inevitable, so attempt to mollify their scientific superego by pretending to themselves that interpretation is the discovery of meaning. Artists and writers, on the other hand, tend to see the interpretation that accompanies their creation as the invention of meaning. But imaginative artists who take the Holocaust as their subject are not as unfettered in their creation as might seem to be the case: they are not free to invent *any* meaning for the world, but instead find themselves constrained by additional, and possibly unique, concerns for truthfulness and authenticity.

At different historical moments, different strictures have been levelled at representation,[14] but one constant factor has been the insistence on the gap or disparity between the art-object and the reality it purports to reproduce or make present for us. It is easy to see how notions of betrayal have become attached to artistic representation, and we need take only one step further to arrive at the guilt which very often attaches itself – often quite subtly – both to the production of artistic representations and to their consumption. Indeed, as Robert Eaglestone reminds us, Levinas flatly refuses to represent, or to attempt to represent the Holocaust, on the grounds that any form of artistic representation cannot but betray the events represented.

Once more there is a relevant parallel in Sartrean aesthetics: the real and the imaginary are denigrated by Sartre with equal force: to stall at the pole of the real implies a failure to transcend what *is* towards what *might be* but is not yet; whereas the imaginary is castigated precisely because it represents a negation of the real, and the real, for Sartre, is the domain of the ethical.[15] Sartre's characteristic double-bind need not detain us too long, but before moving on we should note that his ethical critique of the imaginary closely resembles a common criticism levelled at Holocaust literature and art. It seems that the distinction we made between a historical mode of representation entailing a pact of 'fidelity to the real', on the one hand, and fictional representation in general, on the other, where the pact is of a significantly different kind, is not sufficiently sensitive to account for the specific case of literature (or poetry, or theatre ...) that takes as its subject the Holocaust. The events of the Holocaust make of it a referent quite unlike any other. This point has been well put by Lawrence Langer:

> when the Holocaust is the theme, history imposes limitations on the supposed flexibility of artistic license. We are confronted by the perplexing challenge of the reversal of normal creative procedure: instead of the Holocaust fictions liberating the facts and expanding the range of their implications, Holocaust facts enclose the fictions, drawing the reader into an ever-narrower area of association, where history and art stand guard over their respective territories, wary of abuses that either may commit upon the other'.[16]

Berel Lang, in a piece which stands in an almost prefatory relation to the other essays in this volume, examines the ways in which all Holocaust writing 'turns to history'. Lang cuts through the frequently rehearsed arguments about the intrinsic inadequacy of representation – extended by many modern theorists into a complete incapacity to represent – and asserts that the Holocaust not only can be spoken, but has been and still is spoken. The question which now preoccupies us is how to justify what is spoken. This justification would lie in Lang's hypothesis that 'Holocaust writing characteristically aspires to the condition of history'. This assertion is doing more than claiming that 'serious books about the Holocaust try to get their facts straight'. What is implied here is that history functions both as *terminus a quo* and *terminus ad quem* of such writing: a point of departure, it is also their end, their deepest finality. The Holocaust-as-theme is perhaps unique in our transgressive age in maintaining the integrity of its own boundaries and hence of the limitations it exercises on 'artistic' representation.

Lang enumerates three categories of Holocaust writings that aspire to the condition of history. The first of these contains writings which gesture explicitly towards history and thus make some kind of claim for the veracity of their narratives. At the same time, they mark themselves off from historical writing *per se*. Works such as Anna Gmeyner's *Manja* or Ilse Aichinger's *Die grössere Hoffnung* would doubtless fall into this category. Nevertheless, Andrea Reiter shows that the relation to history of such texts is far from straightforward.

The choice of a child-protagonist as focalizer for their narratives is a strategic one, but it also leaves such narratives treading a sometimes uncomfortable line between avant-gardist defamiliarization and populist sentimentalization.[17]

Testimony – be it oral, or in the form of the memoir or autobiography – certainly belongs in this category of works which 'aspire to the condition of history'. But, here again, in the heretofore rather neglected area of women's testimony, Anna Hardman demonstrates how influential the memoirist's subject-position is in framing the form of the narrative and its explicit or, more often, unspoken assumptions. The distortions, hesitations and ambiguities that entered into the creation of such testimony are also shown to be a significant factor in shaping its reception, with the testimony becoming an object of appropriation for the different contemporary feminist agendas. A kind of critical 'bad faith' can arise, whereby the critic employs the supposed factuality of the testimony under discussion in order to authenticate his/her own assumptions. Once more, the lesson is that history must be taken into account at both ends of the process of representation.

As Aharon Appelfeld remarked, one does not look directly into the sun; and a further category of Holocaust writing – exemplified by the work of Appelfeld himself – appears to have taken this aphorism to heart in that its approach to its subject is marked by obliquity. This is writing in which the Holocaust is implied rather than directly designated; writing where the Holocaust functions as subtext or context. Leon Yudkin's discussion of Appelfeld's 1995 novel *Until the Dawn's Light* deals precisely with this curious strategy of 'non-representation'. The reader of Appelfeld's novels and stories must provide the hidden context himself, for without the assumption of this context, the texts themselves remain, to a significant degree, 'meaningless'. The approach to the events of the Holocaust to be found in the work of Patrick Modiano is no less oblique than that of Appelfeld, but it could perhaps best be described as 'circular' or 'spiralling' – rather than 'tangential'. Modiano was born in 1945, and the whole of his work is a phantasmagorical recreation of memory he, personally, never had.[18] Like water spiralling around a plughole, the works of Modiano swirl around the absence upon which they are constructed. To the extent that Modiano saw his work as responding primarily to an aesthetic imperative, rather than to a concern for historical veracity, it appears to be an exception to the claim that Holocaust writing characteristically aspires to the condition of history. But perhaps Modiano's work

– which appears to be exclusively obsessed with the Holocaust – needs to be understood, counter-intuitively, as entailing the sub- or con-text of the Holocaust: this context must be supplied by a hard-working reader, for its absence from the text is, perhaps, the very condition of that text's existence.[19] For Modiano, the fabrication, or invention, of a falsely 'historical' past (in early works like *La Place de l'Etoile*) – that is, the very avoidance of historical literalness – is the condition for the emergence of some kind of partial truth.

This mention of Modiano has actually led us onto the shifting sands of postmodernity.[20] It is difficult to imagine anything more alien to a postmodern sensibility than an insistence on the ethical imperative of authenticity. The very notion of the *origin* is unthinkable in a post-modern aesthetics: postmodern architecture, literature and art flourishes on the conceit of the copy without an original. This is not to say that the past, as history, is absent from the postmodern universe; on the contrary, it is obsessively present in postmodern literature and art, but always in an ironic mode, never as foundation or origin. The dominant figures of postmodernity are the fake, the forgery and the counterfeit, but no longer considered as travesties of the original, the genuine or the authentic. Now these notions – fake, forgery and counterfeit – with the addition of plagiarism and imper-sonation, burst noisily into the debates surrounding representations of the Holocaust on the occasion of the so-called Demidenko affair in Australia. On the face of it, a novel which turns out to have exten-sively plagiarized other novels, memoirs and historical documents, and which was written by an individual who had usurped the persona of an unreconstructed Ukrainian antisemite for promotional purposes would seem to stand little chance of scoring highly in the 'authentic-ity' stakes. But Sue Vice draws on the work of the erstwhile Russian formalist Mikhail Bakhtin in order to perform a reading of Darville's *The Hand that Signed the Paper* which sees it as utilizing a polyphonic strategy in order to provoke readers and draw them into debate. If the postmodern strategy *par excellence* consists in removing the quotation marks from the quotations, then Vice's reading of Darville's novel restores them and thus restores the text to an audibly polyphonic status. The claim here is that polyphonic texts are better able to provoke the ethical engagement of readers than are monologistic ones which leave little room for moral argument, one way or the other. Vice's thesis finds unlikely echoes in the conclusions drawn by Robert Eaglestone on Levinas's strategy of non-representation. For him, monologism is precisely the technique of the Holocaust deniers – the negationists – whose tactics consist in shouting down the opposition, presenting 'definitive' facts, 'indisputable' historical readings, closing off all avenues of debate and, finally, 'removing the quotation marks from their conversations'. The negationists seek the silence of closure, they refuse the 'infinite conversation'.

With a mention of this 'infinite conversation', we appear to have entered the realm of 'analysis terminable and interminable', the realm of psychoanalysis: are we really claiming that Holocaust-writing in some sense resembles the 'talking cure'? From all that we have discussed so far, a figure is starting to take shape. In the absent origin in Modiano or the sun that cannot be looked at directly in Appelfeld, or the banished representation in Levinas; in the wandering narratives of postmodern fiction, that somehow 'beat about the bush' or 'refuse to get to the point' we can dimly perceive the figures of what could be called 'trauma'. We propose to understand this term, in a broadly Lacanian manner, as that part of the real which resists symbolization.[21] When Lyotard refers to 'Auschwitz' as 'a sign that something waits to be phrased that cannot be … a silence lost to representation',[22] he clearly has in mind this notion of trauma. The essays in this volume by Ann Parry and Martin Crowley – amongst others – are centrally concerned with trauma and the possibility of its working through. Crowley, in particular, analyses the complex relations between Antelme's *The Human Race* and Marguerite Duras's *La Douleur*, paying close attention to the 'sympathetic doubling of the sites of trauma' as a strategy for its representation. In psychoanalysis (viewed as therapy), the aim is to free up fixations and blockages and to help the analysand retrieve more and more of the 'real', of that which would otherwise be lost to words.[23] This is achieved, precisely, through verbalizing (or 'symbolizing') the trauma. Just as there is disagreement between analysts as to the degree to which trauma can ever be verbalized, so writers on the Holocaust perform their work with varying degrees of pessimism or optimism. Saul Friedlander's 1994 piece on 'Trauma, Memory, and Transference' ends with the following words:

> It may well be that for some the trauma, the insuperable moral outrage, the riddle whose decoding never seems to surrender a fully comprehensible text, may present an ongoing emotional and intellectual challenge. However, I would venture to suggest that even if new forms of historical narrative were to develop, or new modes of representation, and even if literature and art were to probe the past

from unexpected vantage points, the opaqueness of 'deep memory' would not be ultimately dispelled. 'Working through' may ultimately signify, in Maurice Blanchot's words, 'to keep watch over absent meaning'.[24]

For our part, we believe in the capacity of literature and art to occupy new vantage points and to invent new modes of representation, but we do not share Friedlander's pessimism regarding the terminal opacity of 'deep memory'. Even if we did, there would be no alternative but to continue 'working through'. Any effort at symbolization, or representation, is necessarily carried out from the vantage point of the already-symbolized, from what we could call, for want of a better term, our 'reality' – and we have seen, at the start of this introduction, some disturbing aspects of our reality today. Any representation of the Holocaust looks both backwards and forwards. It seems to us that the more we are separated in time from the Holocaust, the more difficult the duty we have to the dead becomes to discharge. But we also have a duty to the living, and this duty is more urgent. But it happens that these 'duties' are of a piece: to discharge our duty to the living, we must continue to discharge our duty to the dead. And thus we hope that, through the patient symbolization – or working through – of our collective past, we may also intervene in the present.

Notes

1   Are these events to be referred to as the Holocaust or as the Shoah? Neither term is entirely satisfactory, and both have connotations which some find objectionable. We will not rehearse the arguments here; most contributors have favoured the term 'Holocaust', but we have not sought to impose a 'party line'.

2   It took an outsider – Robert Paxton – to undertake the first serious and sustained questioning of the myths which had been cultivated around the Occupation of France and the Vichy regime. In his *Vichy France: Old Guard and New Order 1940–1944* (New York: Columbia University Press, 1972), Paxton demonstrates how the Vichy government actively sought collaboration with the Nazis, with a zeal which could scarcely be accounted for by the 'traditional' explanations (the best that could be hoped for, the lesser of two evils, damage limitation, etc.). Paxton's book was translated into French and appeared in 1973 as *La France de Vichy 1940–1944* (Paris: Editions du Seuil, 1973). For a fictional 'take' on this period of French history and its reluctant 'working through' see the works of Patrick Modiano, discussed by Samuel Khalifa in this volume, and Didier Daeninckx, *Meurtres pour mémoire* (Paris: Gallimard, 1984). The latter

volume could be described as 'committed detective fiction': the latest genre to take the Holocaust as its subject.

3   Primo Levi, *If This is a Man* and *The Truce* (London: Vintage Books, 1979), p. 381.

4   Geoffrey H. Hartmann, *Holocaust Remembrance: the Shapes of Memory* (Oxford: Blackwell, 1994), p. 5.

5   Robert Antelme, *The Human Race* (Marlboro, Vermont: The Marlboro Press, 1992), p. 289.

6   Roland Barthes, *Mythologies*, selected and translated from the French by Annette Lavers (London: Paladin Grafton Books, 1972), pp. 117–74.

7   The fullest treatment to date of negationism is to be found in Pierre Vidal-Naquet, *Les assassins de la mémoire* (Paris: La Découverte, 1987). This has been translated as *Assassins of Memory: Essays on the Denial of the Holocaust*, translated with an introduction by Jeffrey Mehlman (New York: Columbia University Press, 1992). See also Gill Seidel, *The Holocaust Denial* (Leeds: Beyond the Pale Collective, 1986).

8   This relativizing device is baptized 'The Scales' by Barthes. See *Mythologies*, p. 167.

9   Nadine Fresco, 'Negating the Dead', in Hartmann, *Holocaust Remembrance*, pp. 191–203.

10   See Jean-Paul Sartre, *L'Imaginaire* (Paris: Gallimard, 1940).

11   See Hayden White, *The Content of the Form: Narrative Discourse and Historical Representation* (Baltimore: Johns Hopkins University Press, 1987).

12   See Lawrence Langer, *Holocaust Testimony: the Ruins of Memory* (New Haven: Yale University Press, 1991).

13   See E.M. Forster, *Aspects of the Novel* (1927) (London: Arnold, 1949), pp. 82–4.

14   Representation is, of course, a vast and vastly complex topic. To even begin to give an adequate overview of the subject, one would have to be conversant with a huge body of work form Plato through to Riffaterre. In the light of this, we have chosen here to focus (and even then, quite superficially) on topics which bear directly on the essays presented in this volume. Many works have appeared in recent years dealing with the problem of representing the Holocaust. These include: Lawrence Langer, *The Holocaust and the Literary Imagination* (New Haven: Yale University Press, 1978) and *Admitting the Holocaust* (New York and Oxford: Oxford University Press, 1995); Saul Friedlander (ed.), *Probing the Limits of Representation: Nazism and the Final Solution* (Cambridge: Harvard University Press, 1992); Berel Lang (ed.), *Writing and the Holocaust* (New York: Holmes and Meier, 1988); Efraim Sicher (ed.), *Breaking Crystal: Writing and Memory after Auschwitz* (Urbana and Chicago: University of Illinois Press, 1998).

15   Jean-Paul Sartre, *L'Imaginaire*, pp. 343–61.

16   Lawrence Langer, *Admitting the Holocaust*, pp. 75–6.

17   'Defamiliarization' here in the sense of the Russian Formalists' *ostranenie*, rather than the Brechtian *Verfremdungseffekt*. However, Brecht himself was all too aware of the thinness of the line separating critical detachment from sentimental identification, where audience reaction was concerned.

18   The case of Modiano's countryman, Georges Perec, is even stranger. Perec was born in 1936 in Paris to Polish immigrant parents. His father was killed

at the front shortly before the amnesty in 1940, and his mother was deported to Auschwitz in 1943, never to return. Perec himself lived out the war in children's homes in the Alps. In *W, or the Memory of Childhood* (London: Collins Harvill, 1988) he attempts to retie the threads of his broken childhood. *W* consists of two alternating texts (alternated chapter by chapter, one in roman type, one in italic type); one text is a lacunary autobiography of his first ten or so years, the other is a disturbing fiction set on an island (the eponymous 'W') governed by the Olympic ideal, but which reveals itself gradually to be a ... concentration camp. Not the least strange aspect of the text is the way that Perec 'gets wrong' both personal biographical details and easily verifiable historical facts.

19 The parallel with Perec is, again, striking. His novel *La Disparition* (Paris: Denoël, 1969) is constructed by respecting a crucial constraint: the omission or avoidance of the letter E. So what the reader can see and read (what is *presented*) is entirely determined by an absence, by that which is excluded. The letter E in French is a homophone of 'eux', or 'them', suggesting one obvious interpretation of what has disappeared. Perec's novel has been translated (or rather re-written) by Gilbert Adair under the title *A Void* (London: Collins Harvill, 1994).

20 These 'shifting sands' are becoming increasingly well charted. A significant proportion of Hartmann's illuminating introduction to *Holocaust Remembrance* is devoted to exploring the implications of Baudrillard's theories for future representations of the Holocaust. Similarly, a long chapter in Efraim Sicher's *Breaking Crystal* is concerned with 'The Holocaust in the Postmodern Era'.

21 The 'real' is an elusive concept in Lacan. The real is, roughly, that which pre-dates language, that which precedes the entry into the symbolic order. Thus, it could be the baby's body (in a state of what Freud called 'polymorphous perversity') before it is subjected to toilet training. With the entry into language, the real is progressively 'symbolized' but this process of symbolization is said by Lacan to be unending. Since the real does not really have the status of a 'concept' for Lacan, it is difficult to direct the reader to any one place in Lacan's increasingly voluminous published work where the 'answers' might be found! Short cuts can be found in the form of: Anika Lemaire, *Jacques Lacan*, translated and revised by David Macey (London: Routledge and Kegan Paul, 1977) and Bruce Fink, *The Lacanian Subject: Between Language and Jouissance* (Princeton: Princeton University Press, 1995), see especially Chapter 3: 'The Creative Function of the Word: the Symbolic and the Real'.

22 See Jean-François Lyotard, *The Differend: Phrases in Dispute* (Manchester: Manchester University Press, 1988), p. 148.

23 It is perhaps worth pointing out – to avoid confusion – that this 'real' is *not* that of Sartre referred to earlier in this introduction.

24 In Hartmann, *Holocaust Remembrance*, p. 263.

1
Holocaust Genres and the Turn to History

Berel Lang

The title of our volume seems to me to warrant more than the ritual acknowledgement usually accorded titles. For understood literally, 'Speaking the Unspeakable' is a straightforward contradiction – it *can't* be done – and even if we give the phrase an honorific gloss by calling it a paradox, we only defer the issue of its inconsistency. Maimonides concluded that in a sacred text there can *be* no contradictions – thus, that apparent contradictions must be figurative rather than literal in meaning and so are not, strictly speaking (as we must), contradictory at all. Inconsistencies in secular texts are unlikely to bow to this same principle, but we know enough about the event at the centre of the essays assembled here – an event as close to sacred, after all, as anything in a secular world can be – to know that calling it unspeakable is often also, even always, figurative. In its manner of speaking, it heaps hyperbole atop metaphor, verging on that striking figure of speech, the *praeteritio*, in which a speaker announces that he will not speak about something when what becomes immediately evident is that the purpose of this denial is to do just that.

Most commonly we meet this figure in political discourse – as when a candidate for office declines to violate his listeners' sensibilities by recalling his honorable friend's sordid past; for *our* subject, which involves true moral enormity, we hear it referred to as unspeakable – and usually hear also a fairly detailed description presented to justify that designation. In this way, a 'Negative Rhetoric' emerges along the more traditional side of 'Negative Theology' – both of them so strong and definite in their respective commitments that simple affirmation evidently does not suffice to express them. Surely it is neither accidental nor inconsistent that the best-known statements which place the Holocaust beyond (and so against) representation have come from authors as dissimilar as Adorno, Elie Wiesel and George Steiner – who, through the representations they then allowed themselves, have profoundly influenced the subsequent content of Holocaust discourse.

Thus, I propose at the outset (and if I could, once and for all) to 'de'-figure this figure of the Holocaust; to claim instead that the Holocaust *is* speakable, *has* been spoken, *will be* spoken (certainly here), and, most of all, *ought* to be. Virtually all claims to the contrary – in those variations on the unspeakable which encompass the indescribable, the unthinkable, the unimaginable, the incredible – come embedded in yards of writing which attempt to overcome the inadequacy of language in representing moral enormity at the same time that they assert it; certainly they hope to find for their own assertions of that inadequacy a useful, a *telling* place in its shadow.

It is self-evident, at any rate, that no Holocaust-writing gives preference to silence – although silence is itself, after all, a distinctive literary genre, one that Isaac Babel first named and mastered (and then also, we know, fell victim to). Indeed, silence arguably remains a criterion for *all* discourse (Holocaust or not), a constant albeit phantom presence which stipulates that whatever is written ought to be justifiable as more probative, more incisive, more *revealing* than would be its absence or (more cruelly) its erasure. Put differently, this criterion poses the question of whether the *loss* of any particular text would not, in moral and/or cognitive terms, manifest itself as a gain – a question especially pertinent to Holocaust writing just because of the weightiness of that subject. I concede that, barring the most exceptional instances (like the sub-genre of Holocaust pornography), the price of silence about the Holocaust in lieu of its representation as a *general* principle – that cost inviting the vacuum of forgetfulness – is too high. But even this concession should not cause us to forget that the basic measure also of any piece of Holocaust writing is not the possibility of alternate formulations (which are perhaps beyond its author's ken or will), but the erasure of what he *has* written; that is, silence.

As we assume in any 'representation' a construct which substitutes for an original, then since no representation can ever *be* that original, representations will also never be *quite* 'adequate', however close they come. This is what we might punningly call the 'original sin' of representation – for which Plato, notwithstanding his caricature of it in the *Republic*, provides a ground. And even if we reject the metaphysical framework implicit in this claim of intrinsic inadequacy, it seems clear that now, more than 50 years into the post-Holocaust, the question confronting us is not whether the Holocaust is speakable, but how to justify what *is* spoken. My comments here turn mainly to the latter question, although I defer considering how ethical premises shape (or ought to shape) Holocaust discourse in order to address first the more neutral, descriptive topic of 'Holocaust genres' – moving only after that to examine the relationship between those genres and the ethical imperative that underlies them.

So: Holocaust genres. The inventiveness of twentieth-century history has seen to it that one understanding of this phrase would be that Holocausts themselves may come in 'genres'. My more ordinary interest here, however, is in the kinds of literary representation that consider or assume the Holocaust as a subject – for which representations I propose to detail their distinguishing and common features. On that basis, I later subsume the Holocaust genres identified – certain conventional ones like the diary, the memoir, the novel, together with less conventional ones like oral histories and even the historical treatise – under a single, more inclusive rubric, concluding that Holocaust writing as such has the features of a genre, rooted in its connection (its *moral* connection) to the writing of history.

That discussion is driven by one brief thesis – which comes, however, with a number of corollaries (and strings) attached. The thesis is this: that Holocaust writing characteristically 'aspires to the condition of history' (imposing here on Walter Pater's reflection that 'art aspires constantly to the condition of music'). More fully, my claim is that whether in representation or fact – an ambiguity present, after all, in the very term 'history' which denotes both historical writing and the events written *about* – Holocaust genres are bound (*anchored*) historically, in part because they set out from a particular historical point, but more importantly, because historical authenticity is also what they purport to realize. For Holocaust genres, in other words, history functions not merely as an occasion and a means of measurement, but also as an end – one which affects even the most artful or inventive features of those genres, with the reason for this to be found in an underlying ethical ground.

This is, I realize, a large and amorphous claim requiring elaboration on all its sides. But let me provide a structure for its basic terms by characterizing three divisions in Holocaust writing which serve as evidence for the thesis and which I believe to be intelligible only in light of it: first, the large group of Holocaust writings which at once claim historical veracity and assert or indicate their differences from historical writing as such; second, a smaller but still substantial group of Holocaust writings which presuppose, without asserting, historical veracity – and which disclose that presupposition in their sub-texts or con-texts; and third, the group of Holocaust writings which explicitly present themselves as historiographic, asserting for themselves the status of something like Ranke's ideal of reporting history as it 'actually [*eigentlich*] was'.

The first of these groups includes the large body of Holocaust writings which *profess* historicity, with the exemplary genre here the diary, but encompassing also more mediated forms like the memoir, the autobiography, the 'oral history', the non-fictional fiction (in novels or short stories), all of which evoke and then rely on the reader's belief in their verisimilitude. I refer to the diary as exemplary among these – the Ringelblum or Czerniakow diaries from the Warsaw Ghetto, the (collective) chronicle of the Lodz Ghetto (1941–4), the recently published Klemperer diary from Dresden[1] – inasmuch as the diary includes two elements typical not of historical narrative but of the movement of history itself.

The first of these two elements appears in the direct representation of the contingency of historical time – insofar as the diarist writes in ignorance of what the next moment, let alone any longer period holds for the events he describes or, more pointedly, for himself. The future as thus open and unknown is also incapable of retroactively shaping the events or reactions (or predictions) noted in the diary. Of course, Ringelblum (for example) had few illusions, even early on, about what was in store for either the Warsaw Ghetto or himself. But there is none the less a crucial difference between that anticipation as it entered his diary and the writing, by contrast, in even the sparest or least self-indulgent memoir (like the eponymous *Fragments* of Benjamin Wilkomirski[2]) which none the less reaches into the past from the vantage point of its outcome and, more decisively, of its author's survival. The second element, related to the first, is the exclusion from the writing of the diary of revision – the absence of second or after-thoughts which, were they admitted, would taint or refigure the past, since revision even for 'purely' historical purposes would lose that purity in the process. The diary comes as close as representation can to 'performing' the events it cites rather than to describing them; it is an act in, if not fully of, the history it relates.

The other genres in this first category are more conventional in their representational roles: the memoir or autobiography which depicts the past through the filter of memory – employing that filter tacitly, as Primo Levi's writing often does; or more explicitly, as Saul

Friedlander does in *When Memory Comes*)[3] – in any event viewing the past from a vantage point reached only at a distance from the events cited; the non-fictional fiction which, whether written in the first person or in the third, claims or implies faithfulness to the historical record (at time by reciting the record itself), while simultaneously providing counter-evidence that much else in the text is not, *could* not be factual. So, for widely disparate examples, D.M. Thomas's *The White Hotel*, Leslie Epstein's *The King of the Jews*, Jean-François Steiner's *Treblinka*, Kenneally's *Schindler's List*, Wiesel's *Night*, Hochhuth's *The Deputy*.[4] I quote (as typical of this genre) from the 'Acknowledgements' that precede a lesser known recent 'novel' – *Stones from the River* by Ursula Hegi (1994):

> My godmother, Kate Capelle, had the courage to answer questions I couldn't ask as a child while growing up in the silence of post-World War II Germany.... [She] broke the silence by documenting her memories of the war years on tape for me. Author Ilse-Margret Vogel ... lent me photo albums of her childhood and offered valuable insights on what it was like to live in Germany between the two wars. Historian Rod Stackelberg trusted me with journals he wrote as a boy in Germany. Together with Germanist Sally Winkle, he guided me in my research.... My agent Gail Hochman, helped me with my research of Jewish traditions. Gordon Gagliano ... advised me in matters Catholic and architectural.[5]

If the readers of this preliminary statement did not *know* that a novel was to follow, they could as readily anticipate an historical treatise. And indeed, the writings which constitute this group disclose a common commitment to historicity, whatever other qualities are subsequently built on it – a commitment volunteered *not* for literary reasons (since what could these be?), nor for historical reasons (since then the genres would be quite different), but evidently – the one remaining alternative – for moral reasons asserted out of deference for the subject or in order to preserve history, as the moral ground of memory argues for THAT.

The second category – of Holocaust writing which appears with only a sub- or con-text of historical reference – applies to a smaller but still substantial number of works whose indirection can be understood in terms of Aharon Appelfeld's aphorism that 'one does not look directly into the sun' (that is, of course, *at* the Holocaust). The group of such works are exemplified, in fact, by the best-known of Appelfeld's own books, *Badenheim 1939*.[6] For a reader who does not bring to that book prior knowledge of the Holocaust – the emergent threat of deportation for the Jews, their response of incredulity and denial, and finally the deportations themselves – this book will almost certainly remain opaque, conveying the *sense* of a parable or allegory but evasively and mysteriously – because of the absence of the second, referential term that those literary genres standardly presuppose. *With* such prior knowledge – which Appelfeld thus requires the reader to supply – the work is transformed. (This issue becomes evident in the metamorphoses of the book's title: in the Hebrew original, the title was the ironic *Badenheim, Ir Nofesh* (*Badenheim Spa*, or *Resort*); in the English, we have the quasi-historical *Badenheim 1939*; in the German, just the indefinite *Badenheim*, because Appelfeld's German publisher feared lesser sales if '1939' were attached – exactly the opposite effect assumed for the English or American editions).

To be sure, the diaries or memoirs or novels in the first category mentioned also assume a sub- or con-text – but not so much as a literary or representational device as in the interest of literary economy common to all written discourse; by contrast, in the second group of 'indirect' Holocaust writings, the unconscious of the texts – their repressed past – must be retrieved and articulated by the reader, with these acts themselves then integral in shaping the reader's response. Predictably, the largest proportion of writings here come from poetry – epitomized, it seems to me, in the œuvre of Paul Celan, but also (if less consistently and economically) in writers like Jacob Glatstein or Yehuda Amichai. Because the 'condensation' notable among these (to use Freud's term from his chapter in *The Interpretation of Dreams* on 'The Dream Work') is typical of all poetry, one might object that there is nothing distinctive about its role in Holocaust poetry. But again, the condensation in Celan's 'Todesfuge', for example, ensues then not only in the general referentiality that all discourse presupposes, but in a *specific* historical denotation which, insofar as it is unknown to the reader, must produce a radically different effect for him from the effect of the poem understood as a 'Holocaust poem'. (His readers' emphasis on 'Todesfuge' *as* a Holocaust poem eventually led to Celan's own estrangement from it – and arguably to changes in his shaping of his later poetry.)

The third category of Holocaust genres – historical writing itself – may seem perverse or at best a conceit inasmuch as it characterizes history as a whole as a 'genre.' For then Holocaust history too is tied to the thesis that has been posed – and what could possibly be meant by the claim that Holocaust-*history* aspires to the condition of history? But it is indeed the latter assertion that I would make – in part against the conceptual background that discloses genres not as natural 'kinds', but as themselves historical and conventional; more specifically, as an inference from the varieties of Holocaust history itself.

No one would dispute the large place of historical writing in articulating the complex events known (historically, after all) as the Holocaust. Pick whatever angle of vision you will, and there are for it points of origin and confirmation in historical writing. From Reitlinger's early work on *The Final Solution* to Hilberg's monumental study of *The Destruction of the European Jews* to Hannah Arendt on *Eichmann in Jerusalem* (and the legions of authors who write about Arendt) to Martin Gilbert's compendious geographies (where geography too turns into history), to the *Historikerstreit* of Nolte, Hillgruber, Habermas, Mommsen, Broszat, and others; to Saul Friedlander on the Vatican and Isaiah Trunk on *The Judenrat*, and then to Robert J. Lifton on *The Nazi Doctors* (a plausible metonymy for the virtual library of writings about the conduct of the various professions in Nazi Germany), hardly an issue in the topology of the Nazi genocide and the culture sustaining it has not been worked seriously and deeply in the relatively short period (in historiographic terms) of 50 years.[7] And there should be no doubt either that as the Holocaust fades from first- or second-hand experience, the necessity of this historical writing as a ground for memory as well as knowledge – in effect, for *everything* written or thought about the Holocaust – must become ever more pressing.

Of course, a mere quantity of writing does not itself argue for the distinction of a genre – let alone for applying that term to history as a whole on the basis of the small field of Holocaust history within it. For many historians, furthermore, to find the label of 'genre' attached to their work amounts to an attack on hard-won standards of evidence and proof which (in their view) are not functions of rhetoric or 'style' at all. This is not the place to argue the issues strikingly defined by Hayden White in his study in *Metahistory* of nineteenth-century historiography; sufficient for the moment if we consider only the possibility of conceiving history as itself a genre of writing (as Richard Rorty has provocatively asserted for philosophy and Thomas Kuhn, still more contentiously, for science).[8] To be sure, the evidence for thinking of history as a kind of writing goes beyond that provided by Holocaust history alone – but the evidence is plainly there as well, in certain large differences among the texts of Holocaust history not about the data and events of the Holocaust which in many instances seem beyond dispute, but in the emplotted *representations* of those data and events.

Let me support this claim with two examples – from historians who are equally committed to the view that the Holocaust resulted from the conscious intentions of its perpetrators and who devote much of their work to the evidence leading to this conclusion, but who despite this common ground, none the less appear to inhabit different historiographic worlds. So, consider first Raul Hilberg – a railroad buff in his childhood who would go on to find in the transport system of Nazi Germany a crucial clue to the mechanism and design of genocide. Here he speaks about one element of the transport system, the German Railway's price-schedule for 'passengers' carried to the camps in the East: 'The basic charge was the third-class fare: 4 pfennig per track kilometer. Children under 10 were transported for half this amount; those under four went free.... For the deportees one-way fare was payable; for the guards a round-trip ticket had to be purchased.'[9] A superficially reasonable arrangement presented without commentary or inflection – but not of course without an underlying tone of great intensity. And then, Daniel Goldhagen, stressing the gratuitous, hence intentional brutality applied in the camps, exacerbated by the callousness of the guards:

> The Germans made love in barracks next to enormous privation and incessant cruelty. What did they talk about when their heads rested quietly on their pillows, when they were smoking their cigarettes in those relaxing moments after their physical needs had been met? Did one relate to another accounts of a particularly amusing beating that she or he had administered or observed.... It appears unlikely that these Germans lamented their vicious assaults on the Jews.... This community of Germans, many of whom had paired off in intimate relationships, flourished side by side with the hell for Jews, which these same Germans created and enthusiastically policed.[10]

When I say that historical writing itself aspires to the condition of history, it seems to me that the differences between these two passages provide evidence. There is little question that each of them has a rhetorical or suasive purpose; there may be some question, but none the less substantial evidence that part of this purpose is held by the two authors in common; but there seems to me *no* question that historiographically – in the understanding toward which they urge their readers – the authors diverge sharply: Hilberg aiming to unite the historical representation with history itself, Goldhagen inviting his reader to an imaginary (in the event, prurient, but that's as it may be), if emblematic encounter. The difference here, I believe, is between a conception of historical writing as a function of the understanding, in contrast to the conception that appears in the second, of history as a function of the will. Probably neither account is without some measure of what predominates in the other – but the difference in proportions is evident and, it seems to me, significant. Something in the way of an empirical test can be adduced here – in the prediction I would offer that readers for whom one of these passages carries conviction will be unmoved, even put off by the other. And insofar as this is true, the argument for historical 'styles' and thus also for history (including Holocaust history) as embodying variant conventions of genre becomes compelling. In these terms, then, also history aspires to the actuality of history – since in its formulations not only is there no guarantee of success (and often evidence of failure), but the possibility both of alternate emplotments or causal chains and of different *kinds* of these constructs.

It may be objected that in some sense all literary representation promises allegiance to history – this, because any representation of character or more largely, of human nature, will be measured by what is common and actual in human conduct. Even Aristotle's distinction between an impulse for the universal in poetry and for the particular in history leaves poetry still attached to history insofar as the universal *encompasses* the particular. Furthermore, the 'universal' in this relation can also at times re-enter history, striking as sharply and contingently as any more designedly historical moment. Think, for example, of Lear on the heath carrying the dead Cordelia, as that scene forced even the indomitable Samuel Johnson away from the magic of art and back into the rush and stress of history: 'I was many years ago so shocked by Cordelia's death, that I know not whether I ever endured to read again the last scenes of the play till I undertook to revise them as an editor.' It is impossible to believe that Johnson would have been comforted by a reminder that, after all, Cordelia didn't *really* die because she was 'only' part of a dramatic fiction.

We may be tempted to recall here that in order to make a place for Don Quixote and Gregor Samsa as well as for Lear, the imagination is required to supply much of the grist on which the mills of artistic laughter as well as pain depend. But even here the infringement by history on art does not quite cease. To say that *King Lear* (the drama) is about a king named Lear, or the novel *Don Quixote* about Don Quixote is to say very little, and even that much is misleading. But to say of *Badenheim 1939* that it is about the Holocaust is to say something both true and literarily essential to a reading of the novel, bringing to bear on its understanding extra-literary details of which the novel itself (aside from its title with its own patchwork history) offers hardly a hint.

It might be argued that just *because* of this aura of the text which on my account marks all the Holocaust genres – decisively in *Badenheim* and other works in the second group, but always to some extent – Holocaust writing as such turns out to have the features of a genre, albeit a minor one. The latter qualification precisely reflects – and attests to – that writing's dependence on history – another way, in terms of the account given here, of measuring the moral conditions to which Holocaust writing answers. Such a claim for the genre's minority status strikes more deeply, it should be evident, than the perhaps more typical and certainly more frequent abuses which run through much Holocaust writing of exploitative cant and sentimentality. (No doubt because of the subject, these seem more flagrant in Holocaust writing than elsewhere, but they do not differ in kind.) For Holocaust genres, the imagination is set within the limits of history – and it is constrained there by moral, not aesthetic and not simply historical conditions; they thus join, and for the same reason, other minor genres like the fable or the allegory.

A second objection to the account given might criticize its claims as obvious and, more damningly, trivial. Does not what I have been asserting amount, after all, to the simple tautology that 'Holocaust writing has the Holocaust as its subject'? But this formulation ignores or at least reduces my contention that more than *occasioning* Holocaust representations, the historical Holocaust serves also as their 'final cause', that it is integral to what they aim at *as history*. Arguably, no act of representation or expression occurs except in an extra-representational context; that is, against the background of what in an earlier and easier time would without embarrassment have been called reality. From this point of view, then, there would be nothing distinctive in what has been claimed about Holocaust writing. But the divisions and examples of that writing as I have cited them provide evidence not only that they originate in the Holocaust, but that they conclude there as well, by representing *it*, and doing so constantly under the shadow of a principle of historical authenticity. What stands as a plausible if risky conceit in Baudrillard's book, *The Gulf War Did Not Take Place*, would become something quite different if his title (and work) had instead invoked the Holocaust. This does not mean that 'Holocaust denial' can simply be legislated out of the artistic domain of Holocaust writing – but its absence from the long lists of Holocaust fiction is notable, and even more limited counterfactuals (like George Steiner's discovery of Hitler alive in South America or Anne Frank's escape to a New England village in Philip Roth's *The Ghost Writer*) tread on dangerous ground.

A final and still more serious objection might accept my account (for the sake of argument) and then move to an obvious implication: if Holocaust genres aspire to the condition of history, why would they not do better to *become* history (and their authors, then, historians)? One response to this has already been given: that history itself, even in its own terms, is not so readily actualized, as the differences between Hilberg and Goldhagen, for example, attest. A second response comes from the combination of disinclination and incapacity described in the answer given this question by Cynthia Ozick, herself with the powerful conscience of a Holocaust writer but a non-historian: that she *would* do history if she could but she – the novelist – simply cannot. And a third response, which I only whisper here, half-saying it, half-not, is that indeed (apart from the question of whether they are able to or not), they *should* keep history always before them. On the traditional aesthetic requirement of an internal relation between form and content, is it not plausible to contend that Holocaust, as subject or content, may be more responsive to certain forms – or genres – of expression than to others, and perhaps to some *not at all?*

The dangers of this last response are evident even in its most muted formulation. I don't think that it is exactly *entailed* by anything else I have said, but it obviously has been lurking around the edges. Let me take some of the edge off those edges, however, by suggesting why, if Holocaust genres do, as I have claimed, aspire to historical authenticity, that also *should* be the case. A shift, then, from form to norm, although based on two reasons which serve also as a directive for the Holocaust genres alluded to. The first of these is that the Holocaust *ought to* be written about – not only because it is aesthetically or historically evocative (although the evidence would argue for this as well), but because of a moral ground which also underlies those evocations. The second is that Holocaust writing has not been (and should not be) 'about' the Holocaust by way of the imaginative permutations to which it, like any historical event, is open – but because the events and character of the Holocaust require authenticity in its representation; that is, as history – not as historical or in the light of history or in the 'style' of history. And this, again, neither for aesthetic reasons – since art typically allows itself great latitude in the turns and twists it gives to history, with no possibility ruled out; nor for *merely* historical reasons, since then the Holocaust becomes but one item among an indefinite collection of data, perhaps placed – as it is in one encyclopedic version – between such alphabetically arranged entries as 'Holmes, Sherlock' on one side and the 'Holy Grail' on the other.[11]

Is there such a thing as 'mere' history? Yes and no – with both these characteristics affecting the aspiration of Holocaust writing. Yes, in the sense that for the basic historical unit of the chronicle, all events are equal (thus, mere). No, in the sense that to the moral element of truth ingredient even in 'mere' history is added the moral weight of certain particulars – the Holocaust, for one – which then has a voice, *should* have a voice in their subsequent representations. In this there is not equality but difference, and a difference basic enough to produce deformations when it is denied or overridden. From this perspective, the fact–value distinction celebrated in contemporary scientific and philosophical discourse appears as a fiction – an obvious one even in its own terms once we credit the question of whether the distinction itself is a fact or a value.

There are practical as well as principled dangers in the legislation adopted in a number of countries (Canada, France, Germany) of legally proscribing representations of the Holocaust which deny that any such event occurred. But the moral basis of such legislation is substantial – and it applies with only slight alteration, I should argue, not only to Holocaust denial but to Holocaust distortion, to Holocaust diminution, to Holocaust titillation, to Holocaust kitsch – examples of each of which are only too plentiful (some of them previously mentioned here). Even in the most objectionable of these works, however, the aspiration to historical authenticity is visible – dimly at times, at other times, even here, flagrantly. (Intention may have nothing to do with this; so, for example, the strong commitment to historicity of Holocaust denial, insofar as lying presupposes almost as strong a conception of truth as truth itself.) And, again, it is this impulse for historical reference, I have been suggesting, that *ought to* underwrite Holocaust discourse, with the standard by which it is then to be judged – a necessary if not sufficient condition – that of history as it sets limits for representations of the Holocaust. This, again, as fact and value are intertwined.

Let me bring this ascetic and meta- (in some ways anti-)aesthetic discourse to a suitably reactionary conclusion by citing two statements of testimony from (of all places) the brute world of chemistry. The first statement is by a purveyor of ironies who, so far as I have been able to determine, although living in its time, was largely untouched by the Holocaust – and whose venture into chemistry was that of an urgently curious layman; the second is by a writer who lived directly in the worlds of the Holocaust *and* of chemistry and who, furthermore, discovered a connection between them. So, first, Roland Barthes – as he rejects the standard accounts that claim the historical precedence of painting (or the aesthetic impulse more generally) as inspiration for the 'art' of photography with its indisputable realism: 'I say no, it was not the painters, it was the chemists ... [who] made it possible to recover the rays emitted by ... an object. The photograph is literally an emanation of the referent.'[12] And then, Primo Levi as he reflects on his decision to become a student of chemistry at a time when the impending Holocaust was for him already a presence: 'Chemistry led to the heart of Matter, and Matter was our ally precisely because the Spirit, dear to Fascism, was our enemy' ('Potassium'). 'The nobility of Man acquired in a hundred centuries of trial and error, lay in making himself the conqueror of matter ... and I enrolled in chemistry because I wanted to remain faithful to this nobility' ('Iron').[13]

You may by now anticipate the connection I would draw between these brief allusions to the hard science of chemistry and a science of the no less hard 'matter' of history – the direct touch or 'emanation of a referent' which I would argue is as directly implicated in Holocaust genres as it is, for Barthes, in the 'punctum' of photography. Certainly *The Periodic Table*, and even more severely, his more sustained memoirs of Auschwitz, reflect Levi's attempt to confront the Holocaust in its 'Matter' – that is, from the viewpoint of a chemist of history: laboratory-neutral, but bent fiercely to his analysis of stuff, with the Holocaust the scientific 'unknown' to be broken down into its elements. Indeed, I offer a correspondingly empirical test for the characterization of Levi's writing as chemical: Would it make a large or small or no difference to his readers if they should suddenly learn that his accounts of (or after) Auschwitz were not historically referential, chemical emanations – but imagined; that is, fictional? Surely, it is essential not only to their emotions but to their understanding, that the 'Matter' of his writing – what he alleges *to* have taken place – should in fact have occurred. If what he wrote had not been experience but imagined, the words of his text might not change in the slightest – but can there be any doubt of the difference it would make in the response to his work of his readers?

When added to the other examples cited earlier in this discussion, this glance at chemistry and matter through the eyes of Barthes and Levi underscores the general claim entered here for the historical character – in aspiration and actuality – of Holocaust genres. That account constitutes, I believe, a response (indeed, an answer) to a troublesome inheritance – the still-present anxiety bequeathed by Romanticism that art and its exemplars would not be able to survive the loss of their supposedly ahistorical transcendence. If ever there was a reason for taking matter (including the brute matter of history) seriously in itself and *not* merely as an occasion for moving on to a mystifying Other, surely the events of the Holocaust provide it – not because of the demands made by the writing of history for its own sake, but for the sake of that particular history and *its* demands, which, if not unique, are (I have been claiming) unequivocal.

There is no evidence in the array of Holocaust genres of their governance by an 'invisible hand' which has directed them to a single end of the sort outlined. Yet they exhibit (at times, despite themselves) a common extra-literary conscience – expressed if not in a single voice, with the fine coordination of a chorus. Accidents like this don't just happen, and it is a measure of retributive, although not always poetic justice that we should find in Holocaust genres a transitive principle – representation within the limits of history, history within the limits of ethics – which applies as a basis for judgment even when that judgement then proceeds to treat harshly some of the very works from which the principle itself derives. This is, I suggest, a lesson we can learn from the Holocaust by the *practice* of history rather than by moralizing *about* it. For without history's often narrow, prosaic, non-ironic, non-figurative foundation, visible emblematically in its most rudimentary genre, the much-maligned 'facts' of simple chronicle – who did what to whom and when – Holocaust writing and its genres, individually and collectively, would have been, and *be*, merely imagined. And that, I hope we might at this point agree, is unimaginable. Literally.

Notes

1   Emmanuel Ringelblum, *Notes from the Warsaw Ghetto*, translated and edited by Jacob Sloan (New York: Schocken, 1974); Adam Czerniakow, *The Warsaw Diaries of Adam Czerniakow*, edited by Raul Hilberg, Stanislaw Staron and Josef Kermisz (New York: Stein and Day, 1979); Lucjan Dobroszycki (ed.), *The Chronicle of the Lodz Ghetto 1941–1944* (New Haven: Yale University Press, 1984); Victor Klemperer, *Die unbewaltige Sprache: Aus dem Notizbuch eines Philologen* (Darmstadt: Melzer, 1966).

2   Benjamin Wilkomirski, *Fragments* (New York: Schocken, 1996).

3   Primo Levi, *Survival in Auschwitz* and *The Reawakening*, translated by Stuart Woolf (New York: Summit, 1985); Saul Friedlander, *When Memory Comes*, translated by Helen R. Lane (New York: Avon, 1979).

4   Leslie Epstein, *King of the Jews* (New York: Coward, McCann & Geoghehan, 1979); D.M. Thomas, *The White Hotel* (New York: Viking, 1981); Jean-François Steiner, *Treblinka*, translated by Helen Weaver (New York: Simon & Schuster, 1967); Thomas Kenneally, *Schindler's List* (New York: Simon & Schuster, 1982); Elie Wiesel, *Night*, translated by Stella Rodway (New York: Hill & Wang, 1961); Rolf Hochhuth, *The Deputy*, translated by Richard and Clara Winston (New York: Grove, 1964).

5   Ursula Hegi, *Stones from the River* (New York: Poseidon, 1994), unnumbered acknowledgements page.

6   Aharon Appelfeld, *Badenheim 1939*, translated by Dalya Bilu (Boston: D.R. Godine, 1980).

7   Gerald Reitlinger, *The Final Solution* (South Brunswick, NJ: T. Yoseloff, 1961); Raul Hilberg, *The Destruction of the European Jews* (Chicago: Quadrangle, 1961); Hannah Arendt, *Eichmann in Jerusalem: a Report on the Banality of Evil* (New York: Penguin, 1964); Martin Gilbert, *Atlas of the Holocaust* (New York: Pergamon, 1988); Saul Friedlander, *Pius XII and the Third Reich*, translated by Charles Fulham (New York: Octagon, 1980); Isaiah Trunk, *Judenrat* (New York: Macmillan, 1972); Robert J. Lifton, *The Nazi Doctors* (New York: Basic Books, 1986). For a selection of the original documents of the *Historikerstreit*, see James Knowlton and Truett Cates (eds), *Forever in the Shadow of Hitler?* (Atlantic Heights, NJ: Humanities Press, 1993).

8   Hayden White, *Metahistory: the Historical Imagination in Nineteenth-Century Europe* (Baltimore: Johns Hopkins University Press, 1974); Richard Rorty, 'Philosophy as a Kind of Writing,' *New Literary History* X (1978), pp. 141–60; Thomas Kuhn, *The Structure of Scientific Revolutions* (Chicago: University of Chicago Press, 1970).

9   Raul Hilberg, *The Destruction of the European Jews* (New York: Holmes & Meier, 1985), p. 411.

10 Daniel Jonah Goldhagen, *Hitler's Willing Executioners* (New York: Knopf, 1996), p. 339.

11 E.D. Hirsch, *The Dictionary of Cultural Literacy* (Boston: Houghton Mifflin, 1993).

12 Roland Barthes, *Camera Lucida*, translated by Richard Howard (New York: Hill & Wang, 1981).

13 Primo Levi, *The Periodic Table*, translated by Raymond Rosenthal (New York: Schocken, 1984).

2
Holocaust Writing in Context: Italy 1945–47

Robert S.C. Gordon

If, as Lawrence Langer has written, we are now passing from the 'province of historians of the event' into a phase of imagination and memory in postwar writing on the Holocaust, then part of the critic's task must be to chart the history of our imaginings and memories of the event.[1] One way to write such a history is to recapture the specific contexts within which Holocaust writings and their particular patterns of discourse have been formed, and to reread them in the light of those recovered contexts. Put negatively, this method works against a common tendency to detach Holocaust objects, historical or aesthetic, from the moment of their creation or production, and to be sensitive only to their immediate referent; in other words, to canonize them as transnational, ahistorical, as if thrown up fully formed by the Event. This essay analyses a small homogeneous field of early Italian writing on the Holocaust as a case study in the possible insights afforded by a non-canonical, context-sensitive approach.

The field in question consists in the 55 works in Italian which took as their main subject the experience of deportation to Nazi camps, published in book or pamphlet form between 1945 and 1947, written by Jewish, military and political deportees, or by journalists and novelists, both as direct testimony and fictionalized narrative.[2] Comparable figures for France, as established by Annette Wieviorka, were 'about a hundred [works published] between the liberation of Paris and the end of 1948' ('On Testimony', p. 26). Forty-seven of the 55 Italian works were published in 1945 and 1946, eight in 1947. Not a single text of this kind was published in 1948, and two or fewer in each subsequent year until 1959 (excluding translations and republications), indicating the extent of the sudden dropping away of interest in writing and reading about deportation and the war generally after 1948. Twelve of the 1945–7 texts are by or primarily about Jewish deportees (of which six are by or about women), 19 by or primarily about political deportees, and 11 by or about military internees.[3] Eight are translations. (The shortfall is made up of a number of hybrid texts which do not fit a single category, such as journalistic accounts, and works which I have not been able to consult.)

The only 'canonical' text in the corpus is Primo Levi's account of his deportation to Auschwitz-Monowitz, *Se questo è un uomo* (*If This is a Man*), first published in Turin in 1947. It is an implicit aim of my essay to set that extraordinary work into a largely unknown or forgotten contemporary context, in which many of the motifs of Levi's work find echoes. My primary aim, however, is broader: to examine the ways in which the very first written accounts in Italy of the Nazi camps came to terms with the literary-rhetorical and sociopolitical problems presented by undertaking such a task at such a time. Two areas of interest are particularly illuminated by focusing on such an early period following the war. First, we witness the laying of the seedbed of the 'genre', whether we call it Holocaust literature, literature of atrocity or *littérature concentrationnaire*. We see in embryonic and therefore often relatively unsubtle form the gamut of potential future problems and responses. Second, and in many ways in tension with the first area, we register the hiatus that exists between such early responses and the forms and qualities of Holocaust writing as it grew in its second wave from the mid/late 1950s onwards.[4] Indeed, the transnational, ahistorical canon of Holocaust writing referred to earlier is itself an historically specific symptom of the production, dissemination and reception of that second wave, and is therefore, perhaps, a particularly inapt basis for understanding the early responses.

The historical and cultural context of mid-1940s Italy is that of a devastated post-Fascist nation-in-the-remaking. Between 1943 and 1948, it experienced in rapid succession the fall of the 20-year Fascist régime, a double occupation, a mass anti-Nazi/Fascist Resistance and the building of a democratic, republican Italy around the history and myths of that Resistance, culminating in elections in April 1948.[5] At the same time, there was an extraordinary flowering of creative energy – in writing, visual arts and cinema – conventionally labelled as 'neo-realism', also with its roots and primary subject-matter in the Resistance.[6] The corpus of writings under scrutiny here have these contexts as pressing conditions for their formation, interwoven with and overlaying their function as deportation narratives. And the periodization only goes to underscore the point: the continuity between Resistance (1943–45) – when, among other things, all deportation from Italy took place – and reconstruction (1945–48) indicates that for this period at least, experience and narration or memory belong to the same story. To use Langer's phrase again, the 'province of historians' has not yet been entered. At the same time, deportation is experienced by most of the victims as a traumatic expulsion from the contexts described here, an isolating discontinuity standing against the continuity of collective experience of war and reconstruction. The five features of the corpus discussed and illustrated below come together in this negotiation between contextual continuity and subjective discontinuity. We might say that the desire for context and the fear of its loss are already built into the texts themselves.

Before proceeding to the texts, a cautionary note is necessary: in quantitative terms this corpus is substantial, but production is only one side of the coin. The readership of these texts was very restricted, and their impact minimal, and this aspect too is part of their specificity and their history.[7] Almost all were published by very small, local or politically sponsored publishers, often largely for the benefit of intimate circles of family, acquaintances and fellow survivors. Print runs very rarely exceeded a few hundred. This contrasts with the significant investment in other war and anti-fascist chronicles by the major publishing houses: for example, the Turinese publisher Einaudi sold over 6,000 copies of the then unknown Italo Calvino's first novel, about the Resistance, *Il sentiero dei nidi di ragno* (*The Path of the Spiders' Nests*) in 1947; in the same year, Einaudi turned down Levi's *If This is a Man*.[8] One major publisher, the Milanese Arnoldo Mondadori, did enter the market in 1947, however, so that although there were only eight texts in the year, three of them were published by Mondadori and thus enjoyed substantially greater circulation.[9]

1. Deportation, resistance and the modes of neo-realism

Deportation is experienced in large measure in these texts as resistance truncated. The camp inmate shapes his identity and strategy for survival by holding on to his identity as partisan.[10] Strenuous attempts are made by political deportees in particular to integrate their experience with stories of the Resistance, to draw lines of continuity between the two experiences, and thereby to legitimate themselves – in the postwar context – as contributing actors in the founding of the new Italy. Some of these strategies are simply lexical: Bruno Vasari's 1945 account *Mauthausen bivacco della morte* uses in its title a term – bivouac – which immedately evokes partisan life in the mountainous terrain of Northern Italy. Mauthausen is the natural, or rather unnatural extension of that earlier survival test.[11] Part of Gaetano De Martino's account, *Dal carcere di San Vittore ai 'lager' tedeschi*, amounts to an anthology of Resistance stories as inmates in Milan's infamous San Vittore prison exchange accounts of how they were caught, betrayed, beaten and tortured: 'everyone had their own "story" *(storia)* to tell'.[12] The exchange of stories and the self-effacing giving of voice to others is a key feature of continuity between forms of narrating the two experiences, Resistance and deportation. But if the communal exchange of stories suggests a mutually reinforcing strength derived from the overlap between deportation and Resistance, there is also a quality of uneasiness and anxiety, as evinced by a defensive or over-wrought rhetoric. The following are typical examples:

> I kept thinking of our work left unfinished, of our disgraced Country *(Patria)*, trodden beneath enemy boots.

> A Hero is not only one who enthusiastically gives up his life for his Country *(Patria)*, but also someone who bears up to suffering and privations of all kinds with strength and pride.

> We felt the scent of victory as we marched in the concentration camps just as our partisans felt it as they marched and gathered around the bivouac fires.

> This book intends to make a contribution towards the rebuilding of our Nation *(Patria)*; whilst urging Italians never to forget the Nazi-Fascist scourge ... it wishes to contribute as a document of truth to the struggle for liberty.[13]

There is a form of threatened national identity on display here which recurs again and again in the narratives of deportation. It is particularly striking in the strange, persistent obsession with describing and characterizing the different nationalities in the camps, and with the poor treatment commonly meted out to Italians.[14] The fear implicit in these turns of patriotism is the fear of delegitimation, of exclusion from the 'heroic' war memory of the *Patria,* and from the projection of Resistance memory which will form the very foundations of the new Italy. In the final quotation above, Francesco Ulivelli's socialist publisher makes this clear even at the price of playing down, or at least relativizing, the importance of the testimonial role of Ulivelli's work.

If deportees write their histories using the model of the partisan, it should come as no suprise that they also adopt the narrative and representational strategies of the dominant modes of postwar Resistance writing, the modes of neo-realism. In an influential 1978 essay, Maria Corti established a link between the clandestine Resistance, with its approximately 2,300 different flysheets and pamphlets all with space dedicated to narrative accounts of partisan action, and neo-realist writing after the war. Corti pointed to a new kind of narrative – on the ground, intimate with its readers (with whom it is exchanging stories rather than narrating *ex cathedra*), often self-effacing or anonymous (and thus exemplary in some way), interested in fact and record rather than style or beauty. She also pointed to new modes of writing – localized, with actions and events left to speak for themselves, oral and colloquial language, brevity (notes, fragments, diary entries, intercalated stories, reportage).[15] Almost all of these qualities of narrative and writing also emerge in the deportation literature, sometimes to similar effect, but at other times twisted in their implications by the extraordinary nature of the camp system. In particular, the imperative to record the unimagined depth of the horrors witnessed in the camps lays particular emphasis on the anti-aesthetic claims made by several authors and prefators and shared by partisan-narrators.[16]

A powerful example of a deportee who adopts the modes of neo-realistic writing is Enzo Rava who describes the night following his arrest thus:

> The police station; a filthy cell; they beat me so hard I don't know what's going on any more; I flop down. In a corner someone huddles up. One of the two X crushed my finger with the rifle butt, I'd put my hand on the car door, on a bend, he thought I was trying an escape. For this they beat me up. An awful night.

And then later in the camps, he maintains the same curt, lapidary style:

> Showers. The usual drill. The usual fierce attack. They look at our mouths; do they think there's some gold still left?... Naked in the shower. They give us some rags; a treat ... But in the shower there's always someone bent double from the blows of their rubber canes.[17]

Alba Valech Capozzi writes in a vein which, recalling several of the more experimental neo-realist writers such as Elio Vittorini, embraces the fragmented, modernist potential of this same clipped style. Her memoirs hover between the banal and the poetic:

> The officer started screaming.
> I took fright, but nothing came of it.
> New lorries arrived.
> New tears, news blows, new victims, new insults.
> A soldier had punched me too, and mother too.
> Suddenly a dog sneaked into the hall. It was panting, tongue hanging out. It rushed towards the group of selected Jews, whined, wagged its tail, pawed joyously up at the skirt of its owner.
> A violent kick knocked it to the ground.[18]

All the qualities of writing suggested by Corti are here, as incidentally are echoes of the well-documented influence of contemporary American writers (such as Hemingway, Dos Passos and Faulkner) on the neo-realist generation. Enea Fergnani even provides us with an echo of the neo-realist 'text' *par excellence*, Roberto Rossellini's 1945 film *Rome Open City*: Rossellini's priest Don Pietro (Aldo Fabrizi) pronounces his final lines as he faces the Nazi firing squad: 'it's far harder to live well than to die well'; Fergnani, awaiting deportation to Fossoli and then Mauthausen, meditates 'It's not enough to know how to die, you have to know how to live ... to suffer in order not to die' (*Un uomo*, p. 65). Below we shall see in another context how a related fundamental centre of interest of neo-realism recurs in new light in deportation literature: the nature and definition of man, 'l'uomo'.

2. Genre

The contemporary specificity of the responses to deportation is one key form of context, but other contexts, other histories also impinge. The deportation texts must also be examined for their refashioning of traditional or conventional literary-stylistic forms, since, as Jay Winter has convincingly argued with reference to the First World War, deeply traumatic personal and collective experience stimulates as much a return to traditional responses to loss as it provides an impulse to newly traumatized and unfamiliar forms (although for the latter see section 3 below).[19] Examples of recourse to literary genre and to conventional forms of rhetoric litter these texts, even those which proudly proclaim their anti-literary quality, and in several instances, this provides a subtle means to an intuition of the nascent problems of representation of the Nazi concentration-camp system. Three examples will suffice to illustrate the strategies connected to genre. First, perhaps the most common generic traditional echo is of traditional representations of Hell, and in particular Dante's *Inferno*. Gino Valenzano, for example, entitles his work *L'inferno di Mauthausen* and, perhaps coincidentally, has 34 chapters, the same number of cantos as in Dante's *Inferno*, but otherwise makes little use of the analogy; several texts compare the entry into the camps to the passage through the gates of Hell, with its inscription 'Abandon every hope, who enter here'.[20] Aldo Pantozzi goes on to make the following direct comparison, which is typical of the use made of Dante to draw a line between literary imagination and reality: 'Dante's imagination relegated scenes such as these to the entrails of hell: it has taken six centuries of civilization for them to be removed from the infernal dark up into the sunlight by Nazi barbarity' (*Sotto gli occhi*, p. 68).

Wieviorka ('On Testimony', p. 32), referring to the work of Jacqueline Risset, notes that most references to Dante in Holocaust writing, with the remarkable exception of Primo Levi,[21] are less to a work of literature than to an archetypal imagined place, a correlative of the real camps which rhetorically amplifies the portrayal of the latter. Pantozzi and others confirm this. The generic text thus stands in metonymically for the generic place, which, however, is by definition a non-place, a beyond. In an Italian context there is, of course, a further, cultural act of distinction and authority inherent in the citation of Dante (again bound up with anxiety about legitimation and even about national identity) and this overlays the echo of the universal archetype of Hell at every turn.[22]

A less common convention tapped by a handful of writers is the poetry and prayer genres associated with funerary monuments, canonized in Italy, and bound up with fundamental issues of civility and national identity, through Ugo Foscolo's 1807 poem *Dei sepolcri* (*On Tombs*). It is self-evident that many of the deportation texts act as funerary memorials for those who did not return. Valech Capozzi uses the epigraph to her account to tap into the genre:

> O pitiful traveller who passes through the tragic land of Auschiwitz [sic] in the melancholy night, when you hear in the silence, in the rustling of the trees, a quiet still murmur, stop and pray.
> It is the moaning of so many suffering shadows for the thousands

and thousands of wounds of their martyrdom, it is the still voice of millions and millions of restless ghosts who wander in uneasy search for their dear ones.

Now that the hideous flames no longer glow in the dark nights, and that the perfume of the fields has stretched a veil of oblivion over so many innocent, tortured bodies, may your prayer, o pitiful traveller, assuage the offence and soothe the torment of those pained souls. (Valech Capozzi, *A24049*, p. 1)

Primo Levi, too, famously, had recourse to the poetry of prayer as a model for the epigraph for *If This is a Man*, ironically refashioning the daily prayer of Judaism in his poem 'Shemà'.

A final genre convention used to particularly interesting effect in one text in particular is the novelistic conceit of the found manuscript. The text, called *A Buchenwald Notebook*, is deeply enigmatic: it is presented by a certain Valentino di San Marzano (whose status is unclear in the text, and whose identity I have been unable to establish) who tells of how a mysteriously silent Russian man, Charles Cohen, in his care after the war, left him a pile of notes on his recovery and departure: 'I picked up the various sheets of paper from the floor. Where were they from? Who had written them? Translating and reordering them was no easy task ... They were pages of life and of terror.... The traveller had come from Buchenwald.'[23] The fragmentary notebook goes on to weave a meditation on writing and memory into a narrative of love and deportation, beginning in a Parisian 'pension' reminiscent of Balzac (another genre-piece perhaps), and ending in the Kapo Mitia's cell. Mitia has killed someone else using Charles's name – 'yesterday I died' (p. 30) – and kept Charles hidden, even given him paper to write these notes, in exchange for French lessons. What is particularly striking in the use of the convention of the found manuscript is its uncanny pertinence to the situation of the deportee: as many writers and historians have noted, writing in the camps was all but impossible, certainly for the non-privileged prisoners, including almost all Jews, and this in itself created in many the desperate impulse to write so soon after liberation. Charles's access to pen and paper gives him access to a level of self-knowledge, or acknowledgment of self-forgetting, but only through the absurd whim of Mitia, himself a victim. His rediscovery of writing, like the discovery of the manuscript by Valentino, is a return to selfhood and history but also an horrific turn to their dissolution.

3. Crises in self and writing

The aspects of deportation writing highlighted thus far have tended to draw lines of continuity between this corpus and other forms of writing. But as has been clear throughout, all these lines are drawn in a surrounding field of stark discontinuity and loss: these texts demonstrate the immediate confrontation with the aporia of the world of the various deportation camps, the traumatic crises in selfhood, in representational language, and in both phenomenal and narrative space and time brought about by the camp system. In other words, we are confronted with direct intuitions of many if not all of the range of problems at stake in Holocaust literature. Selected texts can be taken to illustrate briefly four of the different forms of loss which are mourned here.

Cohen's text, for all its generic framing, dwells more than anything on such crises: the narrator is lost to himself, physically and psychically, as when he notes the complete absence of mirrors in the camps, and therefore literally and metaphorically of self-recognition: 'If I touch my face I feel I am touching death ... no-one would recognize me, not even myself. My looks have changed, crumbled from within, like a grand old palace that has become a tomb' (Cohen, *Notebook*, p. 11). Enzo Rava's protagonist shares the sentiment, in his less elaborate language: 'The word "I", "me", is so strange. It feels strange somehow. I am not conscious any more; I don't think any more, I don't think' (Rava, *Martirio*, p. 69).

Cohen's collapsing self also intuits, even as the experience unfolds, the central role to be played by a shattered memory as it will emerge again and again in later works of testimony: 'These lapses of memory are terrifying, I look on my past as though it were a vast plain seen from a flight over windswept banks of cloud' (Cohen, *Notebook*, p. 32).

The loss of self and memory is accompanied, or even preceded by a loss of language: if Rava feels estranged by the single word 'I', many are traumatized further by the senselessness or slippage of all language. To take one example of many: 'Work, hunger, cold, illness, death. They aren't the same words for us as they were before coming to Germany. Here work, hunger, cold, illness, death mean torture, massacre, torment; or worse, hatred, cruelty, violence' (Fergnani, *Un uomo*, p. 188). Once again, it is worth noting in passing how very close indeed this comes to Primo Levi's assertion, 'our way of being cold has need of a new word. We say "hunger", we say "tiredness", "fear", "pain", we say "winter" and they are different things. They are free

words created and used by free men who lived in comfort and suffering in their homes'. Levi typically adds a touch of ironic wisdom in
the last phrase to qualify the point he shares with Fergnani, and this
may be taken as emblematic of what he shares with and what distinguishes him from most of the writers under consideration here.[24]

In other instances, it is not only the loss of the mechanics of
language and its processes of signification, but a more essential frac-
ture in the chain of meaning itself. As Aldo Bizzarri notes in his acute
analytical meditation on his deportation experience, *Mauthausen
Hermetic City*:

> What sense is there to this story?... The reply is *no sense, no reason.*
> That goes for everything at Mauthausen, it is absurd to search for a
> thread of connection, for a logic ... The only fixed point in the
> landscape, behind the constantly changing absurdities of each day,
> is death.... Indeed, as author my task was not so much to show
> how one might have survived it as to recall that everyone was there
> to die.[25]

Bizzarri's emphasis on death as the beginning and end of the camp
world delineates sharply the dark ontology of that world. It also
implicitly acts as a corrective to the very notion of survival and
survival narrative as the dominant model of Holocaust writing, anticipating a key problem of Holocaust representation still at the heart of
its theory and practice (*Schindler's List*).

4. Discourse and narrative: forms of writing

In response to such obstacles, the forms of writing produced vary a
great deal, but the variety seems to address fundamentally the same
issue: how to transmit the experience in all its strangeness – not so
much its unspeakable nature (although such metaphors are much in
evidence), as its unbearable and incomprehensible nature. As we have
seen already, one response to the problem was, at least apparently, to
eschew all style and to reject any notion of literary effect and indeed
of psychology[26] in favour of discursive forms of writing such as analysis, chronicle or history.[27] Others, however, moved in quite different
directions. Many noted, and indeed included in their texts documents, photographs, references to newsreels and newspaper reports
which in themselves served the function of 'proof' or record, explicitly
or implicitly setting up the written accounts as serving some other,

complementary, purpose.[28] The text has the status of something imagined and condensed, in other words of something literary.[29] Rava is, as usual, eloquent on this:

> From the very first days when documents arrived – films, newsreels, radio, official accounts, rumours – it was clear that no human word could speak the horror of the Nazi camps. No number. For several decades perhaps all we shall have will be the camp names, laden by now in all our minds with a sense of horror and anguish.... Hence again the need to get away from the strictly documentary, the need to look on as if from within one of those who suffered those horrors.
>
> Hence the somewhat novelized (*romanzata*) form of the account, a story rather than a report. (Rava, *Martirio*, p. 6)

Frida Misul's studiedly overwrought account of her own deportation to Auschwitz, written with a deliberate sneering or sarcastic tone, takes Rava's intuition – that an aesthetic or at least narrative account comes closer to the unreality of the experience than any document – into her paradoxical subtitle: *The Most Novelesque of Realities The Most Realistic of Novels.*[30] It is worth connecting this notion of a narrative form apt to contain testimony with the tendency mentioned earlier for these texts to contain multiple narratives within them. Acts such as storytelling, anecdote, dialogue are the key means to preserving a sense of subjectivity, of distinction amongst the prisoners in a system of undifferentiated (on an individual level at least) persecution. For if suffering produces solidarity and unity (De Martino, *Dal carcere*, pp. 6, 161; Da Prati, *Triangolo*, p. 207), it also is experienced as a leveller, a destroyer of differences in identity. Rava speaks apologetically of the 'monotony' of the inmates' stories, whose experiences were broadly repetitive and undergone by thousands of others (Rava, *Martirio*, p. 5).

The paradox emerging here is that fiction, fantasy, or at least something more than record, serves better to recall and communicate than bare fact.[31] It is at the root of Rava's careful choice of a fictional protagonist for his otherwise sourced and chronicled text; it is similarly at the root of the forced, but fascinating self-distancing undertaken by Don Paolo Liggeri at the outset of his memoir *Triangolo rosso*:

> These are the memories of a friend, a very dear friend whom I love as myself and who – by a strange coincidence! – is called Paolo like

me, was arrested with me and stuck close by me throughout the stages of our imprisonment until we returned home. A brotherly love, cemented by our common suffering, has brought our souls so close together that even I, rereading these pages, feel I am reading my own words.

Some of you will smile and think of a literary device (*finzione letteraria*). I shall not even try to convince you otherwise....

Now my friend Paolo is no longer with me, I have no idea where he has ended up.... But at least he left me these pages: so that if any reader still thinks that he's just a literary device, and that these are my own memories, so be it, for Paolo and I are but one and the same. (Liggeri, *Triangolo*, p. 7ff.)

Liggeri's awkward confession-cum-disavowal speaks volumes about the precarious status of narrative and selfhood in the face of putting his experiences into a narrated form.

The recourse to 'finzione letteraria', to forms of *récit*, is at the root of the two key test cases in our corpus, Aldo Bizzarri and Giancarlo Ottani, the former an academic and deportee, the latter a journalist. Bizzarri and Ottani stand out in the corpus because they both wrote two separate accounts of the camps, one factual or analytical and the other fictional. Ottani is interesting for his failures and forcings, rather than for any out-of-the-ordinary insights. His work of record, *Un popolo piange*, was the first full account of the Italian-Jewish experience of deportation,[32] and it quotes extensively from primary and secondary sources from press, anecdotes, histories of Jews and of Jews in Italy and other reportage. It is a genuine anthology, written in what he declares as a 'rapid, summary, journalistic style' (p. 5), although it is not without its passionate rhetoric in parts. Its accuracy can be judged by Ottani's final estimate of Jews killed in Europe – 5.5 million. His novel, *I campi della morte*, also published in 1945 (with an epigraph from Hillel used much later also by Primo Levi: 'If I do not help myself who will help me / And if not now when?'), tells the story of a well connected Swiss-Zionist hero and his lover Myriam as the racial laws are passed in Italy in 1938: they are gradually forced into hiding, then arrested and deported, although both survive. *I campi della morte* fails as a novel because it remains dominated by discursive forms of writing: conversations are often set-piece expositions (of Zionism, the war, the camps, key events such as the massacre at the Fosse Ardeatine, and so on), usually narrated by ciphers whom the hero Anthony encounters along the way. In other words, the tension between historical discourse and narrative, *discours* and *récit*,[33] is unresolved on the level of structure and of style, and this creates a sense of detachment precisely where it is unsustainable, in a centred narrative.

Bizzarri, the actual survivor, offers a very different pair of texts indeed. His 'factual' account, *Mauthausen città ermetica*, declares largely similar aims to Ottani's, 'sobriety', 'a dutiful documentary synthesis' (p. 5). But in practice this is a work of sociological analysis, focused more sharply than any other work of this period on the 'system', and as a result a vessel of acute insight into the dynamics of this sealed city. There is personal record and naming and recounting of others here, and the author declares at the end of his strikingly analytical text that writing it has been 'like breaking free from a night-mare: catharsis' (p. 109), but there is also a reserve derived from an understanding that actions in Mauthausen do not directly define their agents, they are not apt for judgement: 'man at Mauthausen was man deformed' (p. 92). When Bizzarri turns to fiction, to complement his analytical/memorial work, he goes further than any other writer of the period again. His 1947 novel, *Proibito vivere*, is a sort of *Decameron* of the camps, set in an unspecified camp in late summer and then winter 1944. On successive Sundays, a group of eight prisoners, from differ-ent countries and backgrounds, take to telling each other stories, just as Boccaccio's brigade tell each other stories to escape from the plague of Florence. Here, however, each meeting is precarious and dangerous, and indeed as the novel proceeds fewer and fewer come to the Sunday gatherings, as the group members are either moved on or killed. The stories are intended as diversions, and they do indeed range widely over genre and tone and setting, but they are constantly and increas-ingly drawn into analogous relationship with the narrators' present situation. Themes such as solitude and dependency, desire for life, fear and violence, time and its measuring out, love, death, and so on resonate in the stories, despite the apparently eclectic, ordinary setting and tone of each. And the lines of continuity are directly evoked by the maverick of the group, Costantino, who finds himself unable to tell diverting stories: instead Costantino writes down his thoughts, and writes them as mournful poetry.

Bizzarri's rich diptych opens up avenues for the fictional represen-tation of the Event without trivializing or schematizing, by using character and characterization in a limited, context-dependent fashion, akin to a Lukácsian realist typology: his fictional narrators are individualized through their 'fictional' *récits* and through the fragments of their 'real' histories which emerge, but the status and meaning of themselves as narrators are wholly determined by their position as concentration-camp inmates. The strength of this balance allows for a literary, often fantastic elaboration without a concomitant diminishing of insight into historical fact. The same dynamic characterizes the (few) successful fictional works which tackled the subject of deportation in these years, of which perhaps the most important was Eduardo De Filippo's extraordinary play *Napoli milionaria* (1945).[34] De Filippo's protagonist, the Neapolitan deportee Gennaro, is a figure, a type of the traumatized Italian returning to find his family and world turned morally upside down and uninterested in his tales of horror from the camps. Gennaro acts as a vessel for a merged vision of national, moral and individual identity in deep crisis, and thus achieves the implicit purpose of so many of the deportation writers noted above, a merging of the experience of deportation with the collective experience of war, occupation, 'liberation' and reconstruction. Indeed, in *Napoli milionaria*, the deportee becomes not the excluded but rather the privileged figure of the national narrative of the years 1943 to 1945 and beyond.

5. Gender

A final area to emerge strikingly in the corpus of texts under examination here is one apparently only obliquely related to the central issues at stake, but which is in reality an intense point of conjunction of many of those other issues: the issue is that of definitions and experiences of gender identity. It was noted earlier that all the 19 major political deportees in the corpus were male, but that of the Jewish-centred texts, half were by women: indeed, of the first-person accounts by Jewish authors in this period, only one, Primo Levi's, is by a man, and five are by women.[35] The historical reasons for this are self-evident – all Jewish women and children were deported as a matter of course (although there were, of course, women Resistance fighters deported also) – but it has an interesting impact on the field of writing, since, with due caution taken over simplistic gender-specific readings, differences of emphasis in these women's writing can be discerned. For example, the issue of national identity is less prominent, as is the tension between soldierly heroism and submission to the camp system; group identities and dynamics loom large as the narratives focus on friendships, childbirth, exchanges and intimate human interrelation and mother–daughter bonds more than strategy and trickery for survival; finally, there is a notable difference in response to the humiliation of the body, to nudity (Tedeschi, *Questo poveso corpo*, pp. 11–20) and sexual degradation in particular. An adequate treatment of these often extraordinary works – Millu and Tedeschi, especially, deserve greater recognition – is not possible here, except to acknowledge the subtlety of their responses to their doubly distinct conditions of imprisonment (as Jews and as women) and also to register certain modes of writing and memory of deportation.

The works by Jewish women stand also in interesting counterpoint to a recurrent, even obsessive – and again apparently gendered – refrain of many of the other texts, one which also synthesizes the problematics of identity, the split from Resistance heroic action and neo-realist writing, and the generic challenge of traditional war literature: the search for a definition of mankind, or simply of man. The titles of Levi's *If This is a Man* and Gino Gregori's *Ecce Homo Mauthausen* are only two of dozens of evocations of and meditations on the term 'uomo'. We have already seen Bizzarri's view of the deportee as 'man deformed'; Camilla Revera, in her preface to Nissim and Lewinska (*Donne*, p. 12), turns the term against the enemy, 'those men who are no longer men (*uomini non più uomini*), the Nazis'; and with a different emphasis again, others see in the camps the uncovering of the essence of Hobbesian man, 'L'uomo lupo all'uomo' (Valech Capozzi, *A24029*, pp. 7–28). This focus takes us back to the affinities of these texts with contemporary neo-realist literature since there too the same refrain is also to be found again and again, in texts such as Elio Vittorini's *Conversazione in Sicilia* (*Conversation in Sicily*) (1938/9) and *Uomini e no* (*Men and Not Men*) (1945) and Carlo Levi's *Cristo si è fermato a Eboli* (*Christ Stopped at Eboli*) (1945). The self-defining, responsible, humane and heroic individual – but also the perhaps suppressed model of the strong Fascist 'man' defined by struggle – is lost, and so too are the archetypal narrative, textual means of representing 'him'. As Tzvetan Todorov has argued,[36] the Holocaust dealt a fatal blow to such received notions of heroism and manhood. The emphases of female authors such as Millu and Tedeschi powerfully underscore the failure of such models – as indeed does the anxiety evident in the persistent return of the term itself.

Examining the field of Holocaust and deportation writing in Italy between 1945 and 1947 gives us an opportunity to recover a very distinct and important phase of response to Nazi oppression.

Although marginal in terms of geography and, relatively, in terms of numbers, the Italian experience of these events threw up a substantial, and substantially ignored body of work in the immediate postwar years. It is work which knows nothing of the canonical criteria of value in judging Holocaust 'literature' as they will be forged over the subsequent decades, which is written as much in a line of continuity with the experience related as in horrific retrospective contemplation of it. It is unfinished business. As such, we commit an error of perspective if we read it as we might read later configurations of the Event, themselves in equally distinct historical relation to their particular referents and contexts. Indeed, we commit an error of this kind as long as we apply an exclusively aesthetic judgement to these works of, or rather in history. Within them, the sociopolitical reality of Italy's reconstruction (and hence of its Fascist past), the cultural energy of a certain mainstream literary current and patterns of genre traditions overlay and interact with intuitions of the specificity of Nazi violence and its aporia. The tools of literary criticism find their most appropriate contribution to Holocaust understanding when used historiographically, to excavate these layers of our historical imaginings.

Notes

1 Lawrence Langer, *Admitting the Holocaust* (New York and Oxford: Oxford University Press, 1995), p. 13.
2 My research was greatly facilitated by the work of Anna Bravo and Daniele Jalla, *Una misura onesta. Gli scritti di memoria della deportazione dall'Italia 1944–1993 (An Honest Measure. Written Memories of Deportation in Italy 1944–1993)* (Milan: FrancoAngeli, 1994) and by the help of the 'Centro di documentazione ebraica' in Milan. Important analogous work on French deportation writing in the immediate postwar period has been done by Annette Wieviorka, *Déportation et génocide (Deportation and Genocide)* (Paris: Plon, 1992) and 'On Testimony', in Geoffrey Hartman (ed.), *Holocaust Remembrance: The Shapes of Memory* (Oxford and Cambridge, MA: Blackwell, 1994), pp. 23–32.
3 Estimates vary but, approximately, there were 8,800 Jewish deportees from Italy; 35,000 political (i.e. Resistance) deportees; and 600,000 Italian army conscripts interned by the Nazis in Italy and elsewhere. Treatment of each group was, of course, very different indeed, but it was precisely a feature of early accounts not to differentiate between genocidal and other forms of deportation.
4 The 1945–7 corpus might already be considered to be a a second wave if one takes those who wrote *during* the war, such as the Warsaw Ghetto chroniclers, as a first wave. For the crescendo of interest, in Italy as elsewhere, in the 1950s and early 1960s, roughly from the publication of Anne

Frank's *Diary* (1954 in Italy) until the Eichmann trial in 1961, see Bravo and Jalla, *Una misura onesta*, pp. 66–72.

5 For a good historical account, see Paul Ginsborg, *A History of Contemporary Italy* (Harmondsworth: Penguin, 1990), pp. 8–120.

6 For a summary account of neo-realism, see John Gatt-Rutter, 'Neo-realism', in Peter Brand and Lino Pertile (eds), *The Cambridge Companion to Italian Literature* (Cambridge: Cambridge University Press, 1997), pp. 535–52.

7 Wieviorka, 'On Testimony', p. 26, contrasts this feature with the equivalent 'survivor's accounts' of the Great War, which found a ready readership of millions of former soldiers. The ignoring of survivor's testimony is thematized by several survivor narratives; for example, Levi, in his identification with Coleridge's Ancient Mariner: one example of many is the title of his collected poems, *At an uncertain hour* (see Primo Levi, *Collected Poems*, London: Faber & Faber, 1988).

8 Levi published his book privately with Editore De Silva in Turin, with a relatively generous print run of 2,500 (1900 were either sold or given away). For Levi and Calvino sales figures, see Bruno Falcetto, 'Se questo non è un classico' ('If this is not a classic'), *L'Indice dei libri dei mese*, XIV, 4, April 1997, p. 7. Ettore Siegrist, *Dachau. Dimenticare sarebbe una colpa* (*Dachau: To Forget Would be a Crime*) (Genoa: Sampierdarena/Stab. grafici Federico Rale, 1945) complains he was turned down by all the major publishers (p. 1). Others, such as Bruno Piazza, were never published in their lifetime: Piazza died in 1946, but his account was only published in 1956: Bruno Piazza, *Perché gli altri dimenticano* (*Because Others Forget*) (Milan: Feltrinelli, 1956).

9 The three published by Mondadori were Aldo Bizzarri, *Proibito vivere* (*Living is Not Permitted*); Anna Seghers, *La settima croce* (*The Seventh Cross*), translated from German; and Ernst Wiechert, *La selva dei morti* (*The Wood of the Dead*) (all Milan: Mondadori, 1947).

10 See Bravo and Jalla, *Una misura onesta*, pp. 17ff.

11 Bruno Vasari, *Mauthausen, bivacco della morte* (*Mauthausen: Bivouac of Death*) (Florence: La Giuntina, 1991; first edition Milan: La Fiaccola, 1945). All translations are my own unless otherwise stated.

12 Gaetano De Martino, *Dal carcere di San Vittore ai 'lager' tedeschi* (*From San Vittore Prison to the German Camps*) (Milan: La Prora, 1955; first edition Milan: Ed. Alaya, 1945), p. 18. I am grateful to John Foot for showing me his unpublished article on San Vittore prison, 'The Tale of San Vittore. Prisons, Politics, Crime and Fascism in Milan, 1943–1946' (forthcoming).

13 From, respectively, Siegrist, *Dachau*, p. 9; Gino Valenzano, *L'inferno di Mauthausen (come morirono 5000 deportati italiani)* (*The Hell of Mauthausen (How 5000 Italian Deportees Died)*) (Turin: SAN, 1945), pp. 109–10; Francesco Ulivelli, *Bolzano: anticamera della morte* (*Bolzano: Antechamber of Death*) (Milan: Edizioni Stellissima, 1946), p. 9 and Preface. See also the Preface to one of the military internees' publications, Marcello Tomadini, *Venti mesi fra i reticolati* (*Twenty Months Behind Barbed Wire*) (Vicenza: Edizione Sat, 1946).

14 For example, see Siegrist, *Dachau*, pp. 143–51; Enea Fergnani, *Un uomo e tre numeri* (*A Man and Three Numbers*) (Milan-Rome: Ed. Avanti!, 1955; first edition Milan: Speroni, 1945), p. 163; Alberto Cavaliere, *I campi della morte*

in Germania nel racconto di una sopravvissuta (*The German Deathcamps in the Account of a Woman Survivor*) (Milan: Casa Editrice Sonzogno, 1945), pp. 91–2. It is interesting to note how some surveys of categories of prisoner find a place for Jews, whereas some ignore the Jews as a specific group altogether.

15   Maria Corti, *Il viaggio testuale* (Turin: Einaudi, 1978), pp. 25–110.

16   See, for example, Valenzano, *L'inferno*, p. 5.

17   Enzo Rava, *Martirio* (*Martyrdom/Torture*) (Genoa: Casa Editrice Mario Ceva, 1945), pp. 14, 68.

18   Alba Valech Capozzi, *A 24029* (Siena: Soc. An. Poligrafica, 1946), p. 22.

19   Jay Winter, *Sites of Memory, Sites of Mourning. The Great War in European Cultural History* (Cambridge: Cambridge University Press, 1995), p. 5 and *passim*. It should be noted that Winter, pp. 8–10, 228–9, discourages analogies between World Wars One and Two in this respect.

20   'Lasciate ogni speranza voi ch'entrate', *Inferno* III, 9, in the version by Allen Mandelbaum, Dante Alighieri, *The Divine Comedy* (London: Everyman's Library, 1995). Examples of references to the gates of Hell in the texts under scrutiny here include Aldo Pantozzi [8078-126520], *Sotto gli occhi della morte. Da Bolzano a Mauthausen* (*In Death's Gaze: From Bolzano to Mauthausen*) (Bolzano: Tip. Pio Mariz, 1946), p. 43; and Giancarlo Ottani, *I campi della morte* (*The Death Camps*) (Milan: Perinetti Casoni, 1945), p. 143. Cavaliere, *I campi* and Fergnani, *Un uomo*, both refer to another area of Dante's Hell, the Malebolge.

21   On Levi and Dante, see, for example Lynn Gunzberg, 'Down Among the Dead Men: Levi and Dante in Hell', *Modern Language Studies*, 16, 1986, pp. 10–28; and 'Nuotando altrimenti che nel Serchio: Dante as Vademecum for Primo Levi', in S. Tarrow (ed.), *Reason and Light* (Ithaca: Center for International Studies, 1990), pp. 82–98.

22   Another echo from the Italian literary canon with a clear patriotic dimension, which is found in more than one text, is reference to the Risorgimento hero, Silvio Pellico, and his account of his imprisonment by Austria-Hungary, *Le mie prigioni* (1832). See, for example, Aldo Bizzarri, *Proibito*, p. 19.

23   Charles Cohen, *Un quaderno di Buchenwald* (*A Buchenwald Notebook*) (Turin: F. Tosco, 1945), p. 10.

24   Primo Levi, *If This is a Man*, translated by S. Woolf (Harmondsworth: Penguin, 1979), p. 129. On Levi's uses of irony, see R. Gordon, '*Per mia fortuna* ...: Irony and Ethics in Primo Levi's Writing', *MLR*, 92, 1997, pp. 337–47.

25   Aldo Bizzarri, *Mauthausen città ermetica* (*Mauthausen Hermetic City*) (Rome: OET/Edizioni Polilibraria, 1946), pp. 87–8, 110.

26   See note 16 above, Valech Capozzi, *A 24029*, preface; and on psychology, Pino Da Prati, *Il 'triangolo rosso' del deportato politico n. 6017* (*The 'Red Triangle' of Political Deportee n. 6017*) (Milan-Rome: Gastaldi, 1946), pp. 277–8.

27   See, respectively, Bizzarri, *Mauthausen*; Fergnani, *Un uomo*; Giancarlo Ottani, *Un popolo piange. La tragedia degli ebrei italiani* (*A People Weeps: The Tragedy of the Italian Jews*) (Milan: Spartaco Giovene, 1945).

28   See, for example, plates in texts by Cavaliere, Da Prati, De Martino, Rava.

It is interesting to note the subtle and complex use of photography in a number of recent historical and narrative works dealing with memory and the Holocaust: see for example, James Young, *The Texture of Memory* (New Haven and London: Yale University Press, 1993) and W.G. Sebald, *The Emigrants*, translated by Michael Hulse (London: Harvill, 1996).

29 A small number of works of the period consisted of drawings of the camps by deportees, and these stand in a similar relation to documentary images as the textual representations: see Franco Brunello, *Stalag 307* (Vicenza: Edizione del Partito d'azione, 1945: Milan; Casa Editrice La Fiaccola, 1945); Gino Gregori, *Ecce homo Mauthausen* (Milan: Ed. Stucchi, 1946); Marcello Tomadini, *Venti mesi*.

30 Frida Misul, *Fra gli artigli del mostro nazista. La più romanzesca delle realtà il più realistico dei romanzi* (*In the Claws of the Nazi Monster. The Most Novelesque of Realities The Most Realistic of Novels*) (Livorno: Stab. poligrafico Belforte, 1946). It is worth noting that sarcasm is not uncommon in these early accounts: it is shared in different ways by Cavaliere, Pantozzi, and also Paolo Liggeri, *Triangolo rosso* (*Red Triangle*) (Milan: La Casa, 1946).

31 A similar case was made by Lawrence Langer's groundbreaking study of Holocaust literature, *The Holocaust and the Literary Imagination* (New Haven and London: Yale University Press, 1975).   ⋅

32 See also Eucardio Momigliano, *40000 fuori legge* (*40000 Outlaws*) (Rome: Carboni, 1945), also published as *Storia tragica a grottesca del razzismo fascista* (*The Tragic and Grotesque History of Fascist Racism*) (Milan: Mondadori, 1946).

33 For these terms used here and in the title to section 4, see Gérard Genette, 'Le discours du récit', translated in his *Narrative Discourse* (Oxford: Blackwell, 1980), p. 29.

34 Eduardo De Filippo, *Napoli milionaria*, in *I capolavori di Eduardo* (*Eduardo's Masterpieces*) (Turin: Einaudi, 1979), pp. 167–252; translated in Eduardo De Filippo, *Four Plays*, translated by Carlo Ardito and Peter Tinniswood (London: Methuen Drama, 1992).

35 These five texts are Liana Millu, *Il fumo di Birkenau* (*The Smoke of Birkenau*) (Milan: Mondadori Arianna, 1957, first edition Milan: La Prora, 1947); Misul, *Fra gli artigli*; Luciana Nissim and Pelagia Lewinska, *Donne contro il mostro* (*Women Against the Monster*) (Turin: Vincenzo Ramella Editore, 1946); Giuliana Tedeschi, *Questo povero corpo* (*This Poor Body*) (Milan: EdIt, 1946); Valech Capozzi, *A24049*. On this issue, see Bravo and Jalla, pp. 58–60, and Hardman (chapter 3 in this volume).

36 Tzvetan Todorov, *Face à l'extrême* (*In The Face of the Extreme*) (Paris: Seuil, 1991).

3
Representations of the Holocaust in Women's Testimony

Anna Hardman

Included in Tadeusz Borowski's *This Way for the Gas, Ladies and Gentlemen*, are his descriptions of women in Auschwitz: those in the camp brothel, the 'Puff girls'; the red-headed block leader who asks, 'Will evil be punished?'; and the women experimented on in a nearby block. His narrator mentions the naked women in trucks who cried for help on their way to the gas chambers as the men in their thousands stood and watched, and the 'young, healthy, good-looking' Jewish woman who, in her desire to live, abandoned her child on the ramp.[1]

Whilst Borowski's mention of these women is 'truthful' in that they represent part of his story, on the whole the stories of such women themselves remain untold. Up until the late 1970s and early 1980s, glimpses such as these and the occasional memoir and diary were the only insights we had into women's experiences of the Holocaust.[2] Such 'insights' inevitably distort and marginalize women's experiences, particularly given that most primary research has focused almost exclusively on male testimony. However, the contemporary scene is changing, with a number of scholars attempting to highlight the voices of women and explore the effect their inclusion has, or does not have, on our understandings of the Holocaust. This focus deserves recognition, if only to gain a more complete picture of aspects of the Holocaust, given the segregation of the sexes at most death and concentration camps.

The entry of such approaches into mainstream Holocaust studies could be said to be marked by the publication of the anthology *Different Voices: Women and the Holocaust* in 1993.[3] This book attempts to identify the particularities of women's experiences, illustrate the quality of writing by women such as Charlotte Delbo, Ida Fink and Sarah Nomberg-Przytyk and bring together a variety of critical studies that attempt to assess the significance of such experiences and writing. However, the very nature of the book is of significance, given that to anthologize is both to canonize and authorize the writers and critical interpretations included. This tendency is reinforced by the publishers' claim that *Different Voices* represents 'the most thorough-going examination of women's experiences of the Holocaust ever compiled', and by the approval of Elie Wiesel on its front cover.

Basic to this anthology is the claim that the specificity of women's experiences needs fuller exploration, which necessarily entails taking gender into account. Joan Ringelheim was one of the earliest thinkers to begin research on women and the Holocaust. She based her work on the assumption that 'no two Jews experienced what is called the Holocaust in quite the same way, even if they were in the same place at the same time. There is no time, there is no place that is the same for everyone, not even in Auschwitz'.[4] The natural implication of such an assertion is that gender is a crucial and obvious difference and, as such, has the significance attributed to other factors which define the self. However, the responses of two contemporaries reflect the antagonism such research has inspired. As noted in *Different Voices*, Helen Fagin claimed that the enormity of the Holocaust would somehow be trivialized or 'made secondary' to a supposed 'agenda' of 'feminism', whilst Cynthia Ozick criticized Ringelheim's work as 'morally inappropriate'. She claimed that 'the Holocaust happened to victims who were not seen as men, women, or children, but as Jews'.[5] This challenge by Ozick encapsulates the widespread feeling that taking account of all voices, not purely Jewish ones, will detract from and distort the uniqueness of the Jewish experience, thus rendering such interpretations 'inauthentic'.[6] Although this area of research might challenge certain arguments about the uniqueness of Jewish suffering during the Holocaust, it does not inevitably obscure its specificity. Whatever the fears of such critics, it has to be said that any exploration of the Holocaust which fails to takes into account the way women figure and interpret their experiences will be incomplete. Although it is generally accepted that factors such as ethnicity, nationality, and cultural background are significant in effecting both the individual's experience and writing, gender is often assumed to be an irrelevancy. However, when one reads women's memoirs it is evident that they reveal different kinds of experience to those reflected in men's testimony. As the title of Myrna Goldenberg's article suggests, exposing the way women were brutalized as compared to men reveals 'different horrors, same hell'.[7]

Given the segregation of the sexes in Auschwitz and other camps, women's physical location has to be taken into account, as this could have a profound effect upon the individual's experience. It is widely acknowledged that, particularly in 1942 and early 1943, the conditions in the women's camp at Birkenau were horrendous, when it was transferred from Auschwitz I. While commandant of Auschwitz, Hoess stated that 'the most wretched conditions prevailed in the women's camp at Birkenau'.[8] The mortality rate during this period was incredibly high, due to lack of water and sanitary conditions. As survivor Seweryna Szmaglewska remembers:

> In the summer of 1942, Birkenau was a swamp fenced off by electrified wire. No roads whatsoever, no paths in between the blocks. Inside dark holes, as if in layered cages, dimly lit by the candles burning here and there, the emaciated apparitions bent double, blue with cold, leaning over a bundle of soiled rags, their shaven heads sunken in between the shoulders, their bony fingers busy catching insects and squashing them on the bunk's edge – this is what the barracks looked like in 1942.[9]

However, one of the questions central to this essay is whether there is, in fact, anything characteristic or distinctive about women's experience of the Holocaust. It falls into two parts: the first will contextualize discussion of women's testimony within a broad overview of the central theoretical accounts; the second will offer a more detailed analysis of these accounts, with particular reference to the nature of survival. This approach will enable me to reflect upon both the possibilities and problems that arise from current scholarship in light of my own reading of a sample of women's memoirs.

There now exists a body of diverse scholarly writing that is contained within the broad description 'Women and the Holocaust'. In the primary instance, historians such as Claudia Koonz and Renate Bridenthal explored the role of women in Germany, especially in relation to Nazi policy,[10] whilst Sybil Milton and Marian Kaplan developed an interest in the specificity of German-Jewish women.[11] Critics such as Gisella Bock have concentrated on the complex relationship between sexism and racism inherent in Nazi policy.[12] Although beyond the scope of this article, awareness of eugenic policy and other critical treatments are crucial if we are to understand more fully the lives of women before, during and – for the survivors – after the Holocaust. Other important areas of research have included the experiences of lesbian women[13] and literary treatments of women's writing.[14]

However, alongside these specific areas of research is a more general discussion relating to women's experiences in the ghettoes, concentration camps and death camps. My interest here relates specifically to these theoretical treatments of women's experiences. For the purposes of this essay, I shall focus on the work of Myrna Goldenberg and Joan Ringelheim, for two reasons. First, they are representative of two broad strategies in this area of research, and secondly, because their work raises significant issues about women's experiences in the Holocaust, especially regarding survival in the death camps. As do most critics in this area, Ringelheim and Goldenberg stress that there are some similarities between male and female experiences – such as thirst, hunger, deprivation and death. However, at the heart of their research is an attempt to highlight what are perceived to be distinctly female experiences. This strategy is two-fold. First, critics focus upon female sexuality, and experiences that are distinctive to them on account of their biology. Thus, Myrna Goldenberg states 'women's narratives frequently acknowledge their vulnerability as sexual beings, and especially as menstruating or pregnant women'.[15]

The presence of these themes in memoirs is cited by Ringelheim and Goldenberg as evidence that women's experience is distinct from that of men, because they were exposed to a 'double vulnerability' both as women and as Jews. This notion of vulnerability as a defining characteristic is extended to experiences assumed to be specific to women, such as the fear of rape, and infertility. Significantly, loss of 'femininity' as figured in women's memoirs is presented as closely linked to this attack upon their sexuality. Given the ways in which Nazi policy distinguished between Jewish men and women, Ringelheim concludes that, 'Jewish women suffered both as Jews and as women from anti-semitism and sexism in their genocidal forms. More women were deported than men. More women were killed than men. Women's chances of survival were simply not equivalent to those of men.'[16] However, more controversial is the second strand of their argument which highlights a broader theme in women's memoirs, namely, that of survival. Whilst claiming that women's chances of survival were worse than men's, it is also asserted that women survived better than their male counterparts because of their uniquely 'female' resources. This, in turn, leads to the assumption that ways of surviving are differentiated by gender: aspects of women's socialization, such as bonding, contributed to their ability to stay alive. By comparison, men are often presented as passive, weak and unable to survive given their social-ization as independent, competitive individuals. These kinds of assumptions are typified by an oft-cited comment by a female survivor of Belsen: 'Men are far weaker and far less able to stand up to the hard-ship than the women – physically and often morally as well. Unable to control themselves, they display such a lack of moral fiber that we cannot but be sorry for them.'[17] After compiling such 'proof texts' from women's memoirs, which demonstrate their superior ability to survive, a variety of conclusions are drawn. Goldenberg is the most forceful, asserting that: 'The experience of women during the Holocaust shows that traditionally feminist values of co-operation and caring are important conditions for the perpetuation of civiliza-tion, irrespective of religious, ethnic, or nationalistic identification.'[18]

The theoretical stance I have outlined above is typical of the posi-tions taken by several scholars involved in this area of research, and provokes questions as to both its appropriateness and validity. It is extended by critics such as Sybil Milton, who promote an 'ethic of caring' particular to women which enabled them to survive.[19] Having said this, there are significant differences between the current approaches of Goldenberg and Ringelheim. The examples of Goldenberg's thesis cited above are drawn from research from both 1996 and earlier work from 1990. Although her most recent writing attempts to address issues relating to the representation and construc-tion inherent to memoirs and other forms of testimony, this makes little if any impact upon her thesis. However, my presentation of Ringelheim's thesis is of her early work. She has since offered a recon-sideration of the direction research on women and the Holocaust has taken. As such, her writing reflects a certain evolution as a theoretical treatment of women's testimony.[20] Her research reflects a welcome self-critical stance, whereby she re-evaluates her previously uncritical use of feminist cultural theory. The implications of this shift have led her to question the widespread reliance upon biological determinism, and address seriously the problems and limitations of this body of crit-ical literature. My intention in the second part of this article is to explore a variety of women's testimonies, in order to determine whether they reflect the stance of Goldenberg, or give grounds for the reservations suggested by Ringelheim. My analysis is restricted to a sample of women's accounts from Auschwitz, primarily the women's camp at Birkenau, in order to provide some kind of context, however fragmented.

Goldenberg's conclusion that the testimony of Jewish women

exposes a 'unique genre' driven by the 'twin circumstances of racism and gender'[21] is typical of this body of critical writing. When we explore a variety of memoirs, her suggestion that they dwell upon themes related to women's biology, such as their perception of motherhood,[22] fear of rape,[23] infertility and loss of attractiveness, or 'femininity' would appear to be justified.[24] For example, the fear of rape by both the SS and liberating Russian troops has a central place in Judith Maygar Isaacson's narrative *Seed of Sarah*. This passage reflects her feelings during one of many selections, 'I shuddered with a sudden insight into our options. Straight ahead – slave labour. To the left – death. To the right – mass rape at the Russian front.'[25] Similarly, in *Auschwitz: True Tales from a Grotesque Land*, Sarah Nomberg-Przytyk describes her memory of arrival at Auschwitz, which, for women, usually included shaving of all body hair, tattooing and sometimes internal examination. The recounting of this experience and the impact it made is present in many memoirs, especially those of women from more Orthodox Jewish backgrounds:

> We ceased to exist as thinking, feeling entities. We were not allowed any modesty in front of these strange men. We were nothing more than objects on which they performed their duties, non-sentient things that they could examine from all angles ... It did not bother them that we were women and that without our hair we felt totally humiliated.[26]

A reading of women's testimonies also reflects the second aspect of Goldenberg's thesis, the theme of mutual support. There are moments in women's accounts that emphasize both their dependence upon and compassion for other women. One of the stories Charlotte Delbo tells, in *None of Us Will Return*, involves the memory of one of her companions, Lulu, who was on a work detail with her. For a short time, she was left alone as her companions moved elsewhere:

> Left alone at the bottom of the ditch, I am filled with despair. The others' presence, the things they said, made it possible to believe we might return. Now that they have left I am desperate. I cannot believe I will ever return when I am alone. With them near me, since they seem so certain of it, I believe it could happen. No sooner do they leave me than I am frightened. No one believes she will return when she is alone.[27]

The episode results in quiet desperation after she is assaulted by a Kapo. However, Lulu gives Charlotte her tools that are lighter and shields her from the Kapo's sight so that she can cry. She remembers, 'It is as though I had wept against my mother's breast.'[28]

Goldenberg and others often draw attention to the special bond between sisters, and their determination to stay together. In Isabella Leitner's memoir, *Isabella: From Auschwitz to Freedom*, she describes a 'pact' she had with her sisters in Birkenau during 1944. The predominant tone of her narrative is one of affirmation and she attributes her survival to her sisters, saying:

> If you are sisterless, you do not have the pressure, the absolute responsibility to end the day alive ... many times when I was caught in a selection, I knew I had to get back to my sisters, even when I was too tired to fight my way back, when going the way of the smoke would have been easier, when I wanted to, when it almost seemed desirable.[29]

Kitty Hart's memoir, *Return To Auschwitz*, is even more specific as to the actuality and significance of women's bonding. Significantly, she expands on this very theme in the revised edition of her book, published in 1997, where she insists that women's bonding provided better chances of survival.[30] In both editions, Hart insists that she survived on account of her relationship with her mother and a group of three or four women, 'little "families" would stick together and organise things together ... Members of the group helped each other and defied the rest.'[31]

It would appear on the basis of such a reading of women's testimonies that the dominant discourse regarding women and the Holocaust, as represented by Goldenberg, is justified. The attack upon women's biology and their greater ability to survive through bonding appears to be a perfectly legitimate reading. However, I would argue that there are a whole variety of problems with such an approach, resulting from a flawed interpretation of Holocaust testimony. This would appear to suggest that Ringelheim's reservations are well founded.

In the first instance, women's testimony will inevitably reflect certain characteristics distinct to them as women, first on account of their biological difference to men, and secondly, in the words of Rittner and Roth: 'Precisely because the Nazis targeted Jews and others in racial terms, they had to see those victims in their male and female particularity.'[32] Although it is vital to address the ways in which the impact of atrocity upon women's bodies and sense of self have been submerged and ignored, to reduce the diversity of women's experience of the Holocaust to its impact on their sexuality may be misguided. Whilst it is crucial we remember the actuality of existence in the camps whereby women were vulnerable, we also need to attempt to make a distinction between this actuality and the way it is figured in their writing. Although we can treat women's writing as a 'genre' given that their biology is a commonality, the problematic implications of this approach can be discerned from the direction current scholarship has taken.

It would appear that when Goldenberg refers to 'women's experience', this understanding is based on certain assumptions about gender difference which go unarticulated. Although it is perhaps inevitable that one's reading of a text is always perspective-ridden, it seems that these narratives have been approached uncritically through reliance on one particular strand of feminist theory. Goldenberg's tendency to homogenize women's experiences runs counter to much contemporary feminist theory, with its emphasis on difference. In this first case, that of women's sexuality, it would appear that for Goldenberg, 'women's experience' constitutes their bodily experience. This in itself may not be problematic, but when women's sexuality is perceived to be a universalizing category, the many differences between women are diminished. Thus, distinctive aspects of the self, such as differences in culture, religion, age, and class, are falsified, which has the potential to negate the diverse interpretation of those experiences and the way they were responded to.

For example, the theme of rape operates in a complex way in Isaacson's memoir. It is evident that one has to allow for the fear of rape as felt in the camp by Isaacson and the process of her remembering and reconstructing that memory. Given the way in which she interpreted selections between women in terms of the likelihood of being raped, it may well have effected the decisions she made at the time. However, beyond this level of remembering, it must be acknowledged that her memory of sexual vulnerability is also dramatized and used as a fictional device. For example, when she is sent to the camp Kommandant's house, she assumes this is for sexual reasons whilst in reality he wants her for domestic duties. The chapter that focuses on this episode is constructed dramatically, so the reader is unsure as to the Kommandant's intentions, with remarks such as, 'I wondered what intercourse might mean in physical terms' and 'I tried to project myself into the role of a concubine'.[33] As we see Isaacson grappling with the memory of sexual vulnerability, it is also clear that this theme becomes a fictional device emphasized for dramatic effect. Although this may be true of all testimony, it is particularly evident in her text, which points to the gulf between the actuality of women's vulnerability and the ways in which it is represented.

Goldenberg's understanding of women's survival in the camps demonstrates how 'women's experience' is also interpreted in gendered terms, as reflecting socialized or essentially 'feminine' experience. These 'traditional women's values' are assumed to include supportiveness, compassion, nurturing, intuitiveness, unselfishness, tenderness, sensitivity, and so on. Consequently, when critics highlight such demonstrations of femininity in testimony, they do so both as proof texts for these theoretical arguments, and as evidence of the superiority of these supposedly 'feminine' characteristics. The result is that we do not hear the multiple voices of these women at all: they are replaced by critics who engage in a highly selective reading of their narratives. For example, one can easily find an alternative reading of Delbo's narrative, *Auschwitz and After*. Although she mentions the support and solidarity she received from a small group of French women, the negation of human solidarity, given the conditions in Birkenau, dominates her writing. On many occasions she expresses memories of numbness or indifference when seeing the impact of atrocity on women around her. She describes her memory of the thirst that plagued her and her ability to do nothing but quench her own:

> I see little Aurore. She is sick, exhausted by fever, her lips discoloured, her eyes haggard. She is thirsty. She does not have the strength to run down to the brook ... She is waiting. Her eyes beg and I do not look at her. I feel upon me her thirsty gaze, the pain in her eyes when I hook my tin cup back on my belt. Life returns to me and I feel shame.[34]

Auschwitz and After reflects a whole variety of contradictory, ambivalent and ambiguous memories of Delbo's relationships with other women, which could support or deny specific theories about gender and survival if taken out of context. For example, in *Different Voices* the editors include Delbo's story, 'Lulu', and present it as an example of 'distinctly feminine qualities' which, in turn, serves to authenticate their assumptions about women's experiences. They cite it to claim that 'not only self-interest but also kinship and friendship, bonding with other women, were the basis for their emotional, and often physical, coping and survival'.[35] Similarly, Goldenberg misrepresents Leitner's narrative by referring to it in a highly selective manner, quoting passages out of context. Whilst she is prepared to refer to the 'pact' which Leitner feels sustained her and her sisters, Goldenberg fails to explore the way Leitner's understanding of her survival is reconstructed within the text in anticipation of the death of her sister Cipi. Such shifting understandings of survival are transparent, and should not be ignored by the critic. At a later point, when transferred to Birnbaumel, Isabella and her sisters were gradually losing hope and realized the futility of their attempting to stay together. She comments 'Our pact must end, else no one will be left … We must make a new pact – each for herself … The old pact must go. A new one must take its place. Somebody will have to live … We cannot all die … Somebody must live to tell the tale.'[36] This kind of ambiguity represents both the conflicting memories and feelings Leitner has about her own survival and the way her account is fictionalized. She dramatizes her understanding of survival early in the text, whereby the 'pact' becomes a fictional device. What is particularly significant is her need to justify her underlying feeling that survival entailed putting her life above her sisters. This self-exposure may conflict with her understanding of what it means to be human, and also reveal a sense of guilt which may transcend gender.

Kitty Hart's memoir demonstrates a similarly ambivalent attitude to survival. Although she insists that 'families' were of crucial importance to women, she acknowledges that 'Outside the family there had to be bribery; within there was love and mutual help.'[37] It would appear that within Hart's memoir, there are a variety of understandings about herself as a survivor. Its dominant discourse appears to be that of 'consolation',[38] as it can be interpreted as a story of affirmation, rather than negation. Hart presents her understanding of survival as a matter of options:

> You could despair, or you could resolve to go along with the system: work up the ranks of privileged prisoners and then turn on your one-time friends and treat them as the SS bullies treated them. Mother would never play this foul game: neither would I. Yet we survived.[39]

One strand of Hart's narrative is concerned with presenting a coherent, reassuring survival narrative, as is evident in her talk of 'families' and the supportiveness which existed therein. This serves several purposes. First, it reaffirms her sense of agency in her own survival. Secondly, it emphasizes continuity between past and present whilst also reinforcing her need to justify her survival. Hart feels the need to state explicitly 'Some death camp survivors didn't want to remember ... because there are things of which they are ashamed ... I'm not ashamed of the things I did there.'[40] However, the other strand in Hart's narrative is the one alluded to in her comment about bribery outside 'the family'. When contextualized within the rest of her narrative and combined with her realization that life under conditions of atrocity was reduced to one's ability to eat, excrete and sleep, there is a self-exposure which remains a sub-text.

There appears to be a simultaneity in some women's memoirs: the affirming memory of relationships coexists with the negation of women outside them. Several also point to the limited nature of these relationships. It is possible that some very positive constructs of survival may represent a form of consolation emphasized by women. Although many survivors may feel what Primo Levi describes as the 'shame' of survival,[41] men and women may well experience this depending upon how the Holocaust affected their understandings of masculinity and femininity. Those testimonies by women that do reflect upon feelings of diminished femininity may feel a particular need to employ consoling devices in order to articulate this sense of loss. However, the gulf between 'masculine' and 'feminine' experiences of survival emphasized by Goldenberg and others may not be what it seems.

When one explores further the complexity of relationships within these 'families' as figured within the text, there exist strong parallels between the ways in which men and women attempted to stay alive. Although detailed comparison cannot be undertaken here, Primo Levi's memoir, *If This Is a Man*, contains certain themes which have been defined by Goldenberg and others as specifically 'feminine'. He mentions his friend, Steinlauf, encouraging him to wash and make an effort to keep clean; and he remembers his relationship with Alberto with warmth. He also mentions three comrades with whom he had some kind of interdependent relationship, although he is prepared to expose the internal divisions within this group and does not sentimentalize or idealize it.[42] Such episodes might challenge assumptions about what constitutes distinctly 'feminine' and 'masculine' survival strategies, and raise questions as to how men and women figure similar experiences differently within the text.

If critics are to take seriously the ambiguities and contradictions inherent in women's narratives, this will involve an alternative understanding of both testimony and the nature of survival. This entails challenging the way certain critics rely on the supposed factuality inherent in testimony in order to authenticate their own assumptions regarding feminist theory and survival. A consequence of this tendency is reflected in Goldenberg's thesis, as she incorporates fragments of Holocaust testimonies into her account, adopting their 'rhetoric of fact'.[43] A more helpful approach might be to explore the complexity and contradictions integral to each narrative. This might allow for a deeper understanding of how women dealt with the impact of the Holocaust, by exploring how this is constructed in the text, rather than selecting details from testimony and presenting them as 'objective fact'.

A discourse that allows for such understandings of the text must also make difficult judgements about the variety of narratives encompassed by the term 'testimony'. It is clear that, in certain respects, Charlotte Delbo's narrative is not equivalent to Kitty Hart's account, and should not be treated as such. As Lawrence Langer points out, Charlotte Delbo makes atrocity the substance as well as the subject of her art.[44] Her writing is complicated by the fact that she speaks with a number of voices throughout her narratives. In *The Measure of Our Days*, the third part of her trilogy, *Auschwitz and After*, she tells the stories of other survivors, and illustrates the impact the Holocaust has had upon their lives. However, this shifting of voices is complicated further in *Days and Memory*, where the narrator recounts conversations with survivors, but there is always an uncertainty as to whose voice we are hearing. By comparison, memoirs such as those by Leitner, Hart and Isaacson are different kinds of narrative, serving many different agendas. However, communicating the 'historical facts' of their experience as opposed to creating a work of art is often the primary intention.

The methodological problems reflected in Goldenberg's research can, in part, be attributed to the failure of different areas within Holocaust studies to engage with each other. These theoretical treatments do not seriously address contemporary debates concerning representation and the Holocaust and alternative understandings of the nature and function of testimony.[45] However, in terms of marketing strategies, evidence of the distorting effect of gender stereotypes can be discerned in the 1990s. Although publication of women's testimonies is now on the increase, there is a tendency to market them in a specific way. For example, Giuliana Tedeschi's memoir, *There Is a Place on Earth*, is described by the publishers' notes on the back cover as reflecting the 'destruction of the feminine personality', 'felt through a woman's sensibility', which reinforces gender stereotypes and may determine what is expected of a memoir by a female survivor.

In conclusion, if rigorous historical research can operate within a discourse that allows for the heterogeneity of women's Holocaust narratives, further insights into both the actuality of their experiences and its representation might be possible. Insights such as those of Lore Shelley, which attempt to interpret women's experiences by contextualizing them in terms of women's specific function in Auschwitz, rather than only their internal understandings of survival, may be helpful.[46] Whilst a gendered interpretation of Holocaust narratives may provide an insight, however partial and incomplete into women's experiences, articulating the relationship between actuality and construction remains ambiguous. As Charlotte Delbo reminds us:

Today, I am not sure that what I wrote is true.
I am certain it is truthful.[47]

Notes

1 T. Borowski, *This Way for the Gas, Ladies and Gentlemen* (Harmondsworth: Penguin Books, 1985), pp. 106, 90–1, 116, 43.
2 For example, *The Diary of Anne Frank* (London: Pan Books, 1954).
3 C. Rittner and J.K. Roth (eds), *Different Voices: Women and the Holocaust* (New York, Paragon House, 1993).
4 J. Ringelheim, 'Thoughts about Women and the Holocaust', in *Thinking the Unthinkable: Meanings of the Holocaust*, edited by R.S. Gottlieb (New York: Paulist Press, 1990), p. 143.
5 Ringelheim, 'Thoughts about Women and the Holocaust', p. 144.
6 See also A. Rosenfeld, *A Double Dying: Reflections on Holocaust Literature* (Bloomington and Indianapolis: Indiana University Press, 1980), p. 160.
7 M. Goldenberg, 'Different Horrors, Same Hell: Women Remembering the Holocaust', in Gottlieb (ed.), *Thinking the Unthinkable*, p. 143.
8 Rittner and Roth, *Different Voices*, p. 157.
9 See I. Strzelecka, 'Women', in *Anatomy of the Auschwitz Death Camp*, edited by Y. Gutman and M. Berenbaum (Bloomington and Indianapolis: Indiana University Press, 1994), p. 401.
10 R. Bridenthal and C. Koonz, 'Beyond Kinder, Küche, Kirche: Weimar Women in Politics and Work', in *Liberating Women's History*, edited by B. Carrol (London: University of Illinois Press, 1976), pp. 301–20; *When Biology Became Destiny: Women in Weimar and Nazi Germany*, edited by R.

Bridenthal *et al.* (New York: Monthly Review Press, 1984); see also U. Frevert, *Women in German History: From Bourgeois Emancipation to Sexual Liberation* (New York: St. Martin's Press, 1990); C. Koonz, *Mothers in the Fatherland: Women, the Family, and Nazi Politics* (New York: St. Martin's Press, 1987); C. Koonz, 'Consequences: Women, Nazis, and Moral Choice', in Rittner and Roth (eds), *Different Voices*, pp. 287–309.

11 M. Kaplan, 'Sisterhood Under Siege: Feminism and Anti-Semitism in Germany 1904–1938', in *The Nazi Holocaust: the Victims of the Holocaust*, edited by M.R. Marrus, vol. II, VI (Westport: Meckler, 1989), pp. 608–29; S. Milton, 'Women and the Holocaust: the Case of German and German-Jewish women', in Marrus (ed.), *The Nazi Holocaust*, pp. 631–67.

12 G. Bock, 'Racism and Sexism in Nazi Germany: Motherhood, Compulsory Sterilization, and the State', in Rittner and Roth (eds), *Different Voices*, pp. 161–86. Compulsory sterilization and forced abortion for all German-Jewish women can be interpreted as preliminary steps in the destruction of 'lives unworthy of life'. This defining of women in biological terms had dire consequences for not only German-Jewish women, highlighting what Bock defines as 'sexist racism', but implicated all Jewish women, in particular. She and others explore how Nazi policy relating to women functioned as a major instrument of social control in Germany and as having massive implications for Jewish women during selection in the death camps. For details of other research regarding Nazi 'race hygiene' policy, see R.J. Lifton, *The Nazi Doctors: Medical Killing and the Psychology of Genocide* (London: Macmillan Press, 1986); R. Proctor, *Racial Hygiene* (Cambridge, MA: Harvard University Press, 1988), pp. 118–30.

13 The subject of lesbianism during the Holocaust, especially in a variety of camps, has been something of a taboo subject. Several women's testimonies associate lesbianism with perversion or regard it with contempt. See I. Leitner with I.A. Leitner, *Isabella: From Auschwitz to Freedom* (New York: Anchor Books, 1994), p. 52; O. Lengyel, *Five Chimneys: a Woman Survivor's True Story of Auschwitz* (Chicago: Academy Publishers, 1995), pp. 197–202. However, critical research into the experience of lesbians and gay men has begun to develop. See C. Schoppmann, 'The position of Lesbian Women in the Nazi Period', in *Hidden Holocaust? Gay and Lesbian Persecution in Germany 1933–1945*, edited by G. Grau (London: Cassell, 1995), pp. 8–15.

14 See M.E. Heinemann, *Gender and Destiny: Women Writers and the Holocaust* (Westport: Greenwood Press, 1986).

15 Goldenberg, 'Different Horrors, Same Hell', p. 151. For examples of these themes in women's memoirs, see L. Adelsberger, *Auschwitz: a Doctor's Story* (London: Robson Books, 1996), pp. 100–1; H. Fried, *Fragments of a Life: the Road to Auschwitz* (London: Robert Hale, 1990), pp. 98–9, 133–4; I. Leitner, *Isabella: From Auschwitz to Freedom*, pp. 32–3, 44; O. Lengyel, *Five Chimneys*, pp. 98–9, 185–93; J. Maygar Isaacson, *Seed of Sarah: Memoirs of a Survivor*, 2nd edn. (Urbana and Chicago: University of Illinois Press, 1990), pp. 71–2; S. Nomberg-Przytyk, *Auschwitz: True Tales from a Grotesque Land* (Chapel Hill and London: The University of North Carolina Press, 1985), pp. 70–1; L. Shelley (ed.), *Auschwitz: the Nazi Administration and SS Enterprises and Workshops,* Studies in the Shoah part I, vol. I (Lanham:

University Press of America, 1992), pp. 14, 78, 128, 152; G. Tedeschi, *There Is A Place on Earth* (London: Lime Tree, 1993), pp. 45, 97.

16 Ringelheim, 'Thoughts about Women and the Holocaust', p. 147.
17 Goldenberg, 'Different Horrors, Same Hell', p. 151.
18 Goldenberg, 'Lessons Learned from Gentle Heroism: Women's Holocaust Narratives', in *The Annals of the American Academy of Political and Social Science*, 548 (1996), pp. 78–93. Quotation is on p.78.
19 S. Milton, 'Women and the Holocaust', in Marrus (ed.), *The Nazi Holocaust*, pp. 645–50.
20 J. Ringelheim, 'Women and the Holocaust: a Reconsideration of Research', in Rittner and Roth (eds), *Different Voices*, pp. 373–418.
21 Goldenberg, 'Lessons Learned from Gentle Heroism', in *AAPSS*, p. 79.
22 See K. Hart, *Return to Auschwitz: the Remarkable Story of a Girl who Survived the Holocaust* (London: Sidgwick & Jackson, 1981), p. 151; Leitner, *Isabella: From Auschwitz to Freedom*, pp. 59, 194–8; Lengyel, *Five Chimneys*, pp. 22–5; Nomberg-Prtzytyk, *Auschwitz: True Tales from a Grotesque Land*, p. 140–1; Tedeschi, *There Is a Place on Earth*, pp. 180, 94–5, 96.
23 See I. Leitner, *Isabella: From Auschwitz to Freedom*, pp. 89–90, 108–11; E. Schloss, with E.J. Kent, *Eva's Story: a Survivor's Tale by the Step-sister of Anne Frank* (Middlesex: Castle-Kent, 1992), pp. 100, 154; Shelley (ed.), *Auschwitz: the Nazi Administration*, pp. 112, 173–4.
24 See C. Delbo, *Auschwitz and After* (New Haven and London: Yale University Press, 1995), pp. 29, 109–14, 117–23, 146; Fried, *Fragments of a Life*, pp. 122, 142, 168; A. Lasker-Wallfisch, *Inherit the Truth 1939–1945: the Documented Experiences of a Survivor of Auschwitz and Belsen* (London: Giles De La Mere, 1996), p. 115; Leitner, *Isabella: From Auschwitz to Freedom*, pp. 19, 98, 121, 133–4, 136–7, 149–65, 169–71, 193; Lengyel, *Five Chimneys*, p. 60; Maygar Isaacson, *Seed of Sarah*, pp. 82, 84, 105; Nomberg-Przytyk, *Auschwitz: True Tales from a Grotesque Land*, p. 29; Tedeschi, *There Is a Place on Earth*, pp. 97–8, 104, 129, 135.
25 Maygar Isaacson, *Seed of Sarah*, p. 85. See also pp. xi, 47, 87–92, 105.
26 Nomberg-Prtzytyk, *Auschwitz: True Tales from a Grotesque Land*, p. 14. See also Adelsberger, *Auschwitz: a Doctor's Story*, pp. 29–30; Lasker-Wallfisch, *Inherit the Truth 1939–1945*, pp. 70–2; Lengyel, *Five Chimneys*, pp. 26–8; Maygar Isaacson, *Seed of Sarah*, pp. 66–8; Schloss, *Eva's Story*, pp. 75–7; Shelley (ed.), *Auschwitz: the Nazi Administration*, pp. 14, 106–7, 166; Tedeschi, *There Is a Place on Earth*, p. 23.
27 Delbo, *Auschwitz and After*, p. 103.
28 Ibid., p. 105.
29 Leitner, *Isabella: From Auschwitz to Freedom*, p. 47–8.
30 K. Hart-Moxon, *Return to Auschwitz* (Laxton: Beth Shalom Limited, 1997), p. 67.
31 K. Hart, *Return to Auschwitz* (1981), p. 91.
32 Rittner and Roth, *Different Voices*, p. 4.
33 Maygar Isaacson, *Seed of Sarah*, pp. 90–1.
34 Delbo, *Auschwitz and After*, p. 72.
35 Rittner, and Roth, *Different Voices*, p. 100.
36 Leitner, *Isabella: From Auschwitz to Freedom*, p. 70.
37 Hart, *Return to Auschwitz* (1981), p. 91.

38   See L.L. Langer, *Admitting the Holocaust: Collected Essays* (Oxford and New York: Oxford University Press, 1995), pp. 13–20.

39   Hart, *Return to Auschwitz* (1981), p. 126.

40   Ibid., p. 226.

41   P. Levi, *The Drowned and the Saved* (London: Abacus, 1994), p. 62.

42   P. Levi, *If This Is a Man* (London: Abacus, 1995), pp. 46, 63, 151.

43   See J.E. Young, *Writing and Rewriting the Holocaust: Narrative and the Consequences of Interpretation* (Bloomington: Indiana University Press, 1988).

44   L.L. Langer, *The Age of Atrocity: Death in Modern Literature* (Boston: Beacon Press, 1978), p. 201.

45   Clearly, this area of critical writing is extensive, but for a general overview see: *Probing the Limits of Representation: Nazism and the 'Final Solution'*, edited by S. Friedlander (Cambridge, MA: Harvard University Press, 1992); *Holocaust Remembrance: the Shapes of Memory*, edited by G. Hartman (Oxford: Blackwell, 1994); *Writing and the Holocaust*, edited by B. Lang, (New York and London: Holmes & Meier, 1988); L.L. Langer, *Holocaust Testimonies: the Ruins of Memory* (New Haven and London: Yale University Press, 1991).

46   For an alternative reading of women's Holocaust writings, see S. Horowitz, 'Memory and Testimony of Women Survivors of Nazi Germany', in *Women and the Word: Jewish Women and Jewish Writing*, edited by J. Baskin (Detroit: Wayne State University Press, 1994), pp. 258–82; R.R. Linden, *Making Stories, Making Selves: Feminist Reflections on the Holocaust* (Columbus: Ohio State University Press, 1993); Shelley (ed.), *Auschwitz: the Nazi Administration*.

47   Delbo, *Auschwitz and After*, p. 1.

4
Between Repulsion and Attraction: George Steiner's Post-Holocaust Fiction

Bryan Cheyette

> When he looks back, the critic sees a eunuch's shadow. Who would be a critic if he could be a writer?... Who would choose to be a literary critic if he could set verse to sing, or compose, out of his own mortal being, a vital fiction, a character that will endure?[1]

There is something singularly paradoxical about George Steiner. An avowed elitist (and champion of the western tradition even while acknowledging its complicity with the Shoah), he is also a tireless popularizer whose literary journalism, in both Great Britain and in the United States, includes hundreds of uncollected pieces in the *New Yorker*, *TLS* and *Sunday Times*.[2] Steiner, the doyen of ineffability and seeker after 'Real Presences', beyond the word, never stops speaking or writing. From his essay 'Postscript' (1966) onwards he tells us – in relation to the Shoah and even culture in general – not to 'add the trivia of literary, sociological debate, to the unspeakable' and, at the same time, endlessly invokes the Shoah and the efficacy of silence. In a recent essay he notes that: 'It is by no means clear that there can be or that there ought to be, any form, style, or code of articulate, intelligible expression somehow adequate to the facts of the Shoah.'[3] And yet, he has lately increased his attempts to formulate, stylize and codify an intelligible approach to the Shoah.

Steiner, the literary journalist, dismisses routinely 'book-chat' journalism. While he upholds the virtues of scholarly 'autism', he also condemns the over-specialization of university research. His cultural criticism continues to be haunted by the opening lines of 'Humane Literacy' (1963), 'When he looks back, the critic sees a eunuch's shadow. Who would be a critic if he could be a writer?' But Steiner goes on writing criticism and adds painfully slowly, at 15-year inter-vals, to his fiction (which he then belittles periodically as 'scripts for thought' or 'allegories of argument').[4] Such contradictions are so blatant and so brazen that while they may be infuriating they are, I believe, symptomatic of a more general fissure.

The George Steiner that I wish to explore is split asunder. Part Rabbi *manqué* – culminating in his *Real Presences: Is there anything 'in' what we say?* (1989) – and part Marxist *manqué* – he has always been Janus-faced, both authoritarian and open. In his spiritualized materialism and his overwrought negative dialectics, his mandarin conservatism, and his avowed distrust of mass culture (along with his location of barbarism at the heart of western humanism), he has turned himself into a more accessible version of Walter Benjamin and Theodor Adorno. Born in Paris to Viennese parents in 1929, his trilingual back-ground – German, French and English – has enabled him to act as an early and welcome 'courier' between the lost world of Central European humanism (Prague, Vienna, Budapest and Berlin) and the parochialism of Great Britain and the United States. In this early role there was always an extraordinary range to Steiner's thought. After three decades, we now take for granted his popularization of the work of Adorno, Horkheimer, and Benjamin, of George Lukács and Franz Kafka, of Schoenberg, Heidegger and Paul Celan.

In one account of the two competing versions of George Steiner, Guido Almansi refers, partly tongue in cheek, to Isaiah Berlin's essay 'The Fox and the Hedgehog' (1979). In this essay Berlin characteristic-ally divides artists, musicians, and thinkers into two categories. He cites a fragment from Archilocus as his starting-point: 'the fox knows many things but the hedgehog knows one big thing'.[5] This distinction enables Berlin to create two versions of the intellectual. On the one hand, the centrifugal fox who chases many unrelated chickens, so to speak, and, on the other, the centripetal hedgehog who subordinates each thought to a central, inexorable vision. Steiner's singular paradox, in these terms, is that he is both a fox and a hedgehog; the fox-like range of his interests have been subordinated increasingly to his lifelong obsessions.

An unmistakably bifurcated George Steiner became most apparent with the co-publication of his latest volume of essays, *No Passion Spent: Essays 1978–1996* (1996), along with his complete fiction, *The Deeps of the Sea and Other Fiction* (1996) (the latter book, I suppose, enabled Steiner to step out from beneath the 'eunuch's shadow'). Reading his recent essays and lectures, there is a sense of them being rather tired, if not exhausted, primarily because of the sheer cussed repetition of familiar themes. Steiner's hedgehog has finally run its course. With his memoir, *Errata: an Examined Life* (1997), Steiner's world of words and his personal history – 'our homeland the text' – have finally become interchangeable.[6] At its most generous, one can view this uneasy shift from the inner life to the life of words as a refusal to write in a too easy confessional mode. After all, Steiner was among the first to point out the dangers of the erosion of privacy in the modern world. Perhaps he is rightly resisting what has been called the 'Oprah-fication' of contemporary life. But the problem for Steiner in his memoir is that his emotional history is often overshadowed by his many textual homelands such as the western canon, or the Jewish question, or the impossibility of translation. In the end, *Errata*, a non-confessional autobiography, is a perfect embodiment of Steiner's psychic division. It refuses to make explicit his inner being by confusing an 'examined life' with the unexamined language of feeling.

But if *No Passion Spent* and *Errata* are rather too comfortable textual homelands, then his complete fiction seems to me to be of a completely different order (and a number of reviewers, such as Antonia Byatt, have explicitly made this point).[7] Being of equal weight to his latest volume of essays (in all senses; the essays and the fiction are around 400 pages long), their joint publication highlighted, I believe, the humility and openness of his fiction when compared to his increasingly closed and orthodox prose. Above all, these two volumes crystallized the two George Steiners, the wily unbounded fox and the one-track hedgehog, who continually and creatively struggle with each other. The George Steiner of *No Passion Spent* is predominantly a monovocal imperial surveyor of the western canon (more Bloomian than Harold Bloom) from the Bible and Homer onwards. The other George Steiner, whom I now wish to explore, is predominantly the multivocal fictionist who writes stories *against* his most sacredly held beliefs and, at his best, turns his own preoccupations on their head to explore his unspoken assumptions.

Steiner's fiction, I want to argue, enacts playfully many different versions of himself, usually from the perspective of the outsider or enemy. To this extent, it has been an internal commentary on his more familiar critical writings and has helped Steiner to think against himself. Put briefly, his first and probably best volume of stories, *Anno Domini* (1964), was published at the same time as Steiner was writing *Language and Silence* (1967) and imaginatively prefigured his lifelong fascination with the slaughter which he managed to escape. The primacy of translation, fathomed at length in *After Babel: Aspects of Language and Translation* (1975), is, crucially, a structuring metaphor in *The Portage to San Cristobal of A.H.* (1981). In this latter novella, with an ambiguity that has always been present in his fiction, Steiner put into the mouth of an aged Hitler ('A.H.') words which he himself had used a decade earlier in his *In Bluebeard's Castle: Some Notes towards the Redefinition of Culture* (1971). His more recent novella and stories, *Proofs and Three Parables* (1992), continues this pattern of creative self-sustenance. Written at about the same time as his *Real Presences*, these fictions make human the 'wager on transcendence' which Steiner has long since called for as an antidote to our current 'post-cultural' nihilism.[8]

While his fiction and essays are intimately allied in terms of their composition, it is hard to gauge what exactly the relationship is between these two modes. With pointed ambivalence, as we have seen, Steiner has routinely deprecated his stories as 'allegories of argument' or 'stagings of ideas' as if they were merely straightforward dramatizations of his intellectual concerns. He has often restated, with relish, the orthodox Jewish disdain for the merely imaginary which is, after all, a form of lying or fabulation; the very opposite of genuine learning or of contributing to a sacred knowledge.[9] In a recent interview, Steiner notes interestingly 'the instrumental collusion between the genres' in his writing and to this extent it might perhaps be a mistake to highlight Steiner's fiction, which he regards merely as an imaginative afterthought mainly contingent on his more familiar critical writings. Most explicitly he has stated that 'I do not possess the inventive innocence, the somnambular immediacy, of the poet and the novelist'. At the same time, he has spoken of the 'threads that unify and make continuous the external diversity of my publications' and the 'interplay between philosophical-critical discourse' and his fiction.[10] In these terms, Steiner, always the self-translator, writes philosophical essays as if they were a species of poetry and fiction as if it were philosophy.

On this level, Steiner's fiction might be said simply to reinforce the strand of cultural pessimism which has always pervaded his work. If language is increasingly diffuse and muddled, and culture remains complicit with mass murder, then history becomes a form of catastrophe (from the crucifixion to the death camps). As Robert Alter has argued, this lethal teleology gives us a simple reading of Steiner's fiction as a form of 'negative transcendence' (a term which was first applied by Erich Heller to the fiction of Franz Kafka).[11] More astutely, as Norman Finkelstein has shown, Steiner's sense of himself as a 'courier carrying urgent letters and signals to the few who might respond' implicitly refers to Kafka's brief parable 'Couriers':

> They were offered the choice between becoming kings or couriers of kings. The way children would, they all wanted to be couriers. Therefore there are only couriers who hurry about the world, shouting to each other – since there are no kings – messages that have become meaningless. They would like to put an end to this miserable life of theirs but they dare not because of their oaths of service.[12]

This parable captures much of Steiner's sensibility. The bellowing rhetoric in which he delivers news from nowhere to the parochial English-speaking world; his abiding sense of pessimism that his message might be unheard and that we live in a world without kings; the suicidal despair of Kafka's meaningless 'couriers' who persist none the less. Alter has rightly noted that of Steiner's nine stories published since 1956, 'two end in suicide, one in the gas chamber, one in deportation to the death camps, one in a trampling to death, and one, an animal fable, in the pet's dream of lunging at the master's throat'.[13] For a writer who has discounted the possibility of modern tragedy (precisely because we live in a world without kings), there is at least an echo in Steiner's fiction of a tragic vision. But I do not believe that his stories are quite as one-dimensional as Alter suggests. To this extent, I take seriously Steiner's description of himself as a Hegelian who, as a writer of fiction, must 'learn to think and feel against [himself]'.[14] In a meaningless world Steiner seems to be saying that what defines us is not culture but the horrors which continue to overwhelm the century. The significance of his fiction is that it need go no further than this sense of futility and masochistic attraction, even desperate need, for that which lies beyond culture. In Steiner's imaginative world, the desire to experience the worst excesses of war and destruction make the received culture seem feeble by comparison.

This sense of being caught between the aesthetic and the barbaric can be found in Steiner's curiously contradictory response to Sylvia Plath's so-called Holocaust poems, 'Mary's Song', 'Daddy' and 'Lady Lazarus' (written between September and December 1962, a few months before her suicide). In his subsequent essay on Plath, 'Dying is an Art' (1965), Steiner reveals the fraught dimensions of his own imaginative dilemma. On the one hand, we have an overly censorious voice which has later been used to police other representations of the Holocaust:

> Are these poems entirely legitimate? In what sense does anyone, themselves uninvolved and long after the event, commit a subtle larceny when they evoke the echoes and trappings of Auschwitz and appropriate an enormity of ready emotion to their own private design?[15]

A few lines before this trenchant dismissal, however, he describes Plath's 'Daddy' as the 'Guernica' of modern poetry; a 'classic' act of translating personal pain into the public realm. The main reason, I believe, for Steiner's ambivalence towards Plath's poetry is that her ultimacies were not unlike his own post-Holocaust stories in *Anno Domini* (written at the same time as Plath's *Ariel* (1965)). This kinship is revealed immediately after his needless reference to Plath's 'subtle larceny' when he asks tellingly: 'Was there latent in Sylvia Plath's sensibility, as in that of many of us who remember only by fiat of the imagination, a fearful envy, a dim resentment at not having been there, of having missed the rendezvous with hell?'[16]

Steiner has always described himself as 'A Kind of Survivor' (the title of his autobiographical 1965 essay) and he is understandably obsessed by his first 11 years in Paris (before being whisked off to America by his father in 1940). Of the Jewish boys and girls in his school class and circle of friends, he has often stated, only two survived (including himself). Steiner's need to surround himself with words (however distrusted), or his seemingly self-destructive personality, which constantly seems to expose itself to ridicule, cannot be separated from this history. With characteristic bombast he has written of the 'unmerited scandal of his survival' and goes on again to note what he calls his 'pathological bent toward some immediate sharing of his school friend's fate – how would I have behaved, how abject would my fears have been', and states that this feeling is 'with me always'.[17] This pathologically envious sense of missing 'the rendezvous with Hell' is the subject of much of Steiner's fiction.

All of the stories in *Anno Domini* are about individuals, or groups of individuals (whether German, American, French, or British) who, like Steiner, are both attracted and repulsed by the horrors which they escaped. All of his protagonists return once more to their 'rendezvous with Hell' and fatally embrace the terrors which, after the war, continue to obsess them. Many of the representative figures of this fatal attraction are non-Jewish so as to place their 'fearful envy' at the heart of their particular national cultures. The life of the mind, in these stories, has been supplanted by the life of the body and the humanizing imperative of postwar culture has been replaced by the lure of death. Thus Steiner's ambiguous relationship to Plath interestingly reveals what Jacqueline Rose has called the 'psychic engendering of history' underpinning Plath's use of Holocaust metaphors. Not unlike his reading of Plath, Steiner's version of Kafka also stresses the 'obscene collaboration between torturer and victim', of one who was not there, and its relation to the Shoah. As he puts it in *Errata*, 'victimisation, ostracism, and torture are dialectic'.[18]

This dialectic is given its most complete portrayal in 'Cake', where an American graduate student from Harvard, the son of an elite family, decides to stay behind in Nazi-occupied France.[19] He acts as a 'courier' for the underground, and, after witnessing the torture of a young woman and her father, begins to fantasize about being captured by the Gestapo. Only under torture can he really know himself otherwise, he fears, he will live, 'as spinsters do, in the brittle familiarity of mere acquaintance' (p. 202). Although his romantic masochism is soon quashed when Steiner's narrator nervously escapes capture, it also becomes the driving force of the story. From the beginning the American is 'gripped' by the image of the girl's abduction which 'brought a queer warmth and drew my skin tight' (p. 200). After this he woke at nights 'shivering with an unclean sweetness' and his perverse jealousy of the old man and the girl 'grew like a cancer' (p. 201). As he walked along the deserted banks of the Loire, his overpowering envy 'became the thing worth living for. At any cost. So I spent my days between fear and desire, between hysterical imaginings of pain, and a secret longing' (p. 203). More than anything else, the American becomes a true 'courier', like Steiner himself, who has 'won remission from hell' (p. 203). Evading torture by the Gestapo, he is smuggled to a sanatorium where he is entrusted with the family history of Rahel Jakobsen, whom he falls in love with, and whom he commemorates after the war.

His abiding role as a 'courier' opens him up in general to experience *in extremis* and, in Steiner's terms, makes him an allegorical or Kafkaesque Jew who eventually internalizes Jewish history. The universalization of Steiner's specific extra-territorial Judaism is, however, fraught with difficulties. In the story the American is also an antisemite who expresses his loathing for a Steiner-like Jewish student in his Renaissance seminar – 'He had been educated in half a dozen countries ("Herr Hitler, you know") and spoke English with flair; but he retained a sugary intonation, part-French, part-German. I detested the fluent acrobatics of his mind' (p. 219). He goes on to argue that – 'by their unending misery, the Jews have put mankind in the wrong. Their presence is a reproach' (p. 219) which is, in short, Steiner's philosophy of antisemitism elaborated in his *In Bluebeard's Castle*. 'Cake', then, elides the distinction between Jew and non-Jew, or even between Jews and antisemites. But this is the imaginative 'dialectic' of one enraptured by the violence inflicted on the victims of Nazism.

Steiner's other two stories in *Anno Domini*, 'Return No More' and 'Sweet Mars', are also written from the point of view of mainstream European culture – in this case postwar France, England and Germany. As with 'Cake', the protagonists of these two stories are suicidally entranced and defined utterly by their wartime experiences. In 'Return No More', the symbolically named Falk, a former German officer, returns in peacetime to the French village which he once occupied. He seeks out the family whose eldest son was publicly hanged by his unit and explains to the sister: 'I know it doesn't make sense. I am like a sleepwalker looking for that which kept me alive in the daytime. Looking for the one door that opens out of night' (p. 167). Later on he talks about coming back to 'hear the silence' (p. 171) and he compares this with the 'stench of forgetting' (p. 176) in postwar Germany. Contemporary Germany wears an 'iron collar so it doesn't look back' (p. 176) and this national amnesia is contrasted with those in France who have an unrelenting memory: 'steep yourself in the remembered horrors. Build them around you like a high safe wall. Is that any less dishonest?' (p. 176). Instead of turning the 'night' into a safe wall of words, Falk is compelled to return once again to the scene of the crime and let the horror engulf him. His death unsettles both an excess of forgetting and an excess of memory.

The last story in *Anno Domini*, 'Sweet Mars', also concerns figures who are unable to leave the past alone to their own suicidal cost. This story is situated in a distinctly British context. Steiner writes surprisingly well on Britishness as can be seen in his fine essay on Anthony Blunt, 'The Cleric of Treason' (1980).[20] He has referred astutely to the general sense of the British 'abstention from public and private encounter' with the Holocaust (with the exception of a few notable individuals in the 1930s such as Storm Jameson, to whom the volume is dedicated). According to Steiner, there is 'a continuum of sanity, of liberal imagining, in British politics' which makes it well nigh impossible for the implications of the Shoah to resonate in British culture.

This too comfortable 'liberal imagining' is addressed specifically in 'Sweet Mars'.[21]

In a pastiche of much British clubland fiction, this story concerns the homoerotic friendship of two army officers, Gerald Maune and Duncan Reeve, whose lives are irrevocably shaped by their wartime experiences. Maune's decision to undergo Freudian analysis, so as to come to terms with the continuing aftermath of the war, is seen by Reeve as an un-English (or Jewish) intervention into the murky depths of the national psyche. Maune's description of his analysis with his therapist, Goldman, sounds not unlike Anthony Blunt's treasonous psychology:

> at best, you will learn to swim with the cold and treasons of the current, rather than against, and you will dive into the deep not for oblivion, but for its secret, nocturnal roots which, when we touch them with salutation and reserve, yield us what power we have to endure on the mutinous waves. (p. 289)

Falk, similarly, in 'Return No More' drowns in a sea of memories: 'the sea was close upon him. He clambered towards the shore. But the tide was quicker' (p. 167). These treacherous 'nocturnal roots' of existence are, in fact, first accounted for in Steiner's defining story, 'The Deeps of the Sea' (1956), published when he was in his late twenties.

'The Deeps of the Sea' concerns an oceanographer who is precisely concerned with the 'cold and treasons of the current' in relation to the depths of the ocean. In an image that reverberates throughout Steiner's fiction, Aaron Tefft, the protagonist of this early story, is obsessed with what he thinks of as the 'inverted everests' which lie below the 'silence of the sea' (p. 1). Like all of Steiner's protagonists, Tefft has a 'brief but terrible vision of the deep' (p. 4) – 'the dark is so absolute that it illuminates, the cold is so intense that it burns' (p. 4) – a vision of an unconquered 'green world', with 'mountain summits reversed' (p. 17) which eventually 'consumed his soul' (p. 12). In the British clubland version of this tale – where the deeps are associated with repressed memory – it is Reeve's fear that Maune's psychotherapy will make explicit their uncharted emotional life. In pained retribution at Maune succumbing to such continental tomfoolery, Reeve insists on writing a series of imagined dreams for Maune to see if his therapist, Goldman, will falsely interpret them. Reeve has a wager with his friend that Goldman will not be able to tell the real thing from his ersatz versions. Maune's duping of Goldman, and the reluctant acknowledgement of his homoerotic relationships in Egypt and Poland – '[He] felt as if he had taken a hammer to his skull' (p. 289) – finally throws the aptly named Maune into irredeemable despair.

By the time of his next fictional work, *The Portage to San Cristobal of A.H.*, Steiner recreates the preoccupations of his earlier volume – concerning an unconquered 'night world' which consumes the inner being of his protagonists – and gives them a specifically Judaic context. In *The Portage* it is 'A.H.' (or Hitler) who is the 'mountain summits reversed' of the contemporary world who represents a 'dark ... so absolute that it illuminates, [a] cold so intense that it burns' (p. 4) to quote from 'The Deeps of the Sea'. The 'green world' of the ocean bed is here replaced by the South American jungle. *The Portage to San Cristobal of A.H.* differs from Steiner's earlier fiction in being explicitly Judaized. But by the late 1970s, when Steiner first published this work in the *Kenyon Review*, the Shoah had become an explicit subject for literary fiction which was a radically different cultural context from the 1950s and 1960s. Unlike the universalized 'deeps of the sea', the search for ultimate meaning in *The Portage* is made manifest by a journey to San Cristobal with Steiner's protagonists, quite literally, carrying the baggage of history on their backs.

As with *Anno Domini*, Steiner in *The Portage* deliberately makes sense of the past in the language of a 'babel' of national cultures – here Israel, Russia, America, Britain, Germany and France. This is a text, in other words, not about the Shoah itself but about the effect that this history has produced on the contemporary world. Ronald Sharp has rightly argued that the issue of translation, as formulated at length in *After Babel*, is at the heart of the novella – after all, a 'portage', like a translation, is a form of transportation, a carrying over from one place to another. In this spirit, the structure of Steiner's novella is a series of 'congruent or discordant translations' of Hitler in the contemporary world by a chaotic variety of national interpreters.[22] The fact that the journey to San Cristobal is unfinished indicates Steiner's refusal to make his story conform to a reality principle or an ultimate translation (the name 'San Cristobal' seems to point towards a Christian transcendence of Jewish suffering). Instead, Steiner offers a range of possible commentaries for the reader to engage with. The helicopters hovering at the end, as Joseph Lowin has argued, indicate the open-endedness of the text (in desperate need of his reader's counter-interpretation) as we are asked to see which national narrative is about to be imposed on history. In his essay, 'Postscript', Steiner stated that after the death camps 'everything is possible'. *The Portage* both attempts to represent this 'everything' and, by doing so, asks the reader (or his theatrical audience) to reject any one version of the past.[23]

The outrageously disturbing voice of 'A.H.' represents the ultimate negative transcendence. Just as 'A.H.' is a master orator, *After Babel* is similarly concerned to show how 'grammar and vocabulary' have become a 'barrier to new feeling' – not unlike the American student in 'Cake' who asks (like his author) whether the humanities have made us less human. Such is the 'night' language of Steiner's 'A.H.' which threatens, once again, to overwhelm Steiner's readers. At the same time, Steiner, in *After Babel*, questions whether 'material reality' can have a history outside of 'language, outside of interpretative belief in essentially linguistic records' as 'silence knows no history'.[24] The divide between a Steinerian Judaic textual homeland – history as, above all else, a function of language and memory – and the theological need to translate language into a higher ineffable realm (whatever that may be) is most obviously figured in *The Portage*. Above all, the contrast between memory and negative transcendence is signified in Leiber, the Judaic remembrancer, and 'A.H.', the failed messiah *par excellence*.

What the crudest readings of *The Portage* have done, is to simply contrast Leiber and 'A.H.' and argue that one is moral and the other is immoral and that Steiner has mistakenly given too much credence to the evil figure. Alvin Rosenfeld contends, somewhat over-generously, that Leiber's fractured and partial testimony is as achieved as a Paul Celan poem while, on the other hand, the last speech of Steiner's Hitler is as kitschy and dangerous as a bad 'B' movie (he invokes *The Boys from Brazil* in this context as an example of the perniciousness of popular culture).[25] But the point is that Steiner is not simply contrasting Leiber and 'A.H.' but is portraying them as part of the same dialectic. Far from being easily containable opposites, these figures are, above all, two different aspects of George Steiner. Just as Leiber tells the story of Steiner's father's escape from Paris, and the slaughter of his friends and family, 'A.H.' has both a 'withered arm' like Steiner and also repeats verbatim much of his philosophy of antisemitism in *In Bluebeard's Castle*. This does not, however, give 'A.H.' the authority of Steiner's criticism – as those who condemned the text have argued – but is, more subtly, Steiner's most profound means of thinking against himself.

Both Steiner and 'A.H.', above all, agree that 'Jews are the conscience of the world' (in the guise of monotheism, Christianity and Marxism) and that this has caused a lethal resentment which culminated in the Shoah. In embodying the redemptive homeland of the text – at its most creative and lasting in an extraterritorial Central Europe – Jews, such as Leiber, personify an essential life-giving cultural transcendence. But this 'blackmail of transcendence' could also take a catastrophic form and become, as 'A.H.' argues, a death warrant for the Jews.[26] This unbearable ambiguity – or dialectic between the aesthetic and the barbaric – is, I believe, at the heart of *The Portage*, which is why 'A.H.' primarily explores the night-side of Steiner's own thinking.

Steiner's protagonists are all attracted to the terrible beauty of war or an absolute knowledge *in extremis* which, in a bitter paradox, defines their humanity at the very point at which they destroy themselves. In *The Portage*, Steiner places his own thinking in this provocative position of negative transcendence. Steiner has long since described our 'post-cultural age' as the time of the after-Word. In his latest restatement of this abiding motif, in his *Real Presences*, he characterized modernity as the 'break between word and world which [for him] constitutes one of the very few genuine revolutions of spirit in Western history'. Once again, he enacts the paradox of modernism, defending traditions which, as Finkelstein argues, 'bear within themselves the potential of their violent unmaking'.[27] Steiner's messianic gesture towards the mending of the vessels – the restoration of the break between word and world – leads, in one direction, to the grotesquely messianic figure of 'A.H.' who claims to have brought about the restoration of the Jewish state. In another direction, it leads to his 1991 novella 'Proofs' which re-examines the messianic impulse generated by Marxism. What the critics of *The Portage* especially objected to was Steiner giving his Hitler-figure the last word in the text and, especially, in the guise of Alec McCowen, in Christopher Hampton's adaptation of the play. But it is precisely Steiner's faith in his readers and audience, that they will offer a counter-interpretation to the language of 'A.H.', which distinguishes his deliberately unfinished dialogue in this work.

It is in these terms that *The Portage* can be related to 'Proofs' which has as its backdrop the rise and fall of Stalinism. Like *The Portage*, 'Proofs' is an extended and many-sided exploration of the grammar of messianism which points both to the Gulag and Steiner's utopian textual homeland. The *Professore*, in this story, is a devoted member of his local Circle for Marxist Revolutionary Theory and Praxis and is also a proof-reader. He wishes to create a perfect textual and material homeland but, at the same time, overflows with self-doubt as he witnesses the fall of Communism throughout Eastern Europe. As the Berlin Wall begins to crumble, the *Professore* discovers that his eyesight is deteriorating rapidly. These two events – public and private – are brought together as he remains a Marxist 'because otherwise I could not be a proof-reader!... Communism means taking the errata out of history. Reading proofs' (p. 350). The messianism, which Steiner has always located within the Socialist project, is not unlike his character's obsessive perfectionism. After all, we learn right at the beginning of the story that the *Professore* is there to 'order the world as only print can' (p. 314).

The duality of his messianic impulse, even at the point at which the *Professore* acknowledges its legacy of mass murder and inhuman oppression, is neatly signified by his growing blindness which is both the blindness of prophecy as well as his inability to see the suffering wrought in the name of his ideals. Just as the early Christians 'panted for the end of time like dogs dying of thirst' (p. 336), it is the Biblical 'prophecy and promise' (p. 337) of Marx which has struggled to accomplish earthly perfection. For Steiner, the Judaic rejection of Christ led directly to the death camps, just as the 'promise' of Marx led to the Gulag. His fiction, I believe, recognizes that this potential for both barbarity and aesthetic perfection continues in his own transcendent philosophy. This is also, most obviously, the imaginative subtext for Steiner's continued preoccupation with Heidegger and his intense empathy in *Errata* for other apologists for antisemitism and Nazism.[28]

Norman Finkelstein has usefully applied Walter Benjamin's account of 'The Destructive Character' to George Steiner. According to Benjamin, this figure 'stands in the front line of the traditionalists.... [he] has the consciousness of historical man, whose deepest emotion is an insuperable mistrust of the course of things and a readiness at all times to recognize that everything can go wrong.' For Benjamin, the destructive character is 'reliabilty itself'.[29] As *Errata* makes clear, there is certainly something profoundly self-destructive in Steiner's refusal to make any one area of expertise his own and to continually question his own reliability in his fiction. On the one hand, Steiner holds up the ideals of pure scholarship or philosophy or poetry, studied in his perfect Platonic University. But, of course, it is this model of scholarship – his father's model above all – that he has failed. Steiner dismisses Freud, where the son wishes to kill the father, and evokes instead the unattainable Classical and Biblical absolute of the

Patriarch. And yet, Steiner can only ever punish himself in these terms. No wonder he thinks of the subtext of his fiction, perversely perhaps, as being about a 'lamed or powerless God'.[30] Those in his fiction who aim for a God-like perfection inevitably destroy themselves.

Like many classical modernists, Steiner invokes the authority of tradition in relation to an apocalyptic present. He is, in Benjamin's terms, in the front line of the traditionalists who recognize that, at any time, 'everything can go wrong'.[31] At one point in Steiner's defining essay, 'Our Homeland the Text' (1985), he speaks of the Jewish cleric 'deranged by some autistic, otherworldly addiction to speculative abstractions and the elixir of truth'; and more recently he has described this 'autistic ubiquity' to be the 'very essence of Judaism'.[32] His use of this term, autism – which also includes bewilderingly God, chess-players, deconstructionists, and himself – points not only to the essence of Judaism but also to the essence of George Steiner. The 'autistic ubiquity' of the diaspora seems to me to be a terribly ambiguous term. All of Steiner's suicidal male protagonists (his destructive characters) can be described as autists who reject modernity for a higher aesthetic order. But such autistic transcendence is, as he says, deranged and redemptive in equal measure.

For this reason Steiner has a stake in the continuation of western culture while also recognizing that it has completely 'gone wrong'. Such is his 'wager on transcendence' where 'diasporic Jews' are both the 'elixir of truth' and embody all of the regimes of thought – Monotheism, Christianity, and messianic socialism – which have supposedly led to their own destruction. In an early uncollected essay Steiner summed up this 'sinister and mendacious dialectic' which has made diasporic Jews both a 'stranger among others' and also a 'stranger' to themselves. It is, he argues, this 'limbo of identity' – in an extra-territorial zone between 'gentile acceptance' and 'transcendental separateness' – which has led both to a 'quantum leap' in Jewish creativity and also to the 'venom of antisemitism'.[33] For all his unceasing provocation, Steiner is above all a 'stranger to himself' in his fiction and, for this reason, his imagination is at its most piquant in relation to his own dearly held beliefs.

Notes

1 George Steiner, 'Humane Literacy', *Language and Silence: Essays 1958–1966* (London: Faber & Faber, 1967; repr. Pelican Books, 1969), p. 21.

2 For a recent account of Steiner's unpublished journalism, see Mark Krupnick, 'Steiner's Literary Journalism: "The Heart of the Maze"' in Nathan A Scott, Jr. and Ronald A. Sharp (eds), *Reading George Steiner* (Baltimore and London: The Johns Hopkins University Press, 1994), pp. 43–57.

3 Steiner, 'Postscript', *Language and Silence*, p. 199 and 'The Long Life of Metaphor: an Approach to the Shoah' in Berel Lang (ed.), *Writing and the Holocaust* (New York: Holmes & Meier, 1988), pp. 154–71. For Steiner's latest account of the Shoah in these terms, see *No Passion Spent: Essays 1978–1996* (London: Faber & Faber, 1996), pp. 328–89.

4 For Steiner's dismissal of his fiction, see 'A Responsion' in Scott and Sharp, *Reading George Steiner*, p. 279 and the book cover of *Proofs and Three Parables* (London: Faber & Faber, 1992).

5 Cited in Guido Almansi, 'The Triumph of the Hedgehog' in Scott and Sharp, *Reading George Steiner*, pp. 58–73.

6 'Our Homeland the Text' (1985) is collected in *No Passion Spent*, pp. 304–27.

7 A.S. Byatt, 'George and his Dragons', *The Independent*, 7 January 1996, Book Section, p. 1.

8 *Real Presences: Is there anything 'in' what we say?* (London: Faber & Faber, 1989) and *In Bluebeard's Castle: Some Notes towards the Redefinition of Culture* (London: Faber & Faber, 1971), pp. 49–74.

9 'A Responsion', in *Reading George Steiner*, p. 279 and 'Literature and the Contemporary Jewish Experience: A Colloquium', *The Jewish Quarterly*, vol. 31, nos 3–4 (1984), pp. 6–19.

10 'A Responsion', pp. 279–80.

11 Robert Alter, 'Against Messiness', *Times Literary Supplement*, 12 January 1996, pp. 23–4.

12 Cited in *George Steiner: a Reader* (Harmondsworth: Penguin Books, 1984), pp. 20–1 and Norman Finkelstein, *The Ritual of New Creation: Jewish Tradition and Contemporary Literature* (New York: SUNY Press, 1992), p. 97 and chapter 6.

13 Alter, 'Against Messiness', p. 23.

14 'The Duellist', *The Guardian Weekend*, 6 January 1996, p. 18 and pp. 16–18.

15 'Dying is an Art', *Language and Silence*, p. 189.

16 'Dying is an Art', pp. 189–90.

17 'A Responsion', p. 276 and 'A Kind of Survivor', *Language and Silence*, pp. 119–35.

18 Jacqueline Rose, *The Haunting of Sylvia Plath* (London: Virago Press, 1991), p. 222 and chapter 6. See also 'K' (1963) in *Language and Silence*, p. 163 and pp. 160–8 and *Errata: an Unexamined Life* (London: Weidenfeld & Nicolson, 1997), p. 52.

19 All references to George Steiner's fiction are to his *The Deeps of the Sea and Other Fiction* (London: Faber & Faber, 1996) and page numbers will be in parenthesis in the body of the text.

20 'The Cleric of Treason', in *George Steiner: a Reader*, pp. 178–204.

21 'Book-Keeping of Torture', *Sunday Times*, 10 April 1988, cited in Tony Kushner, *The Holocaust and the Liberal Imagination: a Social and Cultural History* (Oxford: Basil Blackwell, 1994), p. 19.

22 Ronald Sharp, 'Steiner's Fiction and the Hermeneutics of Translation', in *Reading George Steiner*, p. 208 and pp. 205–29. This is one of the first essays to treat Steiner's fiction with the seriousness it deserves. See also, in this regard, Sara R. Horowitz, *Voicing the Void: Muteness and Memory in Holocaust Fiction* (New York: SUNY Press, 1997), pp. 173–80.

23 'Postscript' (1966) in *Language and Silence*, p. 193 and Joseph Lowin, 'Steiner's Helicopters', *Jewish Book Annual*, vol. 41 (1983–4), pp. 48–56.

24 *After Babel: Aspects of Language and Translation* (Oxford: Oxford University Press, 1975), pp. 21 and 29.

25 Alvin Rosenfeld, *Imagining Hitler* (Bloomington: Indiana University Press, 1985), pp. 83–102. See also Hyam Maccoby, 'George Steiner's "Hitler"', *Encounter*, vol. 58, no. 5 (May 1982), pp. 27–34.

26 This argument was first made in detail in *In Bluebeard's Castle*, p. 40 and pp. 31–48.

27 Steiner, *Real Presences*, p. 93 and Finkelstein, *The Ritual of New Creation*, p. 98.

28 *Errata*, pp. 137–9 and 126–8 and *Martin Heidegger* (London: Fontana, 1975).

29 Quoted in Finkelstein, *The Ritual of New Creation*, pp. 99–100.

30 *Errata*, p. 158.

31 I owe this discussion to Finkelstein, *The Ritual of New Creation*, p. 100.

32 'A Responsion', p. 277 and 'Our Homeland the Text' (1985) in *No Passion Spent*, p. 324.

33 'A View from Without', *The Jewish Quarterly*, vol. 16, no. 4 (1968–9), p. 4 and pp. 3–5 and vol. 17, no. 1 (1969), pp. 3–9.

5
The Holocaust as Seen through the Eyes of Children
Andrea Reiter

A small number of books for an adult readership present the Holocaust or the events leading up to it through the experience of children: for example, Anna Gmeyner's *Manja* (1938), Ilse Aichinger's *Die größere Hoffnung* (1948), Elie Wiesel's *La Nuit* (1958), Ruth Klüger's *weiter leben. Eine Jugend* (1992), Binjamin Wilkomirski's *Bruchstücke: Aus einer Kindheit 1939–1948* (1995), Imre Kertész' *Sorstalanság* (1975).[1] All of the above authors were in one way or another personally affected by the Holocaust, they share the Jewish fate, and their texts share the auto-biographical experience. While it is difficult enough for writers of camp memoirs to present their selves in a different state, it is even more prob-lematic to present the childhood self. It seems almost inevitable that adult views are placed in the children's minds.[2]

As the texts vary in degree of fictionality, the time they were written, and the personal circumstances of their authors, they have in the past been assigned to separate categories such as exile literature (Gmeyner), memoirs (Klüger, Wilkomirski, Kertész) and Holocaust literature (Aichinger, Wiesel). It seems to me, however, that their common denominator, namely the perspective of the child, merits discussing them as a group – in particular as they have a special way of presenting the historical event.

Until now, the difference between fictional and non-fictional repre-sentation of the Holocaust was assumed to be one between innovation and tradition. Memoirists almost invariably follow the form of the report and show little inclination to innovative language, even though in trying to speak the 'unspeakable' they risk trivialization. Only a minority of survivors is concerned about the potential repeat-ability of an event that can be narrated. In contrast, fictional accounts can be more inventive. They may try to find a 'new' language, new forms of expression for the unprecedented experience. They are not constrained by truth, realism and objectivity.[3]

Some memoirs published during the past few years, however, require us to rethink this distinction. These authors, who have reached the age of grandparenthood,[4] had survived the camps as children and now, 50 years on, revisit their childhood experience. Events in the camps have imprinted themselves in many people's minds: documentaries, Hollywood films (such as *Holocaust* and *Schindler's List*) and, of course, the concentration-camp reports themselves have contributed icons through which we remember the Holocaust. Through this a point of saturation has been reached; in other words a climate has been created that gave the publication of a book like Daniel Goldhagen's *Hitler's Willing Executioners* the impact of a bombshell: not that Goldhagen had any new facts, but it was not least the way he expressed them that contributed to the stir.[5]

I would like to argue that this is also true for some of the latest childhood-in-camp memoirs. Like the authentic memoirists, Klüger, Wilkomirski and Kertész tell us the story of their own survival of a camp; but like the authors of fictional accounts they do so in a way that forces the reader to look at the narrated events with new eyes. To all three, perspective is of the utmost importance for its impact on the reader: it is the gaze of the child that allows us to see in a new way that which we think we already know. In psychoanalytic theory the 'gaze' is associated with parental power, which the growing child internalizes but can never really meet.[6] Unlike the authoritarian gaze of the parent, the child's gaze is naïve but accurate. The child's experience with adults in the camps does not invite internalizing the parental gaze. Binjamin Wilkomirski is haunted, even after release, by the betrayals of the adults which he witnessed in the camp. His fundamental trust in them has vanished. On his arrival in Switzerland after the war he draws parallels:

> I gasped for air – more children were led away by grown-ups – and I could not see where they were taken. This was the way it had been before, too. Only then it was gray uniforms that took them away with angry gestures. The gray uniforms carried sticks and whips. The ones they took away never came back.... Maybe this is all just to confuse me; it's dangerous when grown-ups are friendly to children, I say this to myself.... So – careful! The friendly grown-ups are the most dangerous, they are best at fooling you, I thought. (Wilkomirski, *Fragments*, pp. 15–18)

In the camps Wilkomirski has learned that the adults not only betray children but they kill them. Even the apparently friendly ones cannot be trusted – indeed, the child has to be especially wary of them. Nevertheless children who were not in immediate danger such as children in hiding like little Maciek in Louis Begley's *Wartime Lies* did identify with the enemy. A futile battle with bedbugs

> provided, in addition to a temporary material improvement in our comfort, another war game...: in this limited sphere, I could be a hunter and an aggressor, like SS units destroying partisans in the forest, very soon, rebellious Jews in the ghetto of Warsaw. The SS sometimes had to act in secret. So did we. Our landladies resented any mention of bedbugs on their premises....[7]

Children were more likely to be impressed by the smart uniforms of the SS. They were captivated by the position of power their torturers represented. Imre Kertész's narrator reports how he was relieved to see the German soldiers at his arrival at Auschwitz: 'because they looked smart, clean, and they were the only ones in this mess who seemed calm and firm' (Kertész, *Sorstalanság*, p. 91).[8] When he undergoes the infamous selection he feels immediate trust in the doctor, because of his pleasant appearance and his likeable face (Kertész, *Sorstalanság*, p. 98). Watching the doctor 'at work' he quickly realizes the logic behind the exercise: the strong and able-bodied go to the right, while the very young, the elderly and the frail go to the left. Claiming to be older than he actually was, the narrator is waved to the right. The boy identifies with the selector to such an extent that he is annoyed with him when he sends one of the men to the right who he thought was not fit (Kertész, *Sorstalanság*, p. 100).

In their unprejudiced and uninformed attitude, children not only notice details which escape the adult but interpret them in a way which makes them seem even more horrific. Wilkomirski reports an encounter with a rat in a dead woman's body: the child knows the woman's body swells when she carries a baby and he also has vague recollections of having been told that the belly begins to move when the baby is ready to be born; when he witnesses this happening with a dead woman his reaction is puzzlement but also curiosity. Eventually a rat appears from a big wound on the side of the woman's belly. 'I saw it, I saw it! the dead women are giving birth to rats!' (Wilkomirski, *Fragments*, p. 86). He is horrified but not so much at the sight as at its implications. If what he just witnessed was true then mothers did not only bear children but also the worst enemies of their offspring: Wilkomirski relates how the rats bit young children during the night thus inflicting wounds on them that, in the camp situation, meant certain death. Remembering the sight of his dying mother whom he had been able to visit shortly before, he wonders about his own identity: 'I touch my legs again and again. I undo the rags around my calves and feel the skin. Is it skin or do I actually have gray fur? Am I a rat or a human? I am a child – but am I a human child or a rat child, or can you be both at once?' (Wilkomirski, *Fragments*, pp. 86–7). Even much later, when his own son is born, the unexpected sight of hair on the baby's emerging head brings back the painful uncertainty about his own identity.

The child looks with the curiosity of the artist, with the burning eyes of the witness. Jehuda Bacon, who was deported to Terezin at the age of 13 and transferred to Auschwitz a year later, compares himself with other survivors: 'There I realized that – because I was a potential artist – I was seeing things totally differently, perhaps more intensively. Even then I wanted to keep everything in my eyes, I had to keep it. This unconscious: to keep, to remember. Why, I did not know.'[9] The child often does not understand what it sees. And because its mind, unlike the adult's, is not yet guided by logic, it is 'the pictures that remain fixed in your head' as Wilkomirski observed in a recent interview.[10] This inability to interpret and the lack of comprehension have a parallel in the adult's failure to express. The child's situation thus can be used by the adult author to compensate for this shortcoming.[11]

In addition to the problem of comprehension there is the question of memory. It is a recognized fact that even adult survivors remember certain experiences better than others. Some they have forgotten completely. Child-protagonists not only witnessed the camps differently but they also remember them differently. The younger the child during the ordeal, the more gaps in the memory. Wilkomirski, who survived the camps as a very young boy, only recalls glimpses, fragments which consequently also make up his book. He freely admits bouts of amnesia and uncertainty, often switching into the present tense when he wants to relate something that stuck in his mind most clearly. Especially in the early parts of his book, which cover the boy's time in a Swiss orphanage, his memory would be jolted by an event to which he reacted as he would have done in the camp, thus provoking irritation among his carers. Imre Kertész's narrator, on the other hand, never departs from the perspective of the child narrator, nor explains that with hindsight he knows better. 'The *Roman eines Schicksallosen* was not meant to contain a single sentence from beyond [the child's perception]. Only from the perspective of the natural naïveté of man can be told how Auschwitz was possible.'[12] Through this technique Kertész pulls his readers into the closed world he creates in the novel and does not allow them an escape. It is only at a different level – namely the narrator's choice of incidents, some of which have gained archetypal status (like the selection at the *Rampe* of Auschwitz) – that the superior insight of the adult author becomes obvious. Here, the child's perspective works both against and with the knowledge of the reader – the discrepancy between the two creates the charged atmosphere in the book and its impact. We would not be so horrified at the boy's identification with the SS doctor if we did not know already the implications of the selection.

In the *Roman eines Schicksallosen*, the narrator's abstention from qualifying the child's ideas, impressions and judgments thus becomes a literary pose. Additional proof of this pose is found in repeated remarks like 'versteht sich' (it is clear), 'natürlich' (naturally), 'das sah ich ein' (I realized that), etc., which in semantic terms can be called 'supersigns'. Collectively they constitute a meaning in direct opposition to that which the narrator claims to attach to his experiences. The literariness of these supersigns becomes further obvious when one remembers that Kertész has translated the prose writings of the Austrian postwar writer Thomas Bernhard, of which similar supersigns have been recognized as a hallmark.[13]

Literariness was defined by the Russian Formalists as 'a function of the *differential* relations between one sort of discourse and another'.[14] It is the contrast of poetic language to practical language which makes for the status of a text as literature. The Formalists called this technique 'defamiliarization' or 'estrangement'.[15] In poetry, for which Formalist analysis was originally designed, defamiliarization makes familiar words look new, as it were, and thus noticeable. Similarly, a prose text is defined as an assemblage of devices which are seen by both author and reader against the background of the tradition of style and genre. For the reader a genre, for instance, raises certain expectations. In everyday conversation they are usually fulfilled in order to permit the exchange of information. Literary discourse, on the other hand, frustrates these expectations. The degree to which this is the case has been taken as a measure of the literariness and ultimately of the quality of the text. Analogous to the distinction between practical and poetic language in poetry, the Formalists distinguish between the events and their reconstruction in prose: between the *fabula* and the *sujet*. 'The *sujet* creates a defamiliarizing effect on the *fabula*; the devices of the *sujet* are not designed as instruments for conveying the *fabula*, but are foregrounded at the expense of the *fabula*.'[16] This understanding also shapes the Formalists' attitude towards reality: literature is taken to be non-referential, their preoccupation with literariness excludes mimesis; reality, as viewed by the Formalists, is one of the components of the work and not a referent.[17] This is obviously where the writers we have been considering differ in their texts. For them the creation of literariness is not an end in itself. It becomes a means to cast a fresh light on the suffering in the camps during the Holocaust.[18] Certain images – such as the piles of corpses which were filmed by the Allied Forces at the liberation, the shoes, suitcases and other artefacts at the museum in Auschwitz – have, despite their horror, lost their effect because we have become used to them. Film-makers have noticed a similar saturation with certain images. Recent films about the camps thus make a point of avoiding them.[19]

Defamiliarization in Holocaust literature

Linked with the defamiliarizing quality of the Holocaust narrative from the perspective of the child is the presentation of questions hitherto deemed taboo. In Wilkomirski's as well as in Kertész's book, violence – even that perpetrated by Jews – is presented, as are apathy and unwillingness to comprehend. The way in which the stories are told, however, prevents them from slipping into pornography of the kind that is present in John Sack's much condemned journalistic presentation of Jewish revenge in *An Eye for an Eye*.[20] On the other hand 50 years after liberation Jewish guilt is admitted by other survivors; by Roman Frister, for example, who was a boy of about the same age as Kertész when he was deported.[21] He relates his survival as a success story, tainted only by the fact that he caused the death of a fellow inmate by taking his cap after his own was stolen by the Kapo who had raped him. While the child perspective adopted by Kertész leaves no doubt as to who is to blame, even if his juvenile narrator seems to identify with his persecutors, Frister's traditional auto-biographical approach invites the reader to absolve the narrator – which in itself, implies an admission of guilt on his behalf. In other words, where Kertész presents, Frister argues and explains. And this makes for the different literary quality of the two books.

The devices that characterize the concentration-camp texts with a child perspective are, first, the detailed report of specific incidents which shaped the child's view of life even beyond liberation (Wilkomirski, *Fragments*) and, secondly, the naïve interpretation and adoption of a simpleton's attitude towards the experiences in camp, inviting the reader to perceive the presentation as ironic (Kertész, *Sorstalanság*). Both devices violate our expectations as readers. When we dare imagine the fate of children in the camps, we anticipate sentimentality. When a child suffers, the reader sympathizes more readily. A tortured child mobilizes our instincts to protect, to care for, to save. Showing the impact of the persecution of the Jews, or effects of internment and war on the children, thus facilitates a stronger statement. The innocence of the children makes the brutality of the Nazi regime not only more obvious but also more irrational. The sentimental representation, however, distracts from the fact that the child's suffering is not intrinsically different from that of the adult and secondly seems to suggest that adult suffering is somehow more justified. Where the child is, however, presented as naively identifying with the persecutor, as shown in the example from Kertész's novel, the reader reacts with repulsion. Being deprived of sentimental identification and the chance to feel pity causes irritation. It is thus not surprising that the history of publication of Kertész's *Roman eines Schicksallosen* is one of swings and roundabouts. When the novel was finished in 1973 no Hungarian publisher wanted to take it. It was not published until 1975 and it took another 20 years for it to be translated into German. Only then did the book suddenly make an impact, putting Kertész's name on the literary map.[22]

The Viennese-born Ruth Klüger deploys yet another device when presenting herself as a child in Terezin, Auschwitz and Christianstadt (an auxiliary camp of Gross Rosen). Klüger, who is Professor of German at the University of California at Irvine, discovered feminism in the 1960s, and it is with the eyes of a feminist that she views her childhood in camp. This includes a critical assessment of her relationship with her mother, with whom she survived, and of the role of the woman in the Jewish religion ('I do not want to lay tables and light shabbat candles, I want to say kaddish' (Klüger, *Weiter leben*, p. 23)), as well as a controversial defence of the women among the camp orderlies.[23] What is relevant to our discussion is that Klüger, unlike Kertész or Wilkomirski, does not try to speak solely through the mind of the child; rather, she overlays it with the insights she has gained in adult life. Klüger, who since the publication of her memoir has been able to establish herself as a feminist critic,[24] managed to pick up the pieces after liberation and lead a life seemingly untainted by her camp experience. If it had not been for a near-fatal road accident in Göttingen in November 1988 we would not have her account. It was only during her slow recovery that she started writing about her childhood experience.

If one thing unites these three books on childhood in the camps, it is the absence of sentimentality. It is as if the authors could not afford self-pity. They needed to protect their psychological balance by spelling out even the most horrific experiences in ironic detachment, by detailed account or qualified by a theoretical frame. Thus the adoption of a defamiliarizing mode of representation by the survivor-narrator could have personal reasons as well as narratological ones. A famous exception to this is Elie Wiesel's account of his survival. However, Wiesel was one of the very few survivors who successfully turned their experience into an actual novel.

As in the scene in Wiesel's *Night* where the little boy is hanged, sentimentality seems to reign in fiction and turn the books into bestsellers; other examples are Bruno Apitz's *Nackt unter Wölfen* and André Schwartz-Bart's *The Last of the Just*.[25] Anna Gmeyner's *Manja* also belongs to this group, even if it did not achieve the sales of the other two, perhaps because it was published at the wrong time and by the wrong publisher. A notable exception among the fictional concentration camp texts is Ilse Aichinger's *Die größere Hoffnung*, which displays a surrealist approach to the theme. The superficial similarities of the latter two texts on the level of content underline the difference in the narratological approach of the two authors. Hence a comparison of the two novels can further illustrate our argument.

In both texts a group of children is at the centre of the story, with the difference being that Gmeyner also gives us the previous life of the children and the narration does not focus on them until the middle of the book. In both texts the main protagonists are girls (Manja and Ellen) who die on a bridge (Manja drowns, Ellen runs into an exploding shell). These parallels between the two novels, which were published ten years apart, should not obscure the differences: they do not cover the same time period, and the girls die for different reasons. Even the child perspective is used to different ends: Gmeyner presents a sociographic portrait of the interwar years in Germany, Aichinger a surrealist panorama of death and survival in the hinterland during the Second World War. Although the camps feature in both, neither is primarily concerned with them, and for this reason they are perhaps not directly comparable to the camp literature which I discussed above. Where the two novels differ most radically from each other is the way in which they go about telling their stories. Gmeyner does not shrink from employing stereotypes (the beautiful Jewess, the misshapen but intelligent Jew, the successful and sometimes exploitative Jewish businessman, the Nazi caricature – bulldog body, underprivileged but aspiring and cowardly). Because the children in *Manja* are portrayed as the mouthpieces of their parents, Gmeyner undermines the potential of the child perspective. However, this might be explained, at least to some extent, by the circumstances of the book's production and publication. It was written in exile and published by Querido in Amsterdam,[26] its author relying on literary realism not only to depict contemporary history, but also possibly to stir her readers into action.

On the other hand, Aichinger is less concerned with historical details.[27] She does not refer to the facts nor does she use the expected terms (she talks about the Jewish children as those who have 'four wrong grandparents', and the Hitler Youth as those who wear a uniform and carry daggers). Where Gmeyner characterizes the children in a metonymic fashion, through their language and their games, Aichinger shows their unfulfilled wishes in their dreams – the medium through which the adult can represent the child's mind. It is the dreams that demarcate the children from the adults: in children, distinctions between dream and reality are less clear cut:

> 'Dreamt?' Ellen exclaimed. 'No way! I would also have dreamt that the children do not want to play with me, then I would also have dreamt that my mother was expelled, and that I have to stay back on my own, I would have dreamt that nobody guarantees for me, I would have only dreamt that you have hidden the map and that my visa was not granted'. (*Die größere Hoffnung*, p. 10)

The children cling to the dreams because they do not want to know the truth of harsh reality (p. 17); it is only in their dreams that they can cross the borders into safety (chapter 3 'Das heilige Land' ('The Holy Land')). On waking they must realize that the undertaker who took their money has driven them around in circles. Dreams in *Die größere Hoffnung* are not escape routes for the children but constitute their true selves. In them the children are shown as autonomous and not subject to parental guidance and influence.

Aichinger is concerned with language, about which she theorizes in texts written after the novel.[28] Her surrealism is rooted in her critique of a language that had been corrupted by the Nazis.[29] According to Freud, dreams assimilate the poetic process. For Lacan the correspondence of displacement and condensation to metonymy and metaphor ties them in even more closely with literature. In the novel they are associated with ciphers like the visa Ellen tries to obtain, which changes from a means to escape to one that facilitates self-assertion; the star which is at the same time a sign of hope and pride and one of stigmatization and destruction; and Ellen, who stands for a life of self-determination which becomes fulfilled in her death.[30] The author herself has never been in a camp but she witnessed the deportation of her maternal grandmother, incidentally the only event in Aichinger's book (apart perhaps from the children's birthday party) which is depicted in a truly sentimental mode and is thus distinct from the rest of the novel.[31] Hidden in Vienna, Aichinger survived the Nazi regime. But with the experience she gained, hers was obviously a different task from that of Gmeyner's ten years earlier. Ellen, who has only two 'wrong grandparents', is not deported with the other children. And so, after the suicide of her grandmother, she decides to follow them. The incident in which she meets up with one of her friends is depicted in yet another dream in the chapter named 'Flügeltraum' ('Dream of Wings'), which starts off with a typical childish wish-fulfilment dream that the train driver of a Jewish transport forgets where he is supposed to go. In the whole chapter dream and reality merge. Aichinger's poetic imagination shows the influence of Sigmund Freud. Many years later the fusion of dream and reality will be seen as the essence of the cultural scene in Vienna at the turn of the century and referred to in titles of exhibitions and books.[32]

There is one section in her novel which curiously echoes a paragraph in Gmeyner's book. A comparison will, at once, show the differences between the two texts: Ernst Heidemann, a medical doctor and father of one of the five children in *Manja*, through whom Gmeyner herself speaks to the reader,[33] keeps a diary while recovering from tuberculosis in a Swiss resort in which he records the following thoughts:

> I know that this sky, in whose perfect blue I do not tire to look, to follow the course of the birds and clouds, I know that this is the same sky, in which the squadrons of war planes will meet. I see the blue with the knowledge of how poisonous and gray it can darken. (*Manja*, p. 167)

In a more poetic way, the narrator in Aichinger's text expresses a similar insight:

> Skyblue the sky was smiling. But they did not permit themselves to be misled. This clear, frank blue, the blue of the sky, the blue of the gentian and the blue of the *blaue Dragoner* reflected, in the sunlight, the blackness of the universe, this endless, unimaginable blackness, behind the frontiers. (*Die größere Hoffnung*, p. 67)

These two quotations are in their turn paradigmatic of the two texts. Where Gmeyner in a prophetic insight identifies the war machinery as the ultimate threat which the rising National Socialism poses, Aichinger does not actually name the forces that have already begun to destroy the innocence of childhood. The blue of the gentian as well as the blue of the *blaue Dragoner* is reflected by the sun. The sun does not discriminate: hope and desire – represented by the mythical blue flower, the symbol of the German Romantic – as well as of destruction – symbolized by the uniforms of the soldiers (*Die blauen Dragoner* is a soldier's song also popular among Nazi troops[34]) are equally mirrored. While Heidemann's thoughts on the state of the sky in Gmeyner's book give a realistic representation of one character's prophetic insight, and thus have no further structural relevance, the counterpart in Aichinger's text is linked through its symbolism with other parts in the book, indeed it is linked with the theme of the whole work. The quotation appears in the fourth section with the title 'Im Dienst einer fremden Macht' ('in the service of a foreign power') which contains the encounter between the group of Jewish children with the Hitler Youth. Ellen, whose hope of obtaining a visa to follow her mother into the safety of exile has been shattered, now lives for the greater hope which is vaguely but repeatedly connected with the blue of the sky. It can only be a 'greater hope' which the children attach to the blue sky because experience does not allow them any illusion about the treachery of this colour. Its fragility, of which the reader is constantly reminded, prepares her for the end of the text where Ellen, jumping off the destroyed bridge, reaches out for blue sky.

This comparison shows that it is the devices employed by the two authors rather than the content of their works that distinguish Aichinger's *Die größere Hoffnung* from Gmeyner's *Manja*. While Aichinger has used the child-protagonists to give us a child's perspective and thus a strange insight into the Holocaust, Gmeyner did not exploit this potential. Although very different in many respects,

Aichinger's novel has an effect on the reader which is remarkably similar to that produced by the works discussed above. Like their authors she achieves this by defamiliarizing the events. The history of her novel's reception shows some similarities with that of Kertész's and Wilkomirski's. As well as being criticized for its lack of realism,[35] it has been acknowledged as 'literature' through the award of prizes. Nevertheless, the book never gained the recognition and readership it deserves. Choosing defamiliarization rather than sentimental representation can gain the author literary recognition, but is, at the same time, more of a risk in market terms, and it is with the employment of child-protagonists that this becomes more readily apparent.

Notes

1 Anna Gmeyner, *Manja* (Amsterdam: Querido, 1938; repr. Mannheim: Persona, 1987); Ilse Aichinger, *Die größere Hoffnung* (Amsterdam: Bermann-Fischer, 1948; Frankfurt am Main: Fischer Taschbuch Verlag, 1986); Elie Wiesel, *La Nuit* (Paris: Editions de Minuit, 1958) and *Night* (New York: Hill and Wang, 1960); Ruth Klüger, *weiter leben: Eine Jugend* (Göttingen: Wallstein, 1993); Binjamin Wilkomirski, *Bruchstücke: Aus einer Kindheit 1939–1948* (Frankfurt am Main: Jüdischer Verlag, 1995) and *Fragments: Memories of a Wartime Childhood* (New York: Schocken, 1996); Imre Kertész, *Sorstalanság* (Budapest: Szépirodalmi 1975) and *Roman eines Schicksallosen* (Reinbeck: Rowohlt, 1996).

2 For a detailed discussion of this, see Naomi B. Sokoloff, *Imagining the Child in Modern Jewish Fiction* (Baltimore and London: Johns Hopkins University Press, 1992) esp. part I: 'Representing the Voice of the Child'. I also owe important suggestions to Catherine Mowbray's unpublished paper on 'Representing Children in Literature of the Holocaust'.

3 For a discussion of authentic versus fictionalized accounts, see Andrea Reiter, *'Auf daß sie entsteigen der Dunkelheit'. Die literarische Bewältigung von KZ-Erfahrung* (Vienna: Löcker, 1995).

4 On the role of grandparents in the discourse about the Shoah, see *Spuren der Verfolgung. Seelische Auswirkungen des Holocaust auf die Opfer und ihre Kinder*, edited by Gertrud Hardtmann (Gerlingen: Bleicher, 1992).

5 Daniel Goldhagen, *Hitler's Willing Executioners: Ordinary Germans and the Holocaust* (New York: Alfred Knopf, 1996).

6 See Laura Mulvey, 'Visual Pleasure and Narrative Cinema', *Visual and Other Pleasures* (London: Macmillan, 1989), pp. 14–29. The term is actually taken over from the theory of non-verbal communication; see, for example, Michael Argyle, *Bodily Communication*, 2nd edn (London: Routledge, 1988), pp. 161, 164.

7 Louis Begley, *Wartime Lies* (London: Macmillan, 1991; Picador, 1992), pp. 93–4.

8 Where only the German edition has been quoted all translations are mine.

9 Barbara Johr, *Reisen ins Leben. Weiterleben nach einer Kindheit in Auschwitz:*

Mit einer Textliste zum gleichnamigen Film und Beiträgen von Susanne Benöhr und Thomas Mitscherlich (Bremen: Donat, 1997), p. 38.

10 Anne Karpf, 'Child of the Shoah, *The Guardian: G2*, 11 February 1998, pp. 2–6.

11 See Sokoloff, *Imagining the Child*, p. 15.

12 Iris Radisch, 'Hiob von Ungarn', *Die Zeit*, 21 March 1997, p. 13.

13 See Gudrun Kuhn, *'Ein philosophisch-musikalisch geschulter Sänger'. Musikästhetische Überlegungen zur Prosa Thomas Bernhards*, Epistemata. Würzburger wissenschaftliche Schriften. Reihe Literaturwissenschaft 183 (Würzburg: Königshausen und Neumann, 1996).

14 Terry Eagleton, *Literary Theory: An Introduction* (Oxford: Blackwell, 1989) p. 5.

15 See Victor Shklovsky, 'Art as Technique', *Russian Formalist Criticism: Four Essays*, translated and with an introduction by Lee T. Lemon and Marion J. Reis, Regents Critics Series (Lincoln and London: University of Nebraska Press, 1965) pp. 3–24.

16 Ann Jefferson, 'Russian Formalism', *Modern Literary Theory*, edited by Ann Jefferson and David Robey, 2nd edn (London: Batsford, 1986) p. 31.

17 Ibid., pp. 26f.

18 Sokoloff does mention the defamiliarizing effect of the child perspective; however, she does so only in passing (see pp. 26, 35, 109). In contrast, my point here is that the authors, all of whom relate personal experience, chose the point of view deliberately to achieve this effect.

19 Consider, for instance, Thomas Mitscherlich's *Reisen ins Leben* (1996) and Wilhelm Rösing's trilogy on Jewish Exiles (*Ernst Federn*, 1992; *Hans Keilson*, 1996; *Thomas Geve*, 1997).

20 John Sack, *An Eye for an Eye* (New York: Basic Books, 1993).

21 Roman Frister, *Die Mütze oder Der Preis des Lebens. Ein Lebensbericht* (Berlin: Siedler, 1997; original publication in Hebrew, 1993).

22 '"Das 20. Jahrhundert ist eine ständige Hinrichtungsmaschine"': Imre Kertész im Gespräch mit Gerhard Moser', *Literatur und Kritik: Sprache und Verbrechen*, 313/314 (April 1997), pp. 44–9. In comparison it took only four years for Frister's novel to be published in German translation.

23 For a critique of Klüger's feminist stance, see Eva Lezzi: '*weiter leben*: Ein deutsches Buch einer Jüdin?', *Frauen in der Literaturwissenschaft: Rundbrief: Ethnizität*, 49 (December 1996) pp. 14–20.

24 See e.g. Ruth Klüger, *Frauen lesen anders: Essays*, Deutscher Taschenbuchverlag 12276 (Munich: Deutscher Taschenbuchverlag, 1996).

25 Bruno Apitz, *Nackt unter Wölfen* (Frankfurt am Main: Röderberg, 1982); André Schwartz-Bart, *The Last of the Just* (London: Secker & Warburg, 1961).

26 See the preface to *Manja* by Heike Klapdor-Kops, pp. 5–12.

27 See my article 'Narrating the Holocaust: Communicating the End or the End of Communication?', *Patterns of Prejudice*, 29/2–3 (1995), pp. 75–87.

28 See my article 'Ilse Aichinger: the Poetics of Silence', *Contemporary German Writers: Their Aesthetics and Their Language*, edited by Arthur Williams, Stuart Parkes and Julian Preece (Bern, Berlin and New York: Lang, 1996), pp. 209–21.

29 See Aichinger, 'Aufruf zum Mißtrauen', *Aufforderung zum Mißtrauen:*

Literatur, Bildende Kunst, Musik in Österreich seit 1945, edited by Otto Breicha, Gerhard Fritsch (Salzburg: Residenz, 1967) p. 10.

30 See Dagmar Lorenz, *Ilse Aichinger* (Königstein/Ts: Athenäum, 1981) pp. 67–76.

31 Here I disagree with Lorenz who cannot see any sentimentality in the text: see Lorenz, *Ilse Aichinger*, p. 76.

32 Consider, for example, the exhibition *Traum und Wirklichkeit. Wien 1870–1930* (Vienna 28 March–6 October 1985), and Joseph P. Strelka, *Zwischen Wirklichkeit und Traum. Das Wesen des Österreichischen in der Literatur* (Tübingen/Basle: Francke, 1994).

33 See the introduction by Klapdor-Kops.

34 See my article 'Narrating the Holocaust'.

35 See, for example, Lawrence Langer, *The Holocaust and the Literary Imagination* (New Haven and London: Yale University Press, 1975), esp. pp. 124–65; see also John Margetts, 'Hope Unfulfilled: Observations on the Impact of Ilse Aichinger's Novel *Die größere Hoffnung*', *Neophilologus*, 74, 3 (July 1990) pp. 408–25.

6

From behind the Bars of Quotation Marks: Emmanuel Levinas's (Non)-Representation of the Holocaust

Robert Eaglestone

Introduction

Emmanuel Levinas has often been described as a post-Holocaust philosopher. In his very short autobiographical statement 'Signature', he notes that his biography and work are 'dominated by the presentiment and the memory of the Nazi horror'.[1] Why, then, does he refer to the Holocaust so sparingly? And, perhaps more importantly, what does this silence tell us?

Levinas, seen by Zygmunt Bauman as 'the greatest moral philosopher of the twentieth century', is a profound influence on a range of thinkers from Jacques Derrida to Luce Irigaray to John Paul II.[2] He was born in a Jewish family in Kovno, Lithuania and studied in Germany under Husserl and Heidegger. In 1928, he moved to France where he worked as a junior teacher and administrator at the Alliance Israélite Universelle and began to publish philosophical work. These essays, including one on the evils of 'Hitlerism', are credited with having introduced phenomenology to France, to Sartre and de Beauvoir.[3] In 1931 he was granted French citizenship and he married one year later. Having done military service and specializing as a translator of German and Russian, he was mobilized at the beginning of the war. In 1940, with the 10th Army, he was captured at Rennes and transported to Germany, to a camp near Magdeburg. There, with other Jewish military POWs, Emmanuel Levinas spent the war. His wife and daughter were hidden in France by friends and then by St Vincent de Paul nuns. The rest of his family including his parents, parents-in-law and brothers Boris and Aminadab, were murdered in Kovno.[4]

Behind the bars of quotation marks

Levinas writes:

> There were seventy of us in a forestry commando unit for Jewish
> prisoners of war in Nazi Germany ... The French uniform still
> protected us from Hitlerian violence. But the other men, called free,
> who had dealings with us or gave us work or orders or even a smile
> ... stripped us of our human skin. We were subhuman, a gang of
> apes ... we were no longer part of the world. Our comings and
> goings, our sorrow and laughter, illnesses and distractions, the
> work of our hands and the anguish of our eyes ... all that passed in
> parenthesis. We were beings entrapped in their species; despite all
> their vocabulary, beings without language. Racism is not a bio-
> logical concept; anti-semitism is the archetype of all internment ...
> How can we deliver a message about our humanity which, from
> behind the bars of quotation marks, will come across as anything
> other than monkey talk?[5]

In all Levinas's work, the essay from which this half-story is extracted
is the longest account – the longest representation – of the events of
1933–45. This essay will close with the other half of the story. This
brief tale is as close as Levinas gets to representing the Holocaust.

This is not to say that Levinas never mentions the Holocaust. He
talks about it very briefly in interviews. Yet even in these, he avoids
representing the Holocaust as much as possible. A long interview with
him intertwines his biography and philosophical development, but
has a noticeable gap when dealing with the events of 1933–45: Levinas
only mentions that Heidegger 'has never been exculpated in my eyes
from his participation in National Socialism'.[6] Another begins with
the interviewer remarking 'I know that you don't like to dwell on
biographical details' and, here again, Levinas politely avoids discussing
the Holocaust except in philosophical terms.[7]

The Holocaust appears in odd, single sentences in his philosophical,
religious and more general essays.[8] His second major work has two
dedications at the beginning, both invoking victims of the Holocaust.
One is in the vernacular to the memory of those 'assassinated by the
National Socialists' and the 'millions on millions' of other victims of
the 'hatred of the other man, the same anti-semitism'; the other, in
Hebrew, to his murdered family.[9] Yet Levinas is not like the philosophers Emil Fackenheim derides who 'keep on acting as if,

philosophically, there is no difference between the six million and one child dying of cancer'.[10] Indeed, as Maurice Blanchot argues, it is the thought of the Holocaust that 'traverses, that bears, the whole of Levinas's philosophy'.[11] Terms which are central to Levinas's thought, like 'Trauma', 'Persecution' and 'Proximity' are drawn as much from the Nazi horror as from a philosophical vocabulary.[12] The Holocaust is never far from the surface of Levinas's thought. 'The essential problem', he said in interview, 'is: can we speak of an absolute commandment after Auschwitz? Can we speak of morality after the failure of morality?'[13] His philosophical work seeks an answer to this problem.

This answer – which, in a sense, comprises all Levinas's work after 1945 – is not the subject of this essay. This essay is concerned with the status of the representation of the Holocaust in Levinas's work. Since his thought is so involved with thinking after the Holocaust, why is the Holocaust itself not discussed more, why is it not *represented* in more than the odd sentence in Levinas's work? And, more importantly, what does his refusal to represent it mean for contemporary artists, philosophers, critics and historians? How does this refusal contribute to the debates raised in this volume by Berel Lang over the question of 'how to justify what is spoken'?

I suggest that Levinas's reasons for declining to represent the Holocaust are profound and deeply involved with his philosophical project, his desire to understand an ethics outside the 'fundamental conceptual system produced by the Greco-European adventure'.[14] These reasons, which may only be warnings or worries, are, I suspect, important for us today. Levinas declines to represent or to tell stories about the Holocaust because he believes that, in some way, any mode of representation will betray the events of the Holocaust, even to the point of making this event fall into the hands of those who share a philosophical orientation – at some deep level – with its perpetrators. Gillian Rose raises similar objections in her essay 'Beginnings of the day', where she discusses what she names 'the fascism of representa-tion'.[15] She argues that works which lead towards or encourage a spurious or mythological identification offer a dangerous, unreflective 'security'. To explore this, I am going to examine Levinas's under-standing of two modes of representation – art and history – and in turn relate these to the Holocaust.

Levinas, art and the Holocaust: 'feasting during a plague'

Levinas has a profound antipathy to artistic representation of all sorts. His work rejects the Hegelian claim that art has 'the vocation of revealing the truth'.[16] Even more vehemently, he rejects Nietzschean claims that art is worth more than truth, and Heidegger's claim – in 'The Origin of the Work of Art' – that art as poetry is 'founding' or an 'origin'. For Levinas, art can neither have nor reveal a transcendence beyond the ethical. For Levinas, the ethical is 'an irreducible structure upon which all other structures rest' and the aesthetic only *'seem[s]* to put us primordially in contact with an impersonal sublimity'.[17] He argues that the 'aesthetic orientation man gives to the whole of his world represents a return to enjoyment ... every going beyond enjoyment reverts to enjoyment'.[18] Even the most moving art work, which might appear to uncover some profound ethical moment, only moves us as a pleasure. For Levinas, the frisson of horror of *Schindler's List* is exactly that: a frisson from which we can walk away as we leave the cinema. It does not reveal the ethical or teach us about morality.

For Levinas, when we respond to images of suffering in film or in literature, we are not responding to the faces people actually present, to their suffering, but to dead celluloid or to carefully chosen words. The artistic representation is based on the absence of those it represents and, for Levinas, this makes responses to this shadow inauthentic and in bad faith. Art, he writes, 'does not know a particular type of reality; it contrasts with knowledge. It is the very event of obscuring, a descent of the night, an invasion of shadow ... art does not belong to the order of revelation.'[19] He continues, arguing that, in art:

> the world to be built is replaced by the essential contemplation of the shadow. This is not the disinterestedness of contemplation but of irresponsibility. The poet exiles himself from the city ... There is something wicked and egoist and cowardly in artistic enjoyment. There are times when one can be ashamed of it, as of feasting during a plague.[20]

For Levinas, then, representations of the Holocaust that lay claim to being artistic are irresponsible mis-representations, with something wicked and egoist and cowardly about them. In the end, they exist only within an economy of art and its enjoyment.

The work of a philosopher like Martha Nussbaum tests this argument. Unlike Levinas, Nussbaum argues that fiction is ethical because it acts as a dry run for life: identifying with fictional characters 'places us in a moral position that is favourable for perception and it shows us what it would be like to take up that position in life'.[21] Yet this position surely collapses in relation to the representation of the Holocaust. If we identify with a character in a piece of Holocaust fiction, don't we feel, in some way, nauseous, or blasphemous, aware of our inability to imagine the horror? And if we don't, isn't that perhaps in some ways worse? This is the point Gillian Rose makes when she argues that *Schindler's List* 'betrays the crisis of ambiguity in characterisation, mythologisation and identification, because of its anxiety that our sentimentality be left intact'.[22] We are left unreflective, 'piously joining the survivors putting stones on Schindler's grave', as if the Holocaust were a simple thing, about which one could offer sentimental homilies.[23] Moreover, in the end, perhaps we take our reactions to Holocaust fiction as a compliment to the text, to the skill of the writer 'Going beyond enjoyment' returns us to enjoyment, to 'literary appreciation'.

Levinas and Holocaust history

If art, then, proves an unrewarding ground for a Levinasian view of representation of the Holocaust, what about the other mode of representation – history? The representation of the Holocaust has been debated at length by historians in discussions over 'postmodernism'.[24] 'Postmodernist' historians suggest that history is just another genre of representation, 'a verbal structure in the form of a narrative prose discourse' put together following deep-seated ideological, 'epistemological, aesthetic and moral' demands and 'implicit, precritical sanctions'.[25] History, an 'imaginative discipline', in this understanding, cannot represent the truth. However, passing over these acute and important arguments, Levinas's philosophy still finds history deeply problematic as a way of representing the Holocaust.

Levinas's philosophical project is based on the conception of ethics as first philosophy. Underlying all thought and work, all philosophy, is the profoundest ethical relation with the Other, and this relationship is summed up in what Levinas calls the 'face to face'.[26] The Other appears, empirically, before us, and their face 'opens the primordial discourse whose first word is obligation'.[27] This moment of facing interrupts our enclosed self, and opens us to the Other. Our totalizing systems through which we understand the world are interrupted, dislocated by this call to our responsibility for the Other.

There is a problem in this account for Levinas. Where the face is absent, represented in writing or signs, for example, the Other is not encountered, and thus the moment of ethical obligation does not arise. To be expressed by symbols is for Levinas, 'precisely to decline expression'.[28] This problem is perhaps at its most acute in relation to the representation of the past, to history. History passes over the deaths and suffering of individuals.

Levinas writes that history, the construction of historiographers, 'recounts the way survivors appropriate the works of dead wills to themselves; it rests on the usurpation carried out by the conquerors, that is, by the survivors; it recounts enslavement, forgetting the life that struggles against slavery'.[29] Levinas is saying more here than simply 'the victors write the history'. Survivors as well as conquerors write. He is saying that history can account for names, numbers, dates, but not (to put it crudely) the life, the suffering, of the absent Other it names. For Levinas, history is only the outside, the exterior. 'It is not enough that tears be wiped away or death avenged', he wrote in a short book composed mostly during the war, 'pain cannot be redeemed ... no justice could make reparation for it'.[30] History misses the pain. It may recount it but the suffering is lost in the totalizing facts of an historical account of events. The 'I' has been turned into a thing, an event of history: the 'verdict of history is pronounced by the survivor who no longer speaks to the being he judges'.[31] Unable to speak, the absent Other, a suffering being to whom we are obligated before all else, disappears. This is, of course, the position Lyotard analyses in *The Differend*.[32]

The Holocaust, then, which Levinas describes as 'the paradigm of gratuitous human suffering', pre-eminently escapes history.[33] All the historical representations fail to account for the suffering. They fail even to 'represent' the events: rather, they just recite a seemingly endless list of never-living facts, appropriated by the discourse of history. This light makes clear the inadequacy of theories of history like that of Collingwood, outlined in *The Idea of History*.[34] Collingwood argues that the historian's task is to re-enact history in her or his mind. But how, even given exhaustive facts and figures, can the suffering be re-enacted, or even, perhaps, imagined by those who were not witness or victim to it? History cannot but forget 'the life that struggles against slavery'.

Aporias

It seems clear then why Levinas declines to re-tell stories about the Holocaust, why he refuses its representation. The Holocaust can not be represented not because, as Steiner suggests, it is some unutterably evil sublime, but simply because to represent it is to betray the suffering, to be hopelessly inadequate. Yet we are compelled not to forget the Holocaust.[35] How, then, is the Holocaust not to be forgotten?

For Levinas and for other survivors, memory resolves these problems. Memory, he writes, 'realises impossibility: memory, after the event, assumes the passivity of the past and masters it'.[36] That is, memory presents without representing. In this, as Paul Ricoeur remarks in passing, Levinas might be seen to be following the 'biblical watchword (from Deuteronomy) Zakhor, "Remember!"'.[37] Indeed, Levinas cites with approval Fackenheim's work, and his famous 614th commandment forbidding despair over Auschwitz, or its forgetting.[38] However, as Ricoeur points out, remembering 'is not the same thing as a call to historiography'.[39] Testimony, coming from personal memory, might appear also to be a way past this problem of representation. Yet testimony has its own problems. As Gillian Rose writes of Lanzmann's *Shoah*, it 'raises questions of the interestedness of memory and recall on the part of the interviewer and interviewed ... it depends on verbal narrations and representations which raise the same questions of the limit of representation'.[40] Likewise, elsewhere in this volume, Anna Hardman draws attention to the flawed interpretation of women's testimony. Testimony still falls within the purview of representation – either as history or as art. Further, it might be suggested that it is the silent testimony of those who cannot speak which is the more significant.

Does this mean that we – who cannot remember the Holocaust – should follow Levinas and not represent the Holocaust? We are trapped in an aporia: we are unable satisfactorily to represent (re-present) the Holocaust but we cannot let it go unrepresented. If art and history – the only modes of representation open to us – will always betray the suffering of the Holocaust, how can we speak, or at least justify our speech? How can we deliver a message about the victim's humanity which, from behind the bars of quotation marks, will come across as anything other than monkey talk?

A possible answer to this seeming aporia lies, perhaps, in understanding how Levinas understands his post-Holocaust philosophy, and philosophy in general. Levinas sees philosophy as 'a drama between philosophers', made up of interruptions.[41] Each interruption prevents philosophical ideas becoming a totalizing, delimiting dogma, set in stone. For Levinas, as for other postwar thinkers, the whole of western thought is in some way implicated in the Holocaust and his aim is to interrupt not just his philosophical predecessors but the ontological movement of western philosophy itself, to perform 'a dislocation of the Greek logos'.[42] However, this interruption is not achieved easily, because the only way of achieving it is to use as his philosophical tools the tradition – the pre-existing concepts, the ideas, the arguments – he is trying to interrupt. Thus, Levinas's thought is, in his words, 'a fine risk'.[43] To interrupt philosophy after the Holocaust involves doing philosophy, betraying the ethical urge to interrupt at the same time as interrupting. This in turn calls for another interruption and so on, ad infinitum. Levinas cites the Talmud, not as a proof, but as a parallel: 'the doctors of the Law will never have peace, neither in this world or the next; they go from meeting to meeting discussing always – for there is always more to discuss'.[44] There is no last word, no closure or final philosophical resolution for Levinas.

I suggest that, in thinking about the representation of the Holocaust, we take a similar line. The Holocaust must be, for us, represented, either through history or through art. This is an obligation laid on us. Levinas asked how it would be possible to convey a message 'from behind the bars of quotation marks'. His work suggests that the only way to do so would be to understand the quotation marks *as* quotation marks. Quotation marks show that discourse, conversation is taking place. I am suggesting that representation itself has to be understood as 'representation in quotation marks'. It puts itself into a conversation, and so welcomes interruption. Representation in this sense declines to be the last word, the final truth on the subject. Those who create representations – historians, artists, critics – must be acutely aware that their representations are made at the cost of betrayals and consequently must be open to interruption, to disagreement. Rather than hoping to create a final picture, the complete history, the true representation, the Holocaust must be seen as an uncrossable gap, a 'hole in history', in Levinas's phrase, that we cannot fill.[45] This sort of openness is asking for more than historical scepticism, or the openness of the artist to have her or his work criticized and discussed.[46] It demands that we do represent the Holocaust but abandon the nostalgia of a final answer, or the desire for a complete history, for the openness of an infinite discussion. Even representations which seem to call for silence (the remembrance room in the Holocaust Museum in Washington, for example) should call for debate, for speech. They should open and interrupt. Only this way will they fulfil their roles as witnesses.

Interruption does not, cannot lead to silence, or to being silenced. This 'post-structuralist' (for lack of a better word) account of the representation of the Holocaust does not open the door to deniers, as some historians, philosophers and critics have claimed. In addition to all their other faults (bad historical methodology, bad faith, barely concealed ulterior motives) deniers do not interrupt and contribute to an ongoing, infinite conversation. They try to shout down their opposition, and to finish the conversation, to begin a horrible silence by offering final facts and 'indisputable' historical readings. They remove the quotation marks from their conversations.

The aim of this essay has been to problematize the representation of the Holocaust by looking at Levinas's approach to representation. The suggestion has been that representation in general, and representations of the Holocaust in particular, exist as necessary betrayals of the events. In order to redeem themselves from this betrayal, these representations need to be understood not as final words or complete histories, but as contributions to an ongoing conversation about the Holocaust, a conversation which, Beckett-like, can't go on, but must go on. Levinas continues his story:

> And then, about half way through our long captivity, for a few short weeks, before the sentinels chased him away, a wandering dog entered our lives. One day he came to meet this rabble as we returned under guard from work. He survived in some wild patch in the region of the camp. But we called him Bobby, an exotic name, as one does with a cherished dog. He would appear at morning and was awaiting for us as we returned, jumping up and down and barking in delight. For him, there was no doubt that we were men.[47]

Levinas said that his aim was not to outline a system of ethics, but to understand the meaning of ethics. I have tried to outline what conferences and books about the Holocaust are doing: a constant ethical interruption of the necessary historical and artistic Holocaust representations, which can only be failed representations. Our task, like Bobby's, is to try endlessly to recognize the event and its victims' suffering from the failure of representation.

Notes

1 Emmanuel Levinas, 'Signature', in *Difficult Freedom: Essays on Judaism*, translated by Seán Hand (Baltimore: Johns Hopkins University Press, 1990), p. 291; see also pp. 291–5.

2 Zygmunt Bauman, *Modernity and the Holocaust* (Oxford: Polity Press/Blackwell, 1993), p. 214.

3 For Levinas's account of this, see Richard Kearney, *Dialogues with Contemporary Continental Thinkers* (Manchester: Manchester University Press, 1984), p. 52: Levinas says that 'it was Sartre who guaranteed my place in eternity by stating in his famous essay on Merleau-Ponty that he, Sartre, "was introduced to phenomenology by Levinas"'. The essay on 'Hitlerism' dates to 1934 and was reprinted, in a translation by Seán Hand, in *Critical Inquiry*, 17 (1990), pp. 62–71.

4 For a detailed biography, see Marie-Anne Lescourret, *Emmanuel Levinas* (Paris: Flammarion, 1994).

5 Emmanuel Levinas, 'The Name of a Dog, of Natural Rights', in *Difficult Freedom*, pp. 151–3. Quotation is from pp. 152–3.

6 Emmanuel Levinas, *Ethics and Infinity: Conversations with Philippe Némo*, translated by Richard A. Cohen (Pittsburg: Duquesne University Press, 1985), p. 41.

7 Salomon Malka, *Lire Levinas* (Paris: Les Editions du Cerf, 1984), p. 103.

8 See, for example, Levinas's specific discussion of the Holocaust as a philosophical event in 'Useless Suffering', translated by Richard Cohen, in *The Provocation of Levinas*, edited by Robert Bernasconi and David Wood (London: Routledge, 1988), pp. 156–67. Quotation is from pp. 162–3. See also the occasional reference in his collection of essays, *Proper Names*, translated by Michael B. Smith (London: Athlone, 1996). For examples in religious essays, see *Difficult Freedom*.

9 Emmanuel Levinas, *Otherwise than Being; or, Beyond Essence*, translated by Alphonso Lingis (London: Martinus Nijhoff, 1981), frontispiece.

10 Emil Fackenheim, *To Mend the World: Foundations of Jewish Thought* (New York: Schocken Books, 1982), p. 11.

11 Maurice Blanchot, 'Our Clandestine Companion', in *Face to Face with Levinas*, edited by Richard A. Cohen (Albany: SUNY Press, 1986), pp. 41–50. Quotation is from p. 50.

12 Elizabeth Weber, 'The Notion of Persecution in Levinas's *Otherwise than Being, or Beyond Essence*', translated by Mark Saatjian, in *Ethics as First Philosophy*, edited by Adriaan T. Peperzak (London: Routledge, 1995), pp. 69–76.

13 Tamra Wright, Peter Hughes, Alison Ainley, 'The Paradox of Morality: an Interview with Emmanuel Levinas', translated by Andrew Benjamin and Tamra Wright, in *The Provocation of Levinas*, pp. 168–80. Quotation is from p. 176.

14 Jacques Derrida, 'Violence and Metaphysics', in *Writing and Difference*, translated by Alan Bass (London: Routledge and Kegan Paul, 1978), pp. 79–153. Quotation is from p. 82.

15 Gillian Rose, 'Beginnings of the day', in *Mourning Becomes the Law* (Cambridge: Cambridge University Press, 1996), pp. 41–62. Quotation is from p. 48.

16 G.W.F. Hegel, *Introductory Lectures on Aesthetics*, edited by Michael Inwood,

translated by Bernard Bosanquet (Harmondsworth: Penguin, 1993), p. 60.

17 Emmanuel Levinas, *Totality and Infinity: An Essay on Exteriority*, translated by Alphonso Lingis (London: Kluwer Academic Publishers, 1991), p. 79.

18 Ibid., p. 140.

19 'Reality and Its Shadow', in Emmanuel Levinas, *Collected Philosophical Papers*, translated by Alphonso Lingis (Dordrecht: Kluwer Academic Publishers, 1987), pp. 1–14. Quotation is from p. 3.

20 Ibid., p. 12.

21 Martha Nussbaum, *Love's Knowledge: Essays on Philosophy and Literature* (Oxford: Oxford University Press, 1990), p. 162.

22 Rose, 'Beginnings of the day', p. 48.

23 Ibid.

24 For a good introduction to this, see *The Postmodern History Reader*, edited by Keith Jenkins (London: Routledge, 1997). For a further, detailed discussion of postmodernism, the ethics of history and the Holocaust, see articles in the special issue of *Rethinking History*, 'The Good of History', edited by Robert Eaglestone and Susan Pitt, forthcoming.

25 Hayden White, *Metahistory: the Historical Imagination in Nineteenth Century Europe* (Baltimore: Johns Hopkins University Press, 1973), pp. ix, x.

26 This is a (very) brief summary of the core of his first major work, *Totality and Infinity*. His second major text, *Otherwise than Being, or Beyond Essence*, less well known and more complex, redescribes this ethical relationship in terms of language.

27 Ibid., p. 201.

28 Ibid., p. 176.

29 Ibid., p. 228.

30 Emmanuel Levinas, *Existence and Existents*, translated by Alphonso Lingis (Dordrecht: Kluwer Academic Publishers, 1988), p. 91. I am grateful to Petra Newman for pointing out in conversation that this passage is an echo of and response to the Book of Revelations, 7. It is also parallel to a passage in *Totality and Infinity*, p. 238.

31 Levinas, *Totality and Infinity*, p. 240.

32 Jean-François Lyotard, *The Differend*, translated by Georges Van De Abbeele (Manchester: Manchester University Press, 1988).

33 Levinas, 'Useless Suffering', p. 162.

34 R.G. Collingwood, *The Idea of History* (Oxford: Oxford University Press, 1946).

35 The question of why we must not let the Holocaust slip away is too large to be approached here. Indeed, one might argue that it may even be impossible to provide an answer that would be equal to our knowledge that the Holocaust must not be forgotten. It may be that, simply, we have a duty to the dead: this is Paul Ricoeur's position, and this is a constant refrain in his *Time and Narrative*, a work much influenced by Levinas. It may be that we also have a duty to the living and yet to be born. Levinas writes of the Holocaust that there is 'an obligation to speak'. Levinas, 'Poetry and the Impossible', in *Difficult Freedom*, pp. 127–32. Quotation is from p. 132.

36 Levinas, *Totality and Infinity*, p. 56.

37 Paul Ricoeur, *Time and Narrative*, vol. 3, translated by Kathleen Blamey and David Pellauer (Chicago: University of Chicago Press, 1988), p. 187.

38 Levinas, 'Useless Suffering', pp. 162–4.

39 Paul Ricoeur, *Time and Narrative*, p. 187. Ricoeur, following work by Yosef Hayin Yerushalmi, suggests that 'the Jews were able to do without scholarly historiography for centuries to the very extent they remained faithful to the call in Deuteronomy – "Remember!" – and that the shift to historical research in the modern period was in large part an effect of the assimilation of gentile culture' (p. 320n).

40 Rose, 'Beginnings of the day', p. 49.

41 Levinas, *Otherwise than Being*, p. 20.

42 Robert Bernasconi, 'The Trace of Levinas in Derrida', in *Derrida and Différance*, edited by Robert Bernasconi and David Wood (Coventry: Parousia Press, 1985), pp. 17–44. Quotation is from p. 26. For a discussion of Levinas, the Holocaust and the philosophical tradition, see Robert Bernasconi, *Heidegger in Question* (NJ: Humanities Press, 1993), esp. pp. 56–73.

43 Levinas, *Otherwise than Being*, p. 120.

44 Kearney, *Dialogues with Contemporary Continental Thinkers*, pp. 66–7.

45 Levinas describes 1941 like this in 'Meaning and Sense', in Levinas, *Collected Philosophical Papers*, pp. 75–107. Quotation is from p. 93.

46 History is often understood as 'contested'. However, this metaphor assumes that there is a truth than can be won, or at least a method which might win a truth. I am not sure that 'contest' is the right word for a conversation that can or should have no end.

47 Levinas, *Difficult Freedom*, p. 135.

7
Idioms for the Unrepresentable: Postwar Fiction and the Shoah

Ann Parry

> If art persists it is entirely different, outside of taste, devoted
> to delivering and liberating this nothing.
>
> J.-F. Lyotard

> Philosophical reflection and sociological analysis return us ...
> to aesthetic questions, questions of representation.
>
> G. Rose

In 1987 the publication of Victor Farias's work about the relationship
of Heidegger and his philosophy to Nazism became the occasion for a
controversy in which Jean-François Lyotard and Philippe Lacoue-
Labarthe were key figures.[1] The Jew as a signifier and Auschwitz as an
event had previously featured in postmodern debate, but the controversy which erupted in the year when the Berlin Wall came down was
focused unerringly on what National Socialism had revealed about the
trajectory of European culture.[2] Some of the issues raised have been
pursued by scholars in the United States and France who are concerned
with the religious, philosophical and representational implications of
the Shoah.[3] The acceptance of a European identity in Britain is,
however, still variable and often tenuous and the extent to which such
issues are emergent or implicated in postwar cultural forms has proved
of little interest.[4] In an effort to extend critical discussion into the area
this chapter explores some of the arguments put forward in the
'Heidegger Affair' in relation to the ways in which, since the 1960s,
questions about the Shoah and Jewish identity have been negotiated
by writers of fiction in Britain.

My approach has been to take two themes on which the philosophers concentrated and to investigate the representational issues they

have posed for fiction. The themes are their speculations about the ways in which European thought has constructed the Jew, and how the immemoriality of the Shoah has entered European culture. It seemed important to consider the significance of these themes for those who most experience their effects, so the first of the texts to be considered, *The Lost Europeans,* is by an Anglo-Jewish author, Emanuel Litvinoff. It is separated from the others in time – it was published in 1960, and is a 'classic' narrative of journey and quest by a young man.[5] The second text, *Fatherland,* by Robert Harris, belongs to our own decade, though it is set in the 1960s; it appeared in 1992, and is a political thriller and bestseller that makes use of the factional mode.[6] The third text is by a German who has lived and worked in Britain for 30 years. *The Emigrants,* by W.G. Sebald, is a collection of short stories, illustrated by photographs and memorabilia; first published in Germany in 1993 it won several prizes, and, on its appearance in England in 1996 in translation, it was awarded joint first prize at the annual Jewish Book Fair.[7] All three books are, therefore, quite different from one another in formal terms, but are united by their concern about the 'disappearance' of the Shoah. Any choice of texts through which to explore the ideas of the philosophers will, inevitably, seem to be arbitrary and provocative. The selection of a variety of fictional types and forms, united by a common theme, but with different temporal perspectives is an attempt to acknowledge and mediate these limitations. Such a selection provides the means to highlight differences and changes of emphasis in the representation of the issues at stake. Finally, it reveals the attention fiction of various kinds has devoted to subjects that have, as yet, received little critical attention.

In *Heidegger and 'the jews'* Lyotard argues that the actual and representational fate of the latter is crucially related to their being the ever-present but 'unconscious anxiety' of the West. Central to his definition of Jewish identity is the guilt that arises from the unpayable debt he claims that Europe owes to Judaism through its rejection of the original Covenant with God.[8] When the West persecutes 'the Jew' it is in recognition of its own indebtedness, the fact that it is inescapably 'obligated before the Law'.[9] As witnesses to the Covenant, the Jews and their book 'represent something that Europe does not want to or cannot know anything about'.[10] Jews become, therefore, outsiders; in terms of European national identity they are 'unassignable'; without their own language, they are not a nation, they have their roots in a book, not a place. They are on the inside of other nations and yet still separate and different. As such they are threatening, characterized by their capacity to transform themselves; they are 'the very absence of type', not an 'opposition', but a 'contradiction' to the 'Teuton'.[11] Capable of this 'endless mimesis' the Jew carries the potentiality for 'destabilization', the capacity to degrade and then destroy the nation.[12] When viewed from this perspective, 'The Final Solution was the project of exterminating the (involuntary) witnesses to this forgotten event and of having done with the unpresentable affect once and for all ...'.[13] It was the most extreme to date of all the traditional antisemitic adjustments. The Nazis attempted to transcribe the unrepresentable by placing 'outside itself this inexpressible affection by naming it: "the jews" and persecuting it.'[14]

Lacoue-Labarthe's meditations on the Final Solution further those of Lyotard by their concentration on its nature as an historical caesura that reveals the essence of European culture. In Heidegger's 'eternally intolerable' refusal to think the Shoah in his philosophy after 1945, Lacoue-Labarthe finds a reflection of Europe's failure to acknowledge who the largest number of victims of the Shoah were, that it was 'a massacre of THE JEWS'.[15] At 'Auschwitz' the West negated itself in its denial of rational motivation and values that were, supposedly, dearly held.[16] The Jews were no real threat in political, moral or cultural terms. The threat they were deemed to be belonged to the realm of projection; they were 'decreed to be jews' and eliminated as industrial waste. In this 'purely hygienic, sanitary operation' nihilism was accomplished.[17]

The major consequence that arose from this 'accomplishment' was the unrepresentability of the Shoah, and this may not seem an unfamiliar idea. Primo Levi warns us against thinking we can understand it, or ever believing that we can express it; George Steiner refers to it as the 'unspeakable'.[18] But these are essentially responses to the enormity of the event. Lyotard's meditations go in a different direction. Whereas Levi in *If this is a Man* maintains his faith in reason, Lyotard sees 'Auschwitz' as a symbol of its failure, so that the Shoah takes on the status of 'an originary repressed ... that ... cannot be represented', that is – an unconscious without representational formations.[19] The nature of this unrepresentability, as Lyotard conceives it, can be likened to the problematic of the sublime. In Kantian thought the sublime is an excess, an 'unform', which overflows the framing power of the imagination to 'invest, fix and represent'; and such an absolute, which is by its very nature outside time, cannot be remembered. It is a 'presence' which does not leave a mark, something 'which threatens without making itself known, which does not realize itself.'

The paradox is, therefore, that the Shoah, like the sublime, is ever present, but forgotten; it remains 'within' the mind but is both 'infuse and diffuse'.[20] Conceived of in this way 'Auschwitz' becomes the immemorial, that which cannot be remembered, which cannot be represented to consciousness, neither cannot it be forgotten or consigned to oblivion. As an historical differend 'Auschwitz' marks a point of incommensurability, a sign that something waits to be phrased that cannot be; it is a silence, lost to representation.[21] Writing beyond the Shoah is 'outside taste', it is a perpetual struggle with the 'liberation of nothing'.[22] All that can be achieved is 'a degradation of *catharsis*', reason and ethics have been negated, so purgation and renewal are impossible. Writer and reader are located in 'a sphere beyond tragedy'; the enormity and grotesquerie of the Shoah on the one hand exceeds tragedy, but on the other is less than tragedy because 'no (re)presentation of it (i.e. the Shoah) is possible'.[23] All art can do is struggle with and bear witness to the unsayable.

Emanuel Litvinoff's attempt to represent this 'unsayability' in *The Lost Europeans* anticipates Lacoue-Labarthe's suggestion that in the postwar period the trajectory of European culture was at its clearest in its refusal to acknowledge that the Shoah was a massacre of the Jews.[24] The journey that the novel recounts of the protaganist Martin into postwar Europe shows that, whilst the explicit 'othering' of the Jews is 'officially' unspeakable, it nevertheless continues in ways that are muted, but for all that transformed and powerfully active.[25] Furthermore, the inclination to differentiate the Jew from others is as prevalent in Britain as on the continent. In its exploration of Jewish self-identity the novel suggests that the choice between roots and assimilation, which commentators in the 1960s claimed was on 'offer' to Anglo-Jewry, was neither available nor worth having.[26] The 'unassignability' identified as an origin of the Shoah in Europe was present too in postwar Britain. Gradually, the hero of *The Lost Europeans* comes to realize that Jews belonged 'nowhere in the strictly stratified society of England'. Martin reflects that the particular ethnic individualism of his own community in London is neither valued nor recognized. Jews are merely 'one species among a host of refugees' who are 'a burden on the conscience of liberal socialists'. He comes, therefore, to see himself as a part of 'the classic Jewish dilemma', whose inheritance is 'homelessness', and whose tenor is 'bitterness, poverty and rootlessness'. The awareness of this diasporic identity is at its sharpest when he recognizes his exclusion by the nationalist and liberal codes of British society. Liberalism, with its universalist criteria for acceptance, 'the chimerical brotherhood of man', nevertheless leaves Martin, in social terms, an outsider.[27] Nationalism, similarly, excludes those who recognize a community other than the indigenous nation. The ideologies of modern society marginalize the 'stubborn readers of the Book', who represent the denial of the original Covenant.[28] Martin's insight into the position of Jews within British society challenges the assured philosemitism of a complacent liberalism that tended to be self-congratulatory about the role it had played in resisting Nazism.

Yet, when Martin first leaves England to travel to Germany to recover his family's wealth, he feels immured by his English identity; 'England made me', he thinks and believes that this protects him from Europeans. When he meets 'hard grey German eyes' that name him 'Jew' he accentuates his public school 'cultured accent' to ward off their attention. This security is broken down as he realizes that European politics have continued as if nothing had happened. Berlin remains 'the sick heart of Europe'; as the divided city of the Cold War it typifies the uniformity of mass culture, one of whose principal political effects is to ensure the continuation of European antisemitism.[29] So, Hitler men are in high office in the West and East, and Jews suffer. Hugo, rejected by his lover during the War because he was a Jew, at the end of the novel lies dead in the street, murdered by an ex-Nazi disguised variously as an American journalist and diplomat.

The betrayal Hugo had experienced during the war is, therefore, sanctioned in a supposedly regenerate Europe. Litvinoff's novel seems prophetic of Lyotard's 'fear and prejudice' that the 'wound of the Shoah' is being healed without having been 'worked out'; it shows us how the Jews remain an 'unconscious anxiety' threatened by new means of destruction.[30] Martin discovers that 'Mass culture' has produced a particularly ironic and insidious means to give renewed energy to antisemitism: 'by rubbing out national differences', those previously identifiable by their brownshirts now 'looked like fraternity and sorority members of some American university that had opened branches in all the West European capitals ...'. The mimetic capacity which made the Jews a threat is now the means by which those still intent on antisemitic persecution melt into the crowd. This pretended 'absence of type' appears in the novel as the latest deformed manifestation of the deep unconscious need of Europeans 'to destroy something they feared and hated in themselves; their moral inferiority'.[31] It is an inversion that is, indisputably, 'outside taste', and which, at the very least, calls into question the values of the culture of which it is a form.[32] This inversionary mimesis in *The Lost Europeans* reminds us of the inherent instability of identities, including those described by Lyotard: Litvinoff's fictional representations suggest that in postwar/postmodern Europe we are dealing with the rapid disappearance of historical referents and their subjects and that this creates the space for self-fictions that are, in their re-alignments, promiscuous and threatening to 'the Jews'.

Martin, as a result of this insight, concludes that 'all roads led to Auschwitz', but, perhaps not surprisingly, this produces disorientation within his own self-identity. He rejects Europe and any notion of England as home, but he refuses too to identify with the traumatized community of survivors, 'he knew that guilt and punishment were meaningless, life-suffocating, abstractions. They changed nothing...'.[33] Neither is he willing to consider a new life in Israel as an alternative. Such rejections would seem to locate him within a 'degradation of catharsis' in which renewal and purgation are impossible.[34] As he returns to England he knows that 'it is time to move on' and 'Begin again from the beginning....', but neither he nor the reader knows what or where this beginning might be.[35] In the 1960s Litvinoff has not arrived at that positive sense of diaspora that Bryan Cheyette has recently discovered in the latest work of Clive Sinclair and Anita Brookner.[36] His representation of the continuing destructiveness of Europe's definition of the Jew exposes the proximity of philo- and antisemitism and testifies to the continuity of 'the unconscious affect'.

This approximation then and since of supposedly contradictory semitic discourses is manifested more luridly in Robert Harris's dystopian political thriller *Fatherland*, published in 1992, but set in five days in April 1964. To argue that it is possible for a popular text to engage with this issue and some of the others raised in the philosophers' debate about the Shoah is to be at odds with the most respected scholars of the survivor generation. Saul Friedlander, for example, while acknowledging that 'the memory of Nazism and its crimes' are 'directly influenced by global intellectual shifts', has insisted that nevertheless popular fiction is only capable of producing 'a spectacular fusion of kitsch and death'.[37] In a recent article, however, Miriam Bratn Hansen has asked whether the time might not have arrived when this high modernist distaste for the products of mass culture is no longer justified. Soon, she notes, the memory of the Shoah may be dependent upon the complexities of mass mediated forms. As an example of 'aesthetic populism', the characteristic form produced by consumer society, it is at least worth considering, therefore, whether *Fatherland* has produced representations that engage with the 'unsayability' of the Shoah and the persistent 'othering' of the Jews in European society.[38]

A central feature of the plot in this novel is a radical alteration of the course of history, that is then shown to be more apparent than real; the novel both changes and confirms contemporary history. The counterfactuality consists of victory in the Second World War having gone to Germany, the Third Reich still exists, and Jews in Europe have disappeared completely. As to their fate 'nobody knows what's true and what isn't ... most people don't care'.[39] This is another chilling reminder of the failure to acknowledge what the Shoah was. It is a reminder that receives emphasis through the efforts of the German detective, Xavier March, to discover the actual evidence for what happened to Jews and to publish it to the rest of the world. His investigations produce the most discomforting answers to the question that Lyotard asked: 'How does the slaughter ... testify to what it kills?' The elimination of the Jews is shown as not only 'caused by causes one needs to get down to transforming'; it is also the result of 'an unconscious affect' operating 'outside of any status' on the 'inside' of world political and cultural processes before and, more importantly, beyond the Shoah.[40] Joseph Kennedy had advised the Germans in the 1930s how to get rid of the Jews quietly. In the Cold War of the 1960s America accepts any ally that provides a bulwark against the Communist Eastern bloc, so President Kennedy flashes 'his famous smile' and tells Nazi Germany that although their political systems are very different 'we are all citizens of one planet'.[41] This alliance between the 'officially' philosemitic superpower and its opposite suggests an unconscious supra-historical factor at work, so that even when March has discovered the 'facts' he doubts that they will change anything. 'Was history changed so easily?'[42] Ultimately, this is signified by the total absence of Jewish people in the novel; their only presence is as a photographic image of a murdered family and as dust in the destroyed remains of Auschwitz that March reaches, before he too is murdered. Throughout their fate is represented as both known and forgotten.[43] At the centre of the crimes that March investigates is the plan of the Nazi hierarchy to conceal the last evidence of the Wannsee Conference, to forget the forgotten, which, as Lyotard reminds us, 'testifies to the fact that the forgotten is always there ...'.

The re-writing of history in *Fatherland* becomes, therefore, a means of approaching that with which Lyotard believed it was impossible to deal – 'The "politics" of extermination on the political scene'. In spite of the continuance of the Reich, Europe bears an alarming resemblance to the place in which we have lived and still do. The boundaries and distributions of power may be different, but the Cold War is much as it was and postwar culture is developing in familiar ways. The Beatles are in the top ten, 'The permissive sixties are under way' and Britain has faded into irrelevance and insignificance. The pastiche element involved in recapturing the 1960s provides within itself an anticipation of its own future moment too, so that a reader is reminded of the situation in Europe since the fall of the Berlin Wall. The Central European and Eastern power blocs are on the brink of collapse and the degradation and grubbiness of the culture is revealed by explanations and events that have a startlingly contemporary resonance. We encounter a hero who seeks the answer to a mystery he 'had in his heart perhaps always known ... the truth about.' We meet an American who relativizes the fate of the Jews with the explanation that 'wartime is different. All countries do wicked things ... My country dropped an atom bomb ... Remember what the Russians did.'[44] We also recognize quite recent news items – stolen Jewish art treasures and bank accounts come to light. This dual temporal perspectivism in *Fatherland*, that engages with both past and present, becomes an effective representational means with which to 'bear witness to a permanent undertaking ... to banish' the Jews.[45]

And it is supported by a persistent attempt in the novel to implicate that which is both beneath the surface and beyond any familiar temporal dimension. It is perhaps suggested in the œdipal connotations of the title of the novel itself and it is sharply focused in the final betrayal of March to the Nazis by his son Pili. The parallel between the irrationality and cruelty of the boy's motivations and of those who were involved in the elimination of the Jews emerges in the scene in which March tries to say goodbye to his son. As he looks at him he notes 'Those cool eyes' and then what comes to mind is '... all human hair cut off in concentration camps should be utilised. Human hair will be processed for industrial felt and spun into thread.'[46] March sees in Pili those who treated the Jews as 'industrial waste', who did not distinguish between technology and nihilism, between the manufacture of goods and the 'manufacture of corpses in the gas chambers and death camps'.[47] It is impossible to understand why Pili does what he does to his father, 'like the "Jewish threat" it belongs to the realm of projection' and the mixture in this novel of high and low categories, of dystopian form with political thriller, is a provocative means of attempting to portray the timelessness of 'forgetting the forgotten'.[48]

The discourse about the irrepressiblity of the Shoah has its continuity in W.G. Sebald's stories *The Emigrants*, but focus and form are again quite different. As in Litvinoff, Jewish people or themes are at the centre of the narratives though they are not empowered by this centrality.[49] Absence is not signified literally as in *Fatherland*, but it is a central presence in the narratives and it finally absorbs the consciousness of the subjects. The volume comprises four stories which recount the life of a person who escaped the Shoah and went to live in a society that was reputedly free of antisemitism; but the fate of them all turns out to be that of isolation and objectification. Dr Selwyn, having started with a brilliant academic career and lived an exciting social life in the early years of his marriage, is, at the end of his life, 'a dweller in the garden, a kind of ornamental hermit'. He has grown far apart from his wife and has severed his 'last ties with what they call the real world'. Paul Bereyter flees the 'claustrophobia' he feels in contemporary Germany 'convinced that ... he belonged to the exiles and not to the people of S'. Max Ferber lives alone in an abandoned studio-warehouse in 'Manchester ... an immigrant city ... poor Irish, poor Germans, poor Jews.' In the final moments of this story, in looking at photographs of the Litzmannstadt Ghetto at Lodz, 'once known as Polski Manczester', the narrator is able to suggest a continuity in European life that extends into the present.

Time and space, therefore, are again used in these stories to convey the continuing institutionalization of the Jew as 'other'. It is a process with the power to marginalize and reify them and it contributes to their destruction. Two of the subjects of the stories commit suicide, and in ways that deliberately relate to the fate of the previous generation: Selwyn shoots himself, echoing the deaths of many in the early days of the Shoah, and Bereyter lies down on a railway track, which was 'the very image and symbol of Paul's German tragedy'. The deaths of these people, living now in liberal societies, implies that the philosemitism of which such societies are so proud is different from the antisemitism of terror in degree rather than kind. The 'unassignability' of the Jews, in spite of their capacity for an 'endless mimesis' within their national community, remains a powerful and active determinant of their fate.

But it is not in these stories the sole determinant; its peculiar power is related also to the return of history experienced by the characters, the return of their repressed origins. The common theme uniting all those who give the stories their names is the 'tightening ties to those who had gone before', the return of those murdered in the Shoah. Each of the main characters becomes 'obsessive' in their need to explore a 'patchy knowledge of the past', whose immemoriality is a consequence of its traumatic nature. Factual history is replaced by the curious dynamics of trauma. A characteristic feature of trauma is that there is a time-lapse between the horror that is its origin and the first appearance of symptoms, a period of latency during which no trace of the horror is to be found. So, until the ends of their lives, each of the characters pursue their chosen careers in a way that to most is indistinguishable from that of other people. Only the narrators who research their lives become aware of the latency of the trauma that remained suppressed, not only because of its monstrosity, but because too of the disinterest or willed ignorance of the people with whom they lived, reminding us once again of the continuum between philo- and antisemitism.

However, as the subjects of the stories draw closer to death their traumatic experiences emerge from the space of unconsciousness. As this happens they seem to enter the sublime – to which Lyotard compared the unrepresentable. Max Ferber becomes locked in a world in which:

> time ... is an unreliable way of gauging ... things ... There is neither past nor a future ... The fragmentary scenes that haunt my memories are obsessive in character. When I think of Germany it feels as if there were some ... insanity lodged in my head ... I am afraid to find that this insanity really exists. To me you see Germany is ... a curiously extraterritorial place ...

This is the condition of the 'unform', which has overflowed the power of the imagination to fix memories in time and space, and which remains immemorial because the conscious mind fears the terror that would be unleashed. The irony is that in the cases of 'Paul Bereyter' and 'Max Ferber' it is only in and through the inherent forgetting of the trauma that it is finally experienced at all.

The first response of these subjects to the loss of their loved ones back in Germany was to suppress it, so as to avoid any detailed preoccupation with their deaths. Ferber even wonders 'if I have really grasped it to this day'.[50] Paul Bereyter prefers for many years not to enquire too deeply into the fate of his parents and prospective fiancée and this is linked with the conflicts in identity that arise from what Cheyette has called 'the protean instability of the Jew as signifier'.[51]

Thus Paul, who was 'German to the core', returns from France in 1941 and joins the Wehrmacht and then teaches all his life in the town still inhabited by those who caused the deaths of his parents.[52] In the postwar situation the Jew's capacity for mimesis becomes a means of protection, a barrier to keep at bay the originary trauma. The chilling irony is that this is what Europe has always found threatening and the reader is reminded of the ever-present 'unconscious affect'.[53]

The 'forgetfulness' of Bereyter and Ferber was, as their deaths show, partial and temporary, but quite different from 'the systematic thoroughness with which these people [i.e. perpetrators] kept silence ... kept their secrets, and even sometimes ... really did forget'.[54] As in *The Lost Europeans* the places these people inhabit continue to be the same 'miserable hole[s]' they always were 'despite the so-called progress', and this, as one of the narrators comments, is 'an annhilating verdict on the way we lead our life'. A remark that may remind us once again of Lyotard's fear and prejudice that the Shoah is being healed without being worked out, and one that requires, as all these texts have done, a reflection on the nature of art beyond the Shoah. This issue is acutely problematized in the last story when the narrator struggles to write the tragedy of Ferber's youth 'that later shot up again and spread its poisonous canopy'. He describes his struggles with the biographical material with which Ferber provided him in this way:

> Often I could not get on for hours and days at a time, and not infre-
> quently I unravelled what I had done, continuously tormented by
> scruples that were taking tighter hold. These scruples concerned
> not only the subject of my narrative, which I felt I could not do
> justice to, no matter what approach I tried, but also to the entire
> questionable business of writing ... By far the greater part had been
> crossed out ... Even what I ultimately salvaged as a 'final' version
> seemed to me a thing of shreds and patches, utterly botched.[55]

The state described here may seem to confirm Lyotard's hypothesis that art beyond the Shoah would be 'devoted to delivering and liberating nothing'.[56] To rest with such an understanding is, however, to ignore those 'aesthetic questions, questions of representation' to which, as Gillian Rose noted, 'philosophy returns us'. When these questions are considered it becomes clear that these stories remove the conditionality that Lyotard feared hung over the 'persistence of art'. The narrator of the last story, like those in all the others, is an emigrant himself, he may be Jewish, at the very least he identifies strongly with the Jewish tragedy. In his response to Ferber he has travelled from a detachment in which he 'omitted ... to ask the questions he must surely have expected of me' into agonized involvement in which he is 'tormented' by scruples and the inadequacy of his creative abilities.[57] In each of these stories the narrator undertakes such a journey and ends deeply implicated in another's trauma, committed to a struggle to express the unimaginable and perpetuate it: that which was repressed has returned and been memorialized. History has been recovered through a fictional representation of the inaccessibility of its occurrence, which confirms the responsibilities that thought and writing have to the 'forgotten and/as the unrepresentable'.[58] Sebald has achieved, through exploring the dynamics of trauma, a means of representation that allows him to break through the unrepresentability of the Shoah and provide a continuing testimony to its unsayability.

In different ways all of the texts discussed here bear witness to this unsayability by recovering the 'unconscious affect' and testifying to it; in doing so they confirm the significant engagement of 'aesthetics' with the questions that the philosophers addressed in the Heidegger Affair. The fictional representation of issues and events provides the means to realize vividly some of the key concepts of this discourse. In *Fatherland*, within 'the mysterious aura of the political detective story', the complete and unnoticed absence of Jews is the ghastly manifestation of the continuing failure of European culture to acknowledge that the Shoah was essentially 'a massacre of the Jews'.[59] In postwar mass society it appears that the ambivalence of the signifier has become operative throughout the social formation and has produced a confusion in which enemies are able to efface themselves. The conspiratorial nature of international politics draws philo- and antisemitism closer together; and the predominance of relativist discourse encourages the distinction to be occluded between the bureaucratized burning of selected human beings and the organization of the munitions industry. The realization of these issues within the 'aesthetics of populism' and the deliberate rejection of the glamourized version of Nazism allows this post-Cold War thriller to be at least considered as a serious negotiation with the philosophical themes raised in the debate.

The confrontation of this bleak European trajectory by survivors in the work of Litvinoff and Sebald is necessarily more painful by virtue of its being seen in terms of the social and psychological pitfalls to which individual Jewish identities are exposed. There are, however, differences between Martin's final position in *The Lost Europeans* and those of the narrators in *The Emigrants* that suggest the changing impact of the Shoah on Jewish people and on those who try to identify with their continuing nightmare. In Litvinoff's novel Martin retreated not only from the identity offered to him in Britain, but also from his Jewish identity – he refused any relation with the Shoah generation, or Israel, and he even rejected his local community in London. In contrast, all of Sebald's narrators, although somewhat reluctantly, re-engage with the past, accepting that, after the Shoah, history may be the way in which they are implicated in one another's traumas; at the end of the stories each of them discovers that 'they are ever returning to us the dead'.[60] The burden such a 'reintegration' imposes on contemporary Jewish identity is, as some commentators have observed, not without ambivalence; for the non-Jewish it might signal the beginning of an acknowledgment of what the Shoah was. *The Emigrants* offers no remission or alternative to this re-conceptualization of history for either community. Both *The Lost Europeans* and *The Emigrants* conceive of 'Auschwitz' in the way that Lyotard and Lacoue-Labarthe do, as an event which 'opens up, or closes, a quite other history than the one we have known'.[61] It is no longer possible to understand history as a project to liberate humanity from the past. In these circumstances Lyotard has argued that the role of literature is to find an idiom for the 'differend' that is 'Auschwitz', for that which '"asks" to be phrased, but suffers the wrong of not being able to be phrased'.[62] In their various ways the texts discussed here are involved in the search for such idioms.

Notes

1 V. Farias, *Heidegger et le nazisme* (Paris: Verdier, 1987); Philippe Lacoue-Labarthe, *Heidegger, Art and Politics* (Oxford: Polity Press, 1991); J.-F. Lyotard, *Heidegger and 'the jews'* trans. by Andreas Michel and Mark S. Roberts (Minneapolis: University of Minnesota, 1990).

2 Prior to 'L'affaire Heidegger', the Holocaust had been postulated as a break in European consciousness both by scholars who were not and those who were associated with postmodernism. See, for example, George Steiner, *Language and Silence* (London: Penguin Books, 1967) and I. Hassan, 'POSTmodernISM: a paracritical bibliography', in L. Cahoone, *From Modernism to Postmodernism* (Oxford: Blackwell, 1996), pp. 382–400.

3 I am thinking of, for example, S. Friedlander's *Probing the Limits of Representation* (Cambridge, MA: Harvard University Press, 1992) or L.D. Kritzman's *Auschwitz and After* (London: Routledge, 1995).

4 In Britain the terms of the postmodern debate were taken up by

philosopher Gillian Rose: see, for example, essays in *Judaism and Modernity* (Oxford: Blackwell, 1993). In literary criticism little attention has been devoted to the representation of the Holocaust in postwar fiction. Bryan Cheyette's *Construction of the Jew in English Literature and Society 1875–1945* (Cambridge: Cambridge University Press, 1993) is a seminal work that does engage with key notions from the Heidegger debate, but the study terminates in 1945; his most recent collection, *Between 'Race' and Culture* (Stanford, CA: Stanford University Press, 1996) is an exciting continuation and extension of the considerations of his earlier work though few of the British writers discussed are contemporary or popular. In a recent essay Cheyette has explored the way some contemporary Jewish writers have been able to use the postmodern figure of the 'ineffable' Jew to question the English and the Jewish past, see '"Ineffable and usable": towards a diasporic British-Jewish Writing', *Textual Practice*, 10, (2), 1996, pp. 295–313.

5   E. Litvinoff, *The Lost Europeans* (London: Heinemann, 1960).

6   R. Harris, *Fatherland* (London: Arrow Books, 1993).

7   W.G. Sebald, *The Emigrants* (London: The Harvill Press, 1996). W.G. Sebald is Max Sebald, Professor of European Literature at the University of East Anglia. He is not Jewish and, as he tells Carole Angier in a recent interview, he does not feel any longer at home in Germany. He comments that 'In theory I could have had a British passport years ago. But I was born into a particular context and I don't really have an option.' His identification with the Jewish tragedy is clear throughout these stories. See C. Angier, 'Who is W.G. Sebald?', *Jewish Quarterly*, Winter, 1996–7, pp. 10–14; also in this edition a review of *The Emigrants* by G. Josipovici, 'The Forces of Memory', pp. 59–60.

8   Lyotard, *Heidegger and 'the jews'*, p. 11.

9   '*Heidegger and the "jews"*', in J.-F. Lyotard, *Political Writings* (London: UCL Press, 1993) p. 140.

10   Ibid., 'Europe, the Jews and the Book', p. 159.

11   Blanchot too had argued that the Jews, in their rejection of idols and respect for an ethical order that manifested itself in a respect for the law, represented for National Socialism 'the rejection of myths' and intimated a formless, unaesthetic people.

12   Lacoue-Labarthe, *Heidegger, Art and Politics*, p. 96.

13   Lyotard, *Political Writings*, p. 143.

14   Ibid., pp. 27–8.

15   Lacoue-Labarthe, *Heidegger, Art and Politics*, p. 37.

16   He uses the term 'Auschwitz' as Adorno did as a generic name for the Shoah. The quotation is from p. 43.

17   Ibid., p. 37. See also p. 96 and Lyotard, 'Europe, the Jews and the Book', p. 160.

18   See, for example, Primo Levi, *If this is a Man* (London: Abacus, 1987), p. 32 and p. 396; George Steiner, 'The Hollow Miracle', in *Literature and the Modern World: Critical Essays*, edited by D. Walder (Oxford: Oxford University Press, 1990), p. 348.

19   *Heidegger and 'the jews'*, p. 15. Gillian Rose is out of sympathy with Lyotard on this, arguing that despite of the enormity of its failure at Auschwitz it does not justify 'reneging' on reason altogether. See *Judaism and Modernity*,

p. 3. Levi's position in his earliest work on the subject is similar to that of Rose.

20   Lyotard, *Heidegger and 'the jews'*, p. 31.
21   See Bill Readings, *Introducing Lyotard: Art and Politics* (London: Routledge, 1990), p. 126.
22   Lyotard, p. 44.
23   Lacoue-Labarthe, *Heidegger, Art and Politics*, pp. 45, 46.
24   What Litvinoff noted in 1960 was still a feature of British fiction in the late 1970s. David Benedictus's novel *A Twentieth Century Man* (London: Blond & Briggs, 1978) deals with the opening of the camps and the later life of a survivor. She is a Dutch Protestant imprisoned for helping Jews, but their plight in the camps is never mentioned.
25   See Litvinoff, *The Lost Europeans*, p. 9. A German official treats Martin with suspicion as he checks his passport and Martin comments, 'So they still look at a Jew like that ...'.
26   See Efraim Sicher, *Beyond Marginality* (Albany, NY: SUNY Press, 1985). Brian Glanville, writing in *Encounter*, 24, p. 62 in 1960, seemed to suggest that it was just a matter of a Jewish person accepting Englishness; there was no such thing as Anglo-Jewish writing – 'it was all part of one tradition'.
27   Litvinoff, *The Lost Europeans*, pp. 224, 180, 224.
28   Lyotard, 'Europe, the Jews and the Book', pp 161–2.
29   Litvinoff, *The Lost Europeans*, pp. 9, 10, 24.
30   Lyotard, 'Europe, the Jews and the Book' p. 135.
31   Litvinoff, *The Lost Europeans*, pp. 76, 279.
32   Lyotard, 'Europe, the Jews and the Book' p. 44.
33   Litvinoff, *The Lost Europeans*, pp. 224, 294.
34   Lacoue-Labarthe, *Heidegger, Art and Politics*, p. 46.
35   Litvinoff, *The Lost Europeans*, p. 297.
36   B. Cheyette, '"Ineffable and Usable": Towards a Diasporic British-Jewish Writing', *Textual Practice*, 10, (2), 1996, pp. 295–313.
37   See M. Bratn Hansen, *Critical Inquiry*, 22 (Winter 1996), pp. 292–311; see p. 296 for this reference. See also S. Friedlander, *Reflections on Nazism: an Essay on Kitsch and Death* (London: Harper & Row, 1993).
38   In *Twilight Memories* (London: Routledge, 1995) A. Huyssen explores the way in which issues of time and space keep haunting our present, in spite of the decline in historical consciousness noted by the Modernists. The term 'aesthetic populism' is used by Jameson in *Postmodernism, Or the Cultural Logic of Late Capitalism* (London: Verso, 1991) to describe the popular text in which the forms, categories and contents of high culture and mass literature mix. Like Friedlander he too argues that the mixture produces a degraded landscape. Jameson's vision of high and low, popular and quality caught in irresolvable conflict in which the differences between the oppositions are unnegotiable is a long-established and ongoing debate; descending from Adorno, its most recent eruption was in the controversy that grew up around Spielberg's film *Schindler's List;* see the article by M. Bratn Hansen cited previously.
39   Harris, *Fatherland*, p. 210. The irrelevance of the tragedy of the Jews to postwar Europe is also a dominant theme in Philip Kerr's thriller *A German Requiem* (Harmondsworth: Penguin, 1992).

40   Ibid., pp. 28, 26.

41   Ibid., p. 118.

42   Ibid., p. 337.

43   'The Jews had all been evacuated to the east ... Everyone knew that ...' (p. 38); racism 'was all gobbledygook to Xavier March' (p. 98).

44   *Fatherland*, p. 211.

45   Lyotard, 'Europe, the Jews and the Book', p. 160.

46   Lacoue-Labarthe, *Heidegger, Art and Politics*, p. 36 and Harris, *Fatherland*, p. 342.

47   M. Heidegger, quoted in Lacoue-Labarthe, *Heidegger, Art and Politics*, p. 58.

48   Ibid., p. 35.

49   There are four stories in the collection; the first and the last subjects are Jewish; the second is one-quarter Jewish, but is treated before and after the War as if he was Jewish; the third, Ambros Adelwarth, is not Jewish, but the presence of the Shoah is perhaps at its strongest in this story.

50   Sebald, *The Emigrants*, pp. 5, 21, 43 and 59, 191, 235, 61, 166, 54, 181, 191.

51   B. Cheyette, *Between 'Race' and Culture* (Stanford, CA: Stanford University Press, 1996), p. 11.

52   Sebald, *The Emigrants*, p. 55.

53   Throughout the 1950s Paul's pupils always pray for his conversion to Christianity during their classes of Catholic instruction. Although only one of his parents was Jewish his descent was clearly remembered beyond the Shoah.

54   Sebald, *The Emigrants*, p. 50. Lyotard discusses ways in which the Shoah is, by relativization, turned into 'ordinary repression' and easily forgotten (*Heidegger and 'the jews'* p. 44). Sebald seems to indicate something altogether more chilling. The forgetfulness of the people he describes derives from their failure to disavow what had occurred – and in this one is reminded of Heidegger's response.

55   Ibid., pp. 9, 191, 230.

56   Lyotard, *Heidegger and 'the jews'*, p. 44.

57   Sebald, *The Emigrants*, p. 178.

58   Lyotard, *Heidegger and the Jews*, p. xiii.

59   Harris, *Fatherland*, p. 215. These quoted words are Heydrich's and are a reminder of Lacoue-Labarthe's emphasis on 'the aestheticization of politics' in Hitler's Germany. Syberberg made a similar point when he referred to the 'The Third Reich as a total artwork of a perverted West.' See Lacoue-Labarthe, *Heidegger, Art and Politics*, pp. 61–76.

60   Sebald, *The Emigrants*, p. 23.

61   Lacoue-Labarthe, *Heidegger, Art and Politics*, p. 45. Lyotard terms 'Auschwitz' as 'a differend', Lacoue-Labarthe as 'a caesura'.

62   J.-F. Lyotard, *The Differend* (Manchester: Manchester University Press, 1988), p. 148.

8
The Demidenko Affair and Contemporary Holocaust Fiction
Sue Vice

The Demidenko affair caused an enormous furore in Australia in the mid-1990s, following the publication of Helen Demidenko's novel *The Hand that Signed the Paper*. An editorial by Helen Daniel in the *Australian Book Review* of March 1996 concluded, 'It seems to me that the cultural aftershocks of the whole affair will continue for some years, undermining our intellectual, moral, racial and cultural assumptions and leaving us collectively shaken'.[1] There was a breakdown in relations between the Jewish and Ukrainian communities in Australia during this time, and the Ukrainians threatened Alan Dershowitz, the Claus von Bulow lawyer, with legal action over a statement he made on the affair while visiting Sydney. Antisemitic letters and a cartoon depicting the blonde Demidenko roasting over a Chanukah candelabra appeared in national newspapers.[2] This furore is an extreme version of the Holocaust scandals I will be examining, as it unites all of the accusations which have been levelled against other texts – plagiarism, antisemitism, inauthenticity, appropriation and historical revisionism.

The Hand that Signed the Paper was published in 1994 as the first work of a young Australian woman, Helen Demidenko.[3] Her own extra-textual utterances, and, obviously, her surname, allowed it to be assumed that this work was a fictionalized autobiography, and that she was telling the secrets of her own immigrant Ukrainian family. The novel is narrated by a young woman called Fiona Kovalenko, and the similarity of her name to Demidenko's suggests at least an indirect autobiographical link. In the novel, Fiona's uncle, Vitaly Kovalenko, is awaiting trial as a war criminal for his part in the Holocaust in the Ukraine, in particular the massacre at Babi Yar, the ravine outside Kiev where 34,000 Jews were killed over two days in 1941.

Helen Demidenko was awarded three major Australian literary prizes for her novel, and became a celebrity: dressed in Ukrainian peasant blouses and sporting long blonde hair, she appeared on chat shows and was widely interviewed about her family history and her writing. Her statements on her genealogy ranged from relatively harmless anecdotes – her father, a taxi-driver, drove a battered Valiant and could barely read, and at her graduation her family poured vodka over her head – to claiming that almost all of her father's family had been killed in Vinnitsa by 'Jewish Bolsheviks'. The latter tale was supposed to back up the equation made by Demidenko throughout her novel between these two groups.

However, a journalist eventually discovered that Helen Demidenko was the pseudonym of a woman of British descent, Helen Darville, whose mother, Grace Darville, admitted 'We are Poms', who had emigrated from Scunthorpe.[4] Helen Darville's father was neither a taxi-driver nor illiterate, she had no Ukrainian relations and her hair was not really blonde. Thus the opinions of characters in her book – that the majority of Bolsheviks were Jews, and thus Jews were responsible for the terrible famine in the Ukraine in the 1920s – were figments of her own imagination, not ascribable to the antisemitism of unregenerate real-life Ukrainians. Even more damagingly, it turned out that Darville's imagination was not the only moving force of the book and that she had taken material from various sources, including survivor testimonies quoted in Martin Gilbert's history of the Holocaust and S.O. Pidhainy's collection of Ukrainian reports of Soviet atrocities in the 1930s.[5]

An uproar in the Australian literary world ensued. Some claimed that eagerness to celebrate uncritically ethnic minority (and working-class) culture was to blame, and Darville would never have won any prizes if she had published the book under her own name. Others said the novel was a whitewash of Ukrainian participation in the Holocaust; it returned to the old antisemitic link of communism with Judaism, and suggested that Ukrainians were simply avenging themselves for what 'Jewish Bolsheviks' had done during the famine. Darville herself, whose mental health was called into question, went into hiding, after threats that she would stripped of her prizes and sued for breach of copyright. As a result of the furore, the book was still not available in Britain by 1998, even though it was a bestseller in Australia, where it has been reissued under Darville's own name with credit now given to the other works 'quoted' in her novel.[6]

The connection to the events of the Holocaust which Darville invented for herself was, as her critics noted, very significant, as it appeared to give her a position from which to speak, and an 'authentic' take on the Holocaust. The charge of inauthenticity is one which underlies all the other accusations in the scandal surrounding *The Hand*, and the other texts I will discuss. Plagiarism is thought to be inevitable because the writer has no other access to what he or she is trying to portray; antisemitism may be the result of clumsiness, or a secret agenda (as these writers are not survivors, anything is possible); and sensationalism has a similar root – that is, the charge that the Holocaust appears in a text merely to symbolize something else.

It is instructive to examine each of the charges laid against Darville's novel, and what they suggest for any kind of future fictional representations of the Holocaust when there are no longer any 'authentic' voices left. First, 'authenticity' is obviously breached by Darville's assumption of the Demidenko pseudonym. Critics described their reactions to this 'unmasking', ranging from the loss of a frisson at the exposure of a family's secrets, to increased admiration of the book as an imaginative work.[7] Robert Manne suggested that when she took on the Demidenko persona, Helen Darville also took on a discourse of antisemitism, which led her to make certain unwise public pronouncements. In her public apology, she admitted that she had 'said foolish things' while known as Helen Demidenko.[8]

Secondly, plagiarism is seen as a subsidiary attack on authenticity. In Darville's case, plagiarism takes various forms. It seems astonishing that the *nom de plume* Helen Darville chose should be the name of a Ukrainian accomplice in the Babi Yar massacre which appears in Anatoli Kuznetsov's 'documentary fiction', *Babi Yar*, based on eye-witness accounts. Even more extraordinary is the fact that the passage where this name appears is the one D.M. Thomas was accused of plagiarizing for his novel *The White Hotel*.[9] It is as if the name 'Demidenko' signals both authenticity and, at a deeper level, inauthenticity too. Indeed, as Darville's sternest critic Robert Manne points out, the name Demidenko now appears in bold script in Kuznetsov's text to show that originally (in 1966) the Soviet censor cut it out because it revealed Ukrainian participation in the massacre. This is Kuznetsov's version of a part of the story related to him by a survivor, Dina Pronicheva:

> A few minutes later she heard a voice calling from above:
> '**Demidenko**! Come on, start shovelling!'
> There was a clatter of spades and then heavy thuds as the earth and

sand landed on the bodies, coming closer and closer until it started falling on Dina herself.[10]

Even in Kuznetsov's text, the name 'Demidenko' is a complex sign: of a restored textual state, but also of an uncomfortable truth about Ukrainian collaboration with the Nazis. Darville's return to this overdetermined moment may be a part of her project of 'historical revisionism', as it has been called, based on her rather unfortunate comment in an interview that she had sought to reassess the image that Jews are victims, everyone else in Europe victimizers. On the other hand, it may be evidence of a trap set to catch the reader who does not recognize the battle for meaning within the signifier 'Demidenko'.

The real counterpart to Thomas's appropriation of Kutznetsov is Darville's use of an eye-witness account from S.O. Pidhainy's edited volume, *The Black Deeds of the Kremlin*, about the pre-war Ukrainian Famine. This is relatively standard citation, as I would call it, used to give a factual backbone to a work of fiction. It is the method used by Martin Amis in *Time's Arrow*, but Darville was unable to get away with it partly because of her earlier act of plagiarizing an identity for herself. She also took less trouble to make a new aesthetic artefact out of historical material than Amis did with the material he 'borrowed' from Robert Jay Lifton's study, *The Nazi Doctors*. The material thus looks as if it has been lazily transposed by Darville to its new context, like the material Thomas uses from Kuznetsov's *Babi Yar*, with little novelistic amendment. However, even Robert Manne does not spend much time discussing this particular act of appropriation on Darville's part from 'an extremely obscure Ukrainian collection of eye-witness accounts', presumably because it does not appear overtly polemical. Darville borrows from I. Mariupilsky's account of an incident in Mariupil from 1933, entitled 'The Girl who Begged for Bread', in which a zealous communist shopkeeper turns away a starving child who, he says, should be out working. In the version of this incident in *The Hand*, Vitaly relates what happened to the young girl, now his cousin Lara. Although Lara does not die, unlike the girl in the original, the description is not much amended – except to conform to Vitaly's simple, ungrammatical diction, and to make Lara's discourse about the incident Christian.[11]

Darville's publisher, Allen & Unwin, enlisted legal advice on the matter of copyright, and the verdict was that postmodern fiction need not document its historical sources; as long as breach of copyright had not occurred, these instances did not constitute plagiarism.[12] Going as far as literal litigiousness to establish such a critical fact has many implications, particularly for the genre of Holocaust fiction which is likely to rely on anterior sources. Perhaps the most interesting category of plagiarism, if that is still the appropriate word, is Darville's *mis*quotation of her sources. For instance, in Darville's novel, a character sees a sign in a city park that reads, 'No Ukrainians and no dogs allowed'; this is borrowed from Kuznetsov's account of Kiev under Nazi occupation.[13] The shift backwards in time which Darville has effected is primarily rhetorical, to back up the idea that maltreatment of Ukrainians by Jewish Bolsheviks in the 1920s and 1930s was repaid by the enthusiasm of Ukrainians for joining the SS. The transposition of the Nazis' racist sign to an earlier era governed by a different ideology gives this away within the text, once we know the origin of the notice – but it is Darville's extra-textual utterances which sealed the impression of questionable motives. She claimed in an interview that there was a clear 'ratio' between numbers of Jewish commissars present in certain areas of the Ukraine during the Famine, and numbers of Ukrainian volunteers for death-squads during the war.[14]

Again it is not clear what status to give these comments by Darville – especially as she was speaking as Demidenko – other than to observe that they are obviously at least as fictive as her own novel. It seems best to accept the novel's version, despite its occasional lapses of consistency and other breaches of textual decorum, and to see Darville's comments on it as irrelevant curiosities. If we do not make this separation, then all the historical myths which appear in Darville's novel – that Bolsheviks and Jews were the same people, that they caused the Ukrainian Famine, that the Ukrainians therefore had an 'experiential' reason to murder Jews during the Nazi occupation – must be ascribed to the novel's author, rather than to its characters. As the copy-editor of the book aptly put it, 'How do you depict antisemites if they don't act and speak in an antisemitic way?'[15]

The Hand is constructed rather idiosyncratically. It begins with a first-person narrator in the Australian present, Fiona Kovalenko, who has had conversations with her uncle Vitaly and received tapes from her aunt Kateryna, the widow of a member of the German SS. Fiona has transcribed both voices, and the first-person utterances of some other related characters. Thus about half the novel is in the form of first-person accounts by these people. However, interspersed with this, and within the frame of Fiona's narration, is an anonymous third-person narrator.

The most common view of this third-person narrative voice is that it is a technical error on Darville's part. Robert Manne, again putting forward a worst-case scenario, identifies it clearly as Darville's own voice.[16] Manne says that as a matter of simple fact the third-person narrator cannot be Fiona Kovalenko, the first-person narrator, as it knows things she could not (such as details of the relationship between Stalin and Kaganovich, and the psychology of various SS men).[17] There are, of course, other ways of accounting for the third-person narrator in this text. Most narratological theories would have little problem accommodating the unusual but not impossible form used by Darville: a first-person narrator in the present orchestrates and overhears the first-person testimonies of three other characters, who are also intermittently narrated by a third-person voice. In fact, it is a textbook example of Mikhail Bakhtin's concept of polyphony, which he discusses at length in *Problems of Dostoevsky's Poetics*. According to this theory, in contrast to the conventional third-person narrator of, say, George Eliot's novels, where moral and physical facts are told to us over the heads of the characters, in a polyphonic novel the narrator has no such privileged information. Its voice is on the same level as the characters and their voices, and is constructed in the same way; if we learn anything of the moral nature and appearance of the characters, it is through the utterances of the characters themselves, not straightforwardly through the narrator. In the polyphonic novel, Bakhtin says, the author acts as a 'participant in the dialogue without retaining for himself the final word'.[18]

If we see Darville's novel as polyphonic, albeit rather unevenly put together, then accusations of antisemitism can be countered. Antisemitism is a component of the stylized voices we hear, including the voice of the narrator, which is on the same level as those of the characters. This can explain the 'errors' critics have exposed in Darville's text. For instance, the narration concerning Stalin's relationship with Kaganovich is seen by Robert Manne as proof of the presence of an omniscient third-person narrator who must be taken as the moral centre of the text, that is, as the author's voice. The narrator of *The Hand* says this of Vitaly and his wish for vengeance:

> He does not know the truth: Kaganovich only kept his power because he was shorter than Stalin, a good two inches shorter. Vitaly thinks that he kept his power through Jewish cunning.... Kaganovich's reward for his extraordinary loyalty was to be posted to the Ukraine, land of giants. Oh, how it irked him that these

people were taller than he! So he wanted power. Power over this
sullen race that refused to part with its fields.[19]

Manne points out that the only biography of Kaganovich in English
claims he was actually considerably taller than Stalin, and that by the
time of collectivization his Ukrainian posting was over, so he can have
played no direct role in the Famine. Manne takes these inaccuracies to
be evidence of a monologic antisemitic voice in *The Hand*, which
explains 'Kaganovich's powerlust and anti-Ukrainianism as the consequence of the malicious envy of a Jewish dwarf'.[20]
    An alternative way to see the matter is, again, in Bakhtinian terms.
The narrator's voice in the extract above is an example of what
Bakhtin, following the Russian formalists, calls *skaz* – that is, a narra-
torial imitation of an oral utterance. We can see that this is the case
here in such phrases as, 'Oh, how it irked him'. Bakhtin argues that
there are automatically two voices present in any example of *skaz*: the
represented voice, which looks like an oral utterance, and the representing voice, which is responsible for the other voice's presence, that
of the implied author or narrator.[21] Manne's criticism makes the
assumption that these two voices – represented and representing – are
one and the same. The third-person narrator, someone more sophis-
ticated than Vitaly, is capable of seeing through the myth of
Kaganovich's Jewish cunning, but is fallible in other ways. The polyphonic nature of such a narrator is not consistent, as the quotation
above shows; it is a typical 'monologic' move to observe that a character does not know a fact which is available to narrator and reader.
However, elsewhere, in polyphonic patches, the narrator of *The Hand*
simply shows ignorance on the part of the characters, without
commenting on it, and it is these moments which have particularly
exercised Robert Manne.
    Enlisting Bakhtin's notion of polyphony can also help us deal with
the apparent argument of Darville's novel, that Jewish Bolsheviks
were responsible for the Ukrainian Famine, and therefore got what
they deserved later on. Critics have pointed out that this is the very
argument used by the Nazis. However, for critics to argue in such a
way is to assume a monovocal source for these myths within the
novel. Whose opinions are these? As Bakhtin says, in a polyphonic
text 'Fewer and fewer neutral, hard elements ("rock bottom truths")
remain that are not drawn into dialogue'. Bakhtin suggests that, in a
novel, the presence of a 'direct and unmediated' word is so 'imper-
missably naive' that it is at once dialogized by taking on the nature of

'an internal polemic'. That is, an apparently univocal word exists as the representation of such a word, and must interact dialogically with the other words around it, which may contradict it. The same is true even if heteroglossia remains outside the novel and the 'novelist comes forward with his own unitary and fully affirming language'.[22] One could argue that such heteroglossia, in the case of Darville's novel, includes historical and logical correctives to the prejudiced voices we hear in it, correctives helpfully and literally unearthed by Robert Manne. Such correctives are not present within the text, but the voices we do hear require, or even demand, the reader's dialogic response.

For instance, Simon Petlyura, Ukrainian patriot and leader of massive pogroms just after the First World War, appears in *The Hand* described as a champion of 'ethnic peace'. Historically, he was assassinated by Shalom Schwarzbard in Paris in 1926, and Schwarzbard used his trial to reveal the extent of the pogroms in the Ukraine.[23] Schwarzbard appears in *The Hand* as a hired assassin 'under instructions from Moscow' – but these are the words of a character, a student from Lvov. This seems to constitute the novelistic 'testing of an idea', as Bakhtin puts it, rather than a monologic truth. Manne, however, demands a 'clearly identified and morally unambiguous authorial voice' – that is, a non-polyphonic voice – where a subject like the Holocaust is concerned. He argues that if Darville's novel is read 'without knowledge or curiosity', then it may be a very dangerous text; there is 'nothing to suggest that any detail is imagined or false'.[24] This is true, but only within the text. We can argue that the Bakhtinian notion of heteroglossia, a heteroglossia which may well exist only outside the text concerning such subjects as Petluyra's anti-semitism, performs the function of knowledge and curiosity, by providing a context for novels like Darville's and filling the loopholes in it.

This could be a way of accounting for an incident which has troubled several critics. In the part of the novel set in the Ukraine in the 1930s, village life under collectivization is described; the commissar of the village where Vitaly lives is married to a Jewish doctor. She is presented as an ideologically, even selflessly, committed communist, who cannot understand why Soviet policy is leaving the Ukrainian peasants starving. However, her devotion to Stalinism also means that she despises the peasants and accuses them of cattle-like passivity and of breeding like animals; Anatoly Kovalenko's mother begs the doctor to treat her baby son: 'Mrs Kommissar refused. "I am a physician, not a veterinarian", she said softly, enunciating the words with a kind of feral sharpness. "Get away".'[25]

This incident is transcribed by Fiona Kovalenko from her aunt Kateryna's testimony; so it is twice-reported speech. Is the portrayal of this Jewish doctor an antisemitic and Holocaust-denying act, or is it a representation of Kateryna as someone with that cast of mind? As might be imagined, the same defence, that this is a polyphonic text, can be made for the charges of plagiarism. Indeed, as far as the Holocaust-related material in *The Hand* goes, it is hard to see what the future of Holocaust fiction could be if intertextual methodologies were outlawed.

A particularly revealing anecdote about the Demidenko affair is that a troupe of Demidenko lookalikes, men in long blonde wigs, appeared at the 1995 Sydney Gay and Lesbian Mardi Gras, in homage to Helen Darville's literary 'dressing-up'. The critic Sneja Gunew argues that, as Demidenko, Darville was enacting a representation of ethnicity – a category from which, in contemporary Australia, Anglo-Saxon ancestry is exempt – in just the terms we have been schooled to read it: through the superficial cultural details of drink, food and appearance.[26] This explains Darville's success as a novelist of Ukrainian descent, and her abject failure as a 'Pom'. To criticize Darville for the construction or the reception of her novel is to allow oneself to be addressed by only one of the several voices which go to make it up. The literally litigious response to the Demidenko scandal represents a misunderstanding about what a literature of the Holocaust might look like in the next century.

D.M. Thomas's novel *The White Hotel* and Martin Amis's *Time's Arrow* have been taken to task for revealingly different shortcomings. Thomas's novel unites psychoanalysis with the Holocaust: during the 1920s, a young Viennese woman consults Sigmund Freud about debilitating pains in her pelvic region and left breast, which he diagnoses as classic hysterical symptoms. However, it turns out that it is not the woman's past which is thus inscribed on her body, but the future: the pains are proleptic symptoms of the horrific injuries she will suffer, again at Babi Yar. Critics have isolated various problems with this scenario: first, the young woman's hysteria is conveyed by her own diaries and poems, which are pornographic; second, the section of *The White Hotel* which concerns Babi Yar, and which was judged to be the most effective in the novel, turned out to have been borrowed from a survivor account in Anatoli Kuznetsov's *Babi Yar*. Worst of all, although Thomas reproduced Kuznetsov's words almost verbatim, he made the addition of a sadistically pornographic detail of his own to the woman survivor's account: in his version, she does not survive to tell her own tale.

Thomas's case raises the question again of when citation constitutes historical legitimation, and when it is plagiarism. The problem with *The White Hotel* was that while Thomas was fulsome in crediting his debt to Freud, whose case histories and letters infuse the fictional case history, his reliance on Anatoli Kuznetsov's book was signalled only in tiny print on the novel's copyright page.[27] The *Times Literary Supplement* was prompted by the outcry that followed Thomas's 'unmasking' to host a symposium on plagiarism, and among the letters it received on the subject were several which argued that a writer like Thomas has no business dealing with subjects he clearly could not imagine, as he had to appropriate them.[28] As Thomas did not try to pass off Kuznetsov's words as his own, he was not actually plagiarizing; but in this kind of third-generation Holocaust fiction, inauthenticity can be signalled by so many factors that in critics' eyes he might as well have been. The combination of Holocaust plagiarism with pornography is especially potent. In *The Pornography of Representation*, the critic Susanne Kappeler claimed that it made Thomas 'the snuff artist of the cultural establishment', as the woman in *The White Hotel* who dies at Babi Yar 'is not just the fantasized victim of his narrative, the fantasized construction of Freud's case history, but for true literary consummation must be the real victim of authentic history'.[29] This comment sees *The White Hotel* as a patriarchal attack on the feminine, continuing Freudian traditions of misogyny and confusing historical and fictional discourse to do so.

However, I would argue that, as with *The Hand that Signed the Paper*, the reader constructed by the text is more knowing than Kappeler suggests. *The White Hotel* is more self-consciously a 'documentary fiction' than hostile critics have argued. It is also less polemical than well-disposed critics say; these writers read *The White Hotel* as an indictment of psychoanalytic language and practice, which is what makes up the novel's first half in the form of the hallucinations and writings of Freud's fictional patient Lisa Erdman. In this reading, the historical material from Kuznetsov's account of Babi Yar supersedes the fictive psychoanalytic material, and shows that Freud is to blame for not being able to interpret Lisa's symptoms.[30]

Not only does such an argument indict psychoanalysis as ahistorical and unhelpful, it performs the retrospective damage to history that Michael André Bernstein has called 'backshadowing'. Backshadowing sees cataclysmic historical events as inevitable, and their victims are blamed for not seeing what was coming. It is a paradox of backshadowing, as Bernstein says, that the Holocaust is seen as both inevitable and unimaginable.[31] It is very hard to return to a pre-Holocaust era and avoid the temptation to make knowing, melodramatic observations about the little town of Oswiecim, for instance. Yet this is just the temptation Thomas avoids in *The White Hotel*, through his character's forward-looking symptoms; and the one Amis also avoids in *Time's Arrow*, which is narrated backwards. In both cases, the reader's devotion to backshadowing is satirized. Far from blaming Freud for the failure of psychoanalysis to predict Nazi genocide, Thomas shows the violent intrusion Nazism made on its healing impulses, and on what he thinks of as the feminine. This is the force of the following passage from *The White Hotel*:

> Most of the dead were poor and illiterate.... Though most of them had never lived outside the Podol slum, their lives and histories were as rich and complex as Lisa Erdman-Berenstein's. If a Sigmund Freud had been listening and taking notes from the time of Adam, he would still not fully have explored even a single group, even a single person.
> And this was only the first day.[32]

For Thomas, the feminine is a realm of physical 'generosity' and the unconscious, which is why the first half of his text consists of sexual fantasies, and why its central character is, unusually, a female victim of the Holocaust. She dies in the ravine whose name in Russian means 'old woman'. This explains the changes, or rather, superimpositions of material Thomas makes in his treatment of the massacre at Babi Yar.[33]

Susanne Kappeler would presumably interpret the changes Thomas makes to Kuznetsov's account – in the latter Dina's breast and hand are injured, while in *The White Hotel* it is Lisa's breast and pelvis – as part of his pornographic agenda; other critics argue that Thomas shows history has superseded symbolism, as Lisa's symptoms turn out to have a literal meaning. Neither position seems quite right; rather, Thomas's alteration shows that the text is mourning the feminine that Kappeler sees it as destroying.[34] This is especially true of the most horrifying change Thomas makes to Kuznetsov's text; Lisa dies because one of the Ukrainian SS rapes her with his bayonet. (This is not an entirely gratuitous invention by Thomas, but a conflation of episodes from Kuznetsov.[35]) The psychoanalytic discourse of hysteria – a word which means 'flying womb' – is transformed into brutal murder under the Nazis. The polemic, if there is one, is directed at Nazism, not at psychoanalysis.

Interestingly enough, Martin Amis has never been accused of plagiarizing any of his intertexts, which are several, and quite faithfully followed. Some critics grumbled that *Time's Arrow* was typically slick and flashy, simply reproducing a cheap science-fiction gimmick from Philip K. Dick's short story 'Your Appointment Will be Yesterday' (which later formed part of Dick's novel *The Counter-Clock World*). It is true that some of the *tour-de-force* reverse-narration routines in Amis's novel have undeveloped origins in Dick's story: how cooking and eating look backwards, and how conversations between men and women sound backwards (they make no sense either way, as the narrator of *Time's Arrow* tartly observes). The famous reversed bombing of Dresden passage from Kurt Vonnegut's novel *Slaughterhouse 5* is also a ghostly presence in *Time's Arrow*. But the most important influence on the novel is Robert Jay Lifton's history of Nazi medicine, *The Nazi Doctors: Medical Killing and the Psychology of Genocide.*[36] The fact that the section of Amis's novel which deals with the protagonist's time as a doctor in Auschwitz seems like a brief fictionalized version of Lifton's book has not particularly bothered critics, even though on the face of it this is similar to Thomas's reliance on Kuznetsov. I think there are various reasons for Amis' exemption from the 'subtle larceny' slur, in George Steiner's phrase.[37] One is that Amis did not hesitate to credit Lifton in interviews and in his book's Afterword, which lists all the texts he has drawn upon.[38] The second is that the narrative structure of the novel is complex: not only do events go in reverse, but the first-person narrator is an impish, falsely naïve inhabitant of the body of the novel's real hero – Tod Friendly, originally Odilo Unverdorben, one-time Nazi doctor. Both backwards narration and split narration lend themselves to sardonic humour, irony, and general double-voicedness, undercutting the idea that monologic appropriation has taken place.

Amis has taken pains to rearrange his material, at times in a stylized montage, or by the strategic placing of individual details, like the following remark by the narrator on a recurring nightmare: 'I bet [other people] don't have the dream we have. The figure in the white coat and the black boots. In his wake, a blizzard of wind and sleet, like a storm of human souls.'[39] This figure comes from Tod's past, and from Lifton's discussion of the Nazis' pre-war 'euthanasia' project directed against the disabled, and the transportation of patients to killing centres:

> SS personnel manned the buses, frequently wearing white uniforms or white coats in order to appear to be doctors, nurses, or medical attendants. There were reports of 'men with white coats and SS boots', the combination that epitomized much of the 'euthanasia' project in general.[40]

Although the precise meaning of this figure may be lost without a knowledge of Lifton's text, the general sense of someone wearing both a healing medical coat and murderous military boots is quite clear. Most of the factual details in the novel's Holocaust section have similar roots in Lifton's book.

The most significant borrowing Amis makes from Lifton is rather different from the literal citing of individual phrases. This borrowing could hardly be taken for plagiarism, and marks instead the efforts of the fiction to reproduce historical insights using its own generic techniques. Lifton argues that Nazi doctors were subject to what he calls 'the killing–healing paradox'. Instead of using their skills to heal, doctors at Auschwitz used them to kill; the 'medicalization of killing' was crucial to genocide, Lifton argues, and killing was seen as a 'therapeutic imperative', helping to rid the Nazi state of its Jewish bacillus. In an interview, Amis described the effect of reading Lifton's book: 'It's the most extraordinary *donnée* I've ever had as a writer. It all fell into place at once. A doctor at Auschwitz was the absolute example of the inverted world.'[41] Moral reversal becomes, in Amis's novel, narrative reversal.

Lifton argues in *The Nazi Doctors* that this moral reversal was enabled by a process of internal splitting undergone by perpetrators like Mengele, which he calls 'doubling'.[42] Again, this is novelistically reproduced in *Time's Arrow*: the central character, Tod Friendly, is a former Nazi doctor, but he is narrated in the third person by his own conscience or soul. The two entities are really one, just as the Auschwitz self and the ordinary self of the Nazi doctor were one. *Time's Arrow* could be seen as a model for Holocaust fiction: rather than simply backing up a story with historical facts taken from elsewhere, the very structure of the novel is informed and deformed by its subject. This is a rare occurrence, a technique shared only by texts like Louis Begley's *Wartime Lies*, in which the divided survivor-subject is both the character and the means of narration; and Art Spiegelman's

Maus, where the cartoon form is made to do visual duty as both the representation and temporary ironic replenishment of loss.[43]

According to many critics, realism and its postmodern variants are full of pitfalls for Holocaust-fiction writers, but 'beautiful writing' may evade them altogether.[44] My example here is Anne Michaels's 1996 novel *Fugitive Pieces*.[45] Subtle rather than unsubtle larceny seems to be the critical assessment of Michaels's novel, which had very favourable reviews and in Britain in 1997 it won both the Orange Prize and the *Guardian* Fiction Prize. In the *Guardian*, Natasha Walter called it 'an extraordinary piece of work', while the *Toronto Globe* considered it 'exquisitely fabricated':[46] it is interesting that one would not guess from these verdicts that the novel is about the wartime rescue of a Jewish Polish boy, Jakob Beer, by Greek archaeologist Athos Roussos. Crude narration, irony, black humour, appropriation, sensationalism, characters who utter antisemitic slogans: none of these seems quite as bad for Holocaust fiction as exquisite fabrication. All the features of Holocaust novels which create a scandal are characterized by double-voicedness, in contrast to the monologism of Michaels's novel. Why does Jakob's lost sister Bella have to be a talented piano-player *and* beautiful? Why does Athos have to be a saint in human form *and* a paleobotanist? Natasha Walter tempers her enthusiasm for Michaels's novel along such lines: she says Michaels 'is putting literature on a pedestal; it would be wonderful to see her making it a little less polished'. For 'pedestal', one might substitute the term 'single-voiced', and for 'less polished', substitute 'double-voiced'.

Holocaust novels which have caused controversy and even offence may be more interesting and fitting as representations than those which are praised as masterpieces of fine writing. Helen Darville, Martin Amis and D.M. Thomas have each written double-voiced novels which polemicize with readers and draw them into debate. Anne Michaels and others (for example, Caryl Phillips, Cynthia Ozick, David Hartnett[47]), by contrast, have written novels which offer little friction and no scandalous mixture of voices with which to take issue.

Notes

1 Helen Daniel, 'Editorial', *Australian Book Review*, February/March 1996, p. 2.
2 Robert Manne, *The Culture of Forgetting: Helen Demidenko and the Holocaust* (Melbourne: Text Publishing, 1996) discusses the threat of legal action against Dershowitz (p. 85). The cartoon, by Peter Wilkinson and originally

published in the *Australian*, 22 January 1996, is reproduced ibid., p. 177.

3 Helen Demidenko, *The Hand that Signed the Paper* (Sydney: Allen & Unwin, 1994); reissued 1995 with the author's name given as 'Helen Darville'. Except where specified, all references are to the 1994 edition.

4 On 19 August 1995, David Bentley of the Australian newspaper the *Courier-Mail* 'outed' Demidenko as Darville; see *The Demidenko File*, edited by John Jost, Gianna Totaro and Christine Tyshing (Ringwood, Victoria: Penguin Books Australia, 1996), pp. 98–111.

5 Martin Gilbert, *The Holocaust: The Jewish Tragedy* (London: HarperCollins, 1986); *The Black Deeds of the Kremlin: A White Book*, edited by S.O. Pidhainy, I.I. Sandul and A.P. Stepovy, translated by Alexander Oreletsky and Olga Prychodko (Toronto: The Basilian Press, 1953).

6 When Demidenko's novel was reissued in 1995 the following information appeared as an 'Author's Note': 'What follows is a work of fiction. The Kovalenko family depicted in this novel has no counterpart in reality'. Acknowledgement is given to the testimony of I. Mariupilisky from Pidhainy's *The Black Deeds*, and Alexander Donat from Gilbert's *The Holocaust* (*The Hand*, 1995, p. vi).

7 Andrew Riemer, *The Demidenko Debate* (St Leonards, NSW: Allen & Unwin), p. 12.

8 Manne, *The Culture of Forgetting*, p. 20; Allen & Unwin released a statement headed 'Helen Darville Apologises' which was signed by the author and appeared in most newspapers on 25 August 1995 – the text of the letter is in *The Demidenko File*, pp. 208–9.

9 D.M. Thomas, *The White Hotel* (Harmondsworth: Penguin, 1981).

10 A. Anatoli (Anatoly Kuznetsov), *Babi Yar* (London: Sphere Books, 1970), pp. 110–11, author's bold type; see also Manne, *The Culture of Forgetting*, pp. 17–19.

11 *The Black Deeds of the Kremlin*, ed. by Pidhainy, Sandul and Stepovy, p. 284.

12 On 17 September 1995, Allen & Unwin's lawyers Minter Ellison gave their verdict that 'allegations of plagiarism were unsustainable'; quoted in *The Demidenko File*, p. 266.

13 Kuznetsov, *Babi Yar*, p. 253.

14 Manne, *The Culture of Forgetting*, p. 68.

15 Quoted in ibid., p. 45 (interestingly, two earlier copy-editors had refused to work on Darville's typescript).

16 Ibid., pp. 44, 22.

17 Ibid., p. 125.

18 Mikhail Bakhtin, *Problems of Dostoevsky's Poetics*, translated and edited by Caryl Emerson (Minneapolis: University of Minnesota Press, 1984), p. 72.

19 Darville, *The Hand*, p. 96.

20 Manne, *The Culture of Forgetting*, p. 121.

21 Bakhtin describes *skaz* as 'Stylization of the various forms of oral everyday narration'; *The Dialogic Imagination: Four Essays*, translated by Caryl Emerson and Michael Holquist, edited by Michael Holquist (Austin, Texas: University of Texas Press, 1981), p. 262.

22 Ibid., pp. 300, 278.

23 See Howard Aster and Peter J. Potichnyj, *Jewish–Ukrainian Relations: Two Solitudes* (Oakville, Ontario: Mosaic Press, 1987), p. 19, on the debate over

Petlyura's role in Jewish–Ukrainian relations between 1917 and 1921; and Manne, *The Culture of Forgetting*, p. 150.

24   Manne, *The Culture of Forgetting*, pp. 52, 152.

25   Darville, *The Hand*, p. 15.

26   Sneja Gunew, 'Performing Ethnicity: The Demidenko Show and its Gratifying Pathologies', *Australian Feminist Studies*, 11 (1996), pp. 53–63.

27   Thomas claims that the disparity in the paperback edition of *The White Hotel* between his prominent acknowledgement of Freud and scant reference in tiny print to Kuznetsov is not due to a hierarchy of intertexts but to Penguin changing the format of the acknowledgments from the original hardback; see *Memories and Hallucinations* (London: Abacus, 1989), p. 84.

28   'Plagiarism: A Symposium', *Times Literary Supplement*, 28 April 1982; letter from D.A. Kenrick, 26 March 1982. It is worth noting that Thomas's fear, that inventing details about the Holocaust would be less effective than marshalling the words of witnesses, is borne out in his more recent novel *Pictures at an Exhibition* (London: Sceptre, 1994), which seems to me to do what *The White Hotel* was accused of: sensationalize and trivialize the Holocaust.

29   Susanne Kappeler, *The Pornography of Representation* (Cambridge: Polity Press, 1986), p. 93.

30   Laura E. Tanner, 'Sweet Pain and Charred Bodies: Figuring Violence in *The White Hotel*', in *Intimate Violence* (Bloomington: Indiana University Press, 1994); Mary F. Robertson, 'Hystery, Herstory, History: "Imagining the Real" in Thomas's *The White Hotel*', *Contemporary Literature*, 25 (1984), pp. 452–77.

31   Michael André Bernstein, *Foregone Conclusions: Against Apocalyptic History* (Berkeley and London: University of California Press, 1994), p. 23.

32   Thomas, *The White Hotel*, p. 220.

33   Ibid., p. 219; and Kuznetsov, *Babi Yar*, p. 110.

34   I am grateful to Sylvia Kantaris for this insight (personal communication); see also her *Dirty Washing: New and Selected Poems* (Newcastle: Bloodaxe 1989).

35   See Kuznetsov, *Babi Yar*, p. 112.

36   Philip K. Dick, 'Your Appointment will be Yesterday', *The Collected Stories of Philip K. Dick vol. 5: We Can Remember It for You Wholesale* (London: HarperCollins, 1994 [1966]) (I am grateful to Isabelle Doyle for this reference); Kurt Vonnegut, *Slaughterhouse 5* (London: Triad/Granada, 1979 [1969]); Robert Jay Lifton, *The Nazi Doctors: Medical Killing and the Psychology of Genocide* (New York: Bantam Books, 1986).

37   See George Steiner, 'Dying is an Art', *Language and Silence* (Harmondsworth: Penguin, 1979 [1965]), p. 189, where he claims Sylvia Plath's poetry 'commits a subtle larceny'.

38   Martin Amis, *Time's Arrow* (Harmondsworth: Penguin, 1991), pp. 175–6. For a sceptical view of Amis's interest in the formal potential of narrating the Holocaust backwards, see Simon Louvish, 'No business like Shoah business', *New Moon* (November 1991), p. 10. Aviva Kipen is not entirely convinced by Amis's list of acknowledgements and suggests he is overly keen to show that 'some of his best friends might even be Jewish'; 'Hitting and Missing the Mark', *Jewish Quarterly* (Summer 1992), p. 71.

39 Amis, *Time's Arrow*, p. 12.
40 Lifton, *The Nazi Doctors*, p. 70.
41 Quoted in Mark Lawson, 'The Amis Babies', *Independent* Magazine, 7 September 1991, p. 43.
42 Lifton, *The Nazi Doctors*, p. 473.
43 Louis Begley, *Wartime Lies* (London: Picador, 1992); Art Spiegelman, *Maus I* and *Maus II* (Harmondsworth: Penguin, 1987, 1992).
44 The phrase is Claire Kahane's (personal communication).
45 Anne Michaels, *Fugitive Pieces* (London: Bloomsbury, 1996).
46 Natasha Walter, 'Memorable miniatures', the *Guardian*, 20 February 1997, p. 12; in another review Andrew Riemer says that Michaels's 'exquisiteness of language' sits uneasily with 'the probing of moral and spiritual states'; 'Exploring the sad song of humanity', *Sydney Herald*, 30 March 1997, p. 10.
47 Caryl Phillips, *The Nature of Blood* (London: Faber, 1996); Cynthia Ozick, *The Shawl* (London: Jonathan Cape, 1988); David Hartnett, *Black Milk* (London: Jonathan Cape, 1994).

9

Is Aharon Appelfeld a Holocaust Writer?

Leon I. Yudkin

Recent writing

Until the Dawn's Light[1] follows in the tradition of *Katerina*,[2] in its epic scope, its tight, action-packed, sequential narrative, its pace and its violence.[3] Appelfeld's stories have taken two forms; one slow-moving, brooding, with the omniscient narrator passing judgement, and the reader then predicting the inevitable outcome, with the principal protagonists adopting fixed postures. The other moves the narrative on quickly, even impatiently. *Until the Dawn's Light* is of the second type. But here the texture is thicker than the author's earlier fictions of this type, more filled out. It is set in the first decades of the century, in a remote region of Austria. The narrative is filtered principally through the eyes of the young heroine, who was, when young, a brilliant Jewess, outstanding academically in her class of mainly jealous Christians. The atmosphere is one where Christianization is rampant, and indeed seen as the key to success and social acceptability. She too is caught up in the whirl of the times, evincing contempt for an outworn faith, and putting a misplaced reliance on a plodding classmate who cannot cope with Latin or Mathematics. She, out of social conscience and empathy, seeks to help this inarticulate brute, and then accepts his offer of marriage.

This is the source of her tragedy. She converts, and becomes his house slave, violently exploited and beaten. She has a child, Otto, who becomes the focus of her whole life, and for whom she is writing her memoirs. At first, she accepts her lot passively, partly out of the recognition that her fall stemmed from her own mistaken notions and gullibility, and partly out of terror. She even takes an outside, menial job, which entails leaving her home throughout the week, virtually abandoning her beloved child, and surrendering her husband to a local wench, who fills in, looking after the child and the house – that is to say, stripping her of her last remaining hold on life. All builds up to the violent climax within a violent setting.

The story is told on two time-scales. One is the present, ongoing time, with the heroine in desperate straits, fleeing the law after murdering her husband, taking her child with her, but then leaving him to the care of a benign educational institution. The other scale is of the material of the journal, which she wants to entrust to her son. This is a description of how she arrived at this condition, her sympathy for her boorish husband, the entrapment, the denial of her Jewish roots, the hostility of the alien environment, and, finally, the despair leading to murder and flight. She had not been able to care for her helpless father, and she is determined now to do her best for her little boy. She has reached the stage where she hankers for her roots, in the place of her birth, that region where the Baal Shem flourished (as she learns from Buber's *Tales*), the Carpathians. And it is in the course of her flight, which is accompanied by increasingly violent behaviour, that she is finally caught by the police. But, at this point, she is virtually indifferent to her present condition, and only longs for her father and the cafe where they used to sit.

In a recent study, Yigal Schwartz has categorized Appelfeld's work under three headings.[4] These are: the attempt to recapture and restore the author's childhood; the 'broad expanse of a literary kingdom'; the religious stance of the narrator, the relationship between the Jewish world (that of the tribe and its faith) and the encroaching gentile world. *Until the Dawn's Light* belongs to the third category. Its main theme, obsessively recurrent, is the immutable and persistent character of an ancient kernel of Jewishness, which is always at the back of the mind of the chief protagonist, however difficult its satisfactory formulation. This sense is indeed the common theme of all Appelfeld's fiction, whatever the place or time setting, and however the narrative is filtered.

Appelfeld's subject

Whatever the apparent setting of the author's fiction, whatever the decade, there persists a consistent view of the subject. The settings do indeed vary, from the central Europe of the first decade of the century, to the Austria of the 1930s, from the period immediately preceding the war and the Holocaust, to the transit following the war for the survivors. Pre-Israeli Palestine and Israel are also the scenes for the setting of some of the stories. But there is a remarkable indifference to external realia, to the current scene, to the concerns of other sections of the population. In the postwar setting, the protagonists remain frozen in the attitudes, psychic and mental, that had been acquired earlier. The Holocaust has frozen them into fixed positions. But we also find that the Holocaust has not, so it seems, wrought a fundamental transformation of postures, only confirmed them. The typical Appelfeld protagonist learns from his experience in the world that his encounter can only bring about rediscovery of the Jewish element, whatever that may be and however it may be seen. Thus, ironically, although the Holocaust has cast its shadow both forwards, where the survivors are now transfixed, and backwards, to those who operate within the framework of an impending doom, one known at least to the reader, it does not change the situation, but only confirms it. Appelfeld in fact never treats directly of the period between 1939 and 1945. He rather assumes it as an entity known. The representation of the documentary truth, the factual account of the horror, can be left to others, to historians, to chroniclers, to writers of different types. Appelfeld perceives his function differently. It seems to be to get under the skin of the historical personality of the Jew in the modern world, to discover the psychic reality of the 'tribe'. It may be ironic that the writer who is known as the Holocaust writer *par excellence* should, in fact, never have touched it directly, but rather skirted round delicately, leaving the horrific crassness to others. What an author of this special character might be able to achieve instead is a penetration into this permanent reality, living in the shadow of a world, where the Holocaust is only the most horrific and ultimate manifestation, but not one unique, unprecedented, or indeed perhaps, unrepeatable.

Variations in technique

Time is a significant operative in Appelfeld's stories. Some of the stories cover a very brief span, focusing on figures found in a given situation and frozen in them. Others cover a lifetime. *Katerina*, for example, is narrated by the central figure, and conveys the essence of her very long and eventful life. *Until the Dawn's Light* is proclaimed by the dust-jacket to be of that mould, rich in incident and external plot development. It is also a violent story, as we have seen. But there is a message in the tale, and the sting is in the violence. There is the violence perpetrated on the brutal husband, who is himself violent, and there is the violence done to the heroine brought on by her own denial; the lack of recognition of her own essence. As a result of the violence done to her, she herself becomes violent. But the initial action was her own, and it lay in a sort of self-deception. And this misunderstanding too came about as a result of circumstances, to a large extent historically conditioned. Blanca is a Jewess, living on the borders of non-Jewish society, seeing in her Jewish element merely negative connotations. From the standpoint of her parents' negative assessment of the Jewish part of her being and from her own assessment of the rights of man and the current situation, it would mean little to her, apparently, to sacrifice that small Jewish part, which, for her, was just an irritation. In this sense, the story line represents a further stage in the line of tradition of Enlightenment literature, and particularly of what is known as Vitalism, influenced, directly or indirectly, by Nietzsche. In Adolph, Blanca discerns the lad for whom she evinces sympathy and whom she is later to marry. She sees in him power and vitality. He is strong and untroubled by intellectual doubts and physical weakness. Just as the pathetic Jew emerging from the Pale was attracted to the natural rootedness of the gentile native, to his unencumbered physicality and free sexual expression, so is Blanca drawn to the apparently untroubled Adolph. These traits are apparent in his lack of academic prowess, which becomes, for Blanca, a virtue rather than a failing, and her liberal sympathies allow her to view him as at least an equal. That this 'vitality' is actually antisemitism, and that this was always present as an essential element of his makeup and culture would only become fully apparent in their life together. By denying her historical place, she is also denying herself. The tale thus unfolds as a necessary retribution, determined and justified by her wilful blindness. She goes to her fate, at the enigmatic and problematic conclusion of the novel, willingly. There is to be inherent justice in what awaits her. She has to suffer shame, the shame of a daughter not taking in her 53-year-old father, the shame of a Jewess hating her Jewishness, the shame of a person not defending herself until she takes the drastic and ultimate step of killing her husband. No moderate way out was offered as a possibility. The shame of her non-recognition led to the shame of her conversion, to the shame of her betrayal and to the crime of murder. In the meantime, she takes revenge by burning down churches, whilst writing her memoirs (this book) for her child, whom she has protected above all else. The novel is a tale of return. Here, the Carpathian mountain region represents the actuality of her origins, and it is to that Land of the Baal Shem, founder of the Hasidic sect, an authentic tendency of Jewish revivalism, that she would return. But, before that can be achieved, she must pay the price both for her own shame and for the crime committed by society. As in Dostoevsky's *Crime and Punishment*, the criminal gives himself up. Self-surrender is more effective than discovery, because it involves self-knowledge and a willingness to put what has been learned into effect. The heroine offers a message in this version of the *Bildungsroman*, and there the story ends.

This novel obviously contains no reference to the Holocaust, and any implications for that event, or knowledge derived from it, would necessarily be indirect. It is set in the first decades of the century, before the First World War. Historically, we know that the Jewish communities of Europe still flourished, although, to some extent, their spiritual life was residual. Enlightenment had drawn the Jewish and Gentile worlds together, and there seemed little intelligent option for the smaller element than to be absorbed into the larger. But, if our claim is true, and the Holocaust is not the defining event in Jewish history, but rather the ultimate metonymy of loss, this account can be seen as an illustration of the depradation brought about by the modern situation. Our subject then is less clearly demarcated than might be thought. Denial can lead to hostility and to the violence of mutual destruction.

Post-Holocaust fiction

One of the effects of the Holocaust on literature has been that it has brought about a situation which transcends the possibility of any sort of adequate representation. Any mimetic effort true to its subject would cease to be aesthetic production, literary material, and become gruesome chronicle. The literature that takes in the Holocaust – and any serious contemporary literature must take it in, in the sense that it remains at the base of its assumptions – has to go beyond representation of the facts, whilst, of course, still acknowledging their veracity. The Holocaust in Appelfeld, and as conveyed by the author himself in his own person, is the Holocaust of the child, without concrete memory. And, as there is no concrete memory, the traces cannot be erased.[5] Much of Appelfeld's fiction, as we have seen, is set in the postwar world, in the world of survivors, where these are the chief figures and the exclusive focus.

Does this make Appelfeld a Holocaust writer? Certainly, this is how he is regarded, although many take issue with this blanket categorization, and hedge it with qualifications, even when partially accepted.[6] In the Foreword to the collection of essays entitled, appropriately, 'Essays in the First Person', the author does specifically denote his theme as being 'the relationship to the Holocaust'. Indeed, this is one of the few occasions where this stance is explicitly invoked. But then, the genre is different, and so demands and creates patterns of its own. The title of the essay collection conveys this essential distinction. 'The first person' is what it declares. This is no longer a fiction, where a world separate from the author is created, but the revelation of immediate and personal experience in relation to the Holocaust. The testimony is of the individual, the only one valid. Gershon Shaked has argued that the world of the author is indeed populated by figures who have emerged directly from the cauldron, not filtered by imagination nor by empathy, as is the case with other Israeli writers who have entered this territory.[7] But fiction is what it makes claims to be, an imaginative penetration into the world of the other. This is surely why fiction of any kind, but specifically that relating to the Holocaust, is placed in disparate settings and in various periods. Even when the author deploys the first-person narrator, it must clearly be grasped as a fictional device; that much can be seen by the crude device of checking such fictions against the author's own biographical data, and coming up with clear discrepancies. Autobiographical essays are in a different category from fictional narrative, and the reader response generated therefore varies in accordance with the nature of the expectations raised.

But again, in spite of the necessary caution that we must exercise in making a distinction between autobiography and fiction, even the fictionalized work remains close to a tapestry, a portrait of tribal Jewry, of which the author is part. He is witness to a scene, the portrait of a residual and terrorized people attempting to come to terms with the shock and trauma before moving on to wherever. The immediate postwar phase is a vital element in this overall panorama. The individuals and the collective bear the effects of what has passed, but they must also consider what is to come, and make preparation. This can be called the Italian phase, as it was in southern, coastal Italy that a small group assembled, an assortment of survivors, supported by the 'Joint', and described in important stories, such as '1946'.[8] In this camp, near Naples, a cross-section of this battered population awaits its fate. The story is saved from excessive metaphorization by the narrative thrust. There is still a tendency to compare everything to something else, to characterize the 'mournful melody' as being 'full of evening', to picture the 'striped coats' as 'startled waves', but there is an urgent story to tell. We want to know about these people, how they have been affected, how they plan to shape their future, and where they are going to go.

But are they separate individuals, or do they constitute an indistinguishable mass? We read that: 'The warm darkness wiped all individuality from their countenances'. Of course, within the group people have names. There are adults, old and young, children, entertainers, the sick, the adventurers. And there are also the outsiders. An attractive woman is brought in, Stella, a local. Lump, through his infatuation, becomes young again. In the meantime, she is fascinated by the fate of the Jews.

We are immediately struck, in terms of narrative technique, by the fact that we are not taken up specifically with any particular individual's fate or story. As in *Badenheim,* the first of the two stories in the volume, we are presented with a section of a population, here, the tribe, and move from one to the other, as though dealing with a representative sample. The year, 1946, becomes a metaphor, and stands, together with the location, Italy, for the beginnings of the recovery (for the residue only, obviously). Italy in 1946 represents a kind of halfway point between the terror of repression and obliteration on the one hand, and the possibility of recovery, on the other. The people still bear the marks of the terror. Like animals, they still carry the traces of being hunted, and have not yet made their way back into human specificity. Appelfeld often characterizes the unit as a 'tribe'. They stick together. Stella, the outsider, attempts to get hold of the nature of the collective, not of each individual. Lump, in his responses to her (she, after all, is his girlfriend), stresses the unique talents of each separate person. They had education, which means background and a private history. We are at a transitional stage between the undifferentiated animal horde and the normality of separate humans coming together voluntarily, but also going their own ways at will. Lump also sees himself as an animal in relation to Stella, and asks her why she ties him up when he wants to leave the camp. His freedom is expressed precisely in not knowing when he will return; that is the human element in his being, not to be bound like a dog. But what a motley crew is here in this random sample of few survivors; smugglers, illegal traders, and also, by the way, a rabbi, held up as a model, and worshipped as a symbol. There is, however, an even deeper source of malaise. Any sign of life that is to be found in Lump now comes to him exclusively from the outside:

Sometimes he felt that his existence was light as a feather. True life was embodied in Stella. As long as Stella stays with him he will live. At night Stella would withdraw to the side, kneel down and pray. Lump knew suddenly, that everything in him had died. Maybe he was just a metamorphosis, a shadow attached for a moment to a live body. (p. 116)

A central feature of the survivor, picked up time and again in the literature, is the sense of death in apparent life.[9] The Italian camp acts as a staging post on the way back to some sort of re-entry into a new phase. There is little sense of contemporary reality within the group. Even when the place name, Palestine, begins to be heard within the camp, those who hear it do not relate to it as an actual place in the world, but only as a sound composed of syllables. The thought too that they might conduct a trial of two men who had probably betrayed them to the police (for smuggling) is thought to be virtually inconceivable. So rather than get down to the projected 'trial', they just hold them, tied up. The question to be raised is: what is the Law, and what constitutes justice? Rather than confront the difficulty, they become virtually paralysed.

So, to what extent are Appelfeld's narratives populated by survivors specifically marked by the Holocaust? It is said of two of the young women that they are becoming more and more beautiful: '"The war has not changed them in the least. They have the memory of ants."' (This speech is unattributed, so presumably belongs, like so many of the utterances made in the stories, to the general collective.) And the reply comes back, from another unattributed source: '"So what do you want them to do? Cry?"' (p. 129). An emergent view is that the events of the war are best forgotten, even at this early stage, as the memory of them can achieve nothing positive. Another response is to prepare in the direction of collective strength, for possible self-defence and even Nationhood. This is under the direction of the charismatic Franck, an outsider from what had been the Austrian army, held in suspicion as well as in awe by the Jews. He can restore some measure of self-respect. If only that had existed a little earlier, they perhaps would not have been led like sheep to the slaughter! But it is too late now. In any case, it all belongs to the past, just as Judaism itself seems to belong to the past. Not unnaturally, they sometimes speak of the Jewish episode in history as though it is all over now. So, even if the Holocaust is not represented or even invoked directly, it remains a constant presence by implication.

We must return to the question of what the term 'Holocaust writer' means. It can carry with it the connotations of direct description of the physical act of destruction and extermination. That clearly does not happen here. On the other hand, it can also be interpreted as transmitting the effect of the event, its implications for what has gone before it, and what is to come in its wake. The fact of the Holocaust can modify our understanding of the Jewish situation preceding it, as well as shaping the fate of the remnants beyond. Much of Appelfeld's writing in this respect is indirect. It involves the reader, who must know more than what is starkly set down on the page. But does not all writing carry certain shared assumptions and knowledge with the reader? In this instance, the reader is presumed to know what has happened. The Hebrew reader, certainly, bears it on his skin. '1946' transmits the implied heritage of the six previous years, and takes us beyond, into the collective psyche, where not all is overtly stated. But it still must be understood as Holocaust writing in this enlarged sense of the term. The two opposed views put forward by the protagonists in the story are: first, that the past should be remembered, recovered and revived; and second, that it is just as well to forget it all, with its misery, humiliation and suffering. Meanwhile, the remnants are few, and such as are left may well soon be dispersed, or disappear like water in the sand. Again, one possible reaction to this, as expressed here, is that this would be a positive upshot, as 'everyone bears within him the sting of poison' (p. 136). And the reaction expressed to the articulation of that tendency, is that there is no necessity to take steps to achieve that, as the disappearance will take place willy nilly. We do not have to bring it about. This is but one tendency among several; the respect due to the Rabbi, the pleasant, if rather vague connotations of Palestine, the awareness of the Day of Atonement, the new self-respect that is now being acquired under the direction of Franck. But this is all in a state of flux, and may shift once more, as the foundations of such attitudes are so shaky. It is a decadent and almost extinct society, that can only be redeemed, and that in very small part, by the allure of a way out. The whole situation is interim. The respite is not decisive, but offers a pause following catastrophe, but before the unknown future. We have here the partial story of a group. As with *Badenheim*, there is no hero, no central figure, but the remnants of a society, the residue of the tribe. The story ends when the camp is dissolved, and they are picked up by boat to go on to the new destination. But, by the time they leave, they are severely depleted and reduced in every sense. Some had gone to other places in Europe, some to Australia, and others had mysteriously disappeared. It is a ragged medley, but one that suffers in its separate parts, dissolving into a mixture of despair and Messianic hope. By this time, there are only 32 people left, including children and the sick, and they have nothing, no possessions of any kind. There is no resolution at the story's conclusion, although there is a demarcation of the end of a process.

Witness to disaster

In order to grant a perspective to the events that dominate Appelfeld's opus, *Katerina* is narrated, unusually, by a gentile woman, who tells her story at the age of 80. The perspective on the total narrative is gained by the fact that, within a relatively brief fictional space (132 pages of Hebrew text), a time span of several generations is covered, as well as a large geographical area. The story also takes us from the inter-war period, when *stetl* life still existed, although under threat, as far as the present moment, which means, through the most violent and destructive episodes of Jewish history. And all this is viewed both from within and without; from the standpoint of a participant and one who was involved, but also who was not actually Jewish. The author has adopted in this novel an unusually heavy disguise, an invention and imagined situation that adds to the power of the fiction. But we are back in the Land of the Cattails (Land of the Reeds), a characteristically Appelfeld locus, a very Jewish, primal and tribal scene. She, Katerina, has come to play out her last, and recall times past, for herself, and incidentally, for the reader too. Her story is full of incident and violence. So this is a family saga on an epic scale, compressed, where the narrator comes full circle, returning to the source of her life. The author returns to the cruelty and viciousness displayed towards women in his later novel, *Until the Dawn's Light*. But whereas that is a story about a highly educated Jewess, whose conscience leads her to assimilationist tendencies, here we have the gentile narrator actually attempting to get under the skin of her Jewish associates. The similarity between the two works lies in their scale, pace and variety; strong narrative features not always evinced in the author's work. There is a strong sense of locale, of association with the ethnic environment, and, especially in old age, with their religious roots. Here the tribe becomes manifest in individual sentiment, obliterating accumulated baggage and increments. The dead indeed exercise maximum control. The generations past necessarily tighten their hold over the present.

Initially, she left home in order to escape the primitive domination of her father and, especially, of her new stepmother. What really preserves Katerina is her belief in manifest destiny and in ultimate retribution. Everything that is done on earth will find its inevitable consequence. So, even if evil is done, it will be seen by God, who will exact recompense. When she left her home, she set out on what was known as 'the Jewish path', a side road, and this seemed to confirm her fate as interlocked with that of the Jews, despite the general hostility evinced towards them on the part of her own people. They were associated with devils and feared as cheats. For example, it was not regarded as wrong to steal from them; her mother would tell her that you could steal from a thief with impunity. The Jews were another species, something derived from the fact that they had murdered Jesus. Her own life was to be one of degradation in the primitive rural heartland of the Ukrainian regions, starting out amongst the down-and-outs and beggars at the Strasov railway station, learning to steal and subsist as far as possible, like her associates there.

But Katerina is extricated from this life by a Jewish woman who takes her into her employ. It is from this point on that the absolute division between Jew and Christian begins to break down for her, and that she can begin to cross this terrifying divide. She moves into that other territory, and so can offer something of a dual perspective that marks out this narrative. She observes that on the part of the Jews too, the sense of otherness is perceptible and total. It is as though there are two quite distinct human species that eye each other with suspicion and loathing. She bears a child by a man whom later she can scarcely remember, suffers in childbirth, and struggles to nurse the baby. So her life now enters a new phase, and she succumbs more and more to the Jewish influence. She says that she became associated with them, without paying due attention to the fact (p. 26). Although we still have a narrative transmitted from both sides of the fence, the gravity of sympathy shifts, and the narrator is now further entrenched in the Jewish camp, with all the guilt necessarily flowing from that self-identification with the Christ killers. A duality was to enter her soul, and divide her permanently. She no longer belongs unambiguously to one category or the other, and she is thus no longer capable of enjoying the simple pleasures that she once had experienced so vividly. She becomes even more attached to the family when, first the father, Benjamin, with whom she had fallen in love, and then, Rosa, the mother, were murdered by hooligans and mobsters. She devotes herself to the two children, who are later forcibly removed by

Ruthenian agents of the relatives of the late mother. Now she has lost almost everything. She has abandoned her own baby, her protectors have been murdered, her charges have been snatched away, and she is alienated from her own origins. But now she is redeemed for a second time by another Jewess, this time by one non-observant, one of the 'modern' variety. But her stay there is brief, and again she returns to the inn, her first port of call, where she made her initial contact with the outside world. However, she is by this time so 'infected' by her Jewish influence that she can no longer be absorbed into that earthy and primitive community. She must travel on, and so she continues to Czernowitz, whence her most recent employers had made tracks. But their ways part again, and again Katerina is left alone. It is a new Katerina and also a new environment. As one familiar and sympathetic, and specifically as a Yiddish speaker, she wants to and can mix freely with the down-at-heel Jews of this city, capital of the province of Bukovina. We are in the underbelly of urban life, amongst drunkards and beggars, amongst whom are many Jews, including her new comrade, Sammy. They drink together, live together, and soon she finds herself, much to Sammy's regret, pregnant. Her whole being is now bound up with her lovely little boy, whom she has circumcised and calls Benjamin, after her true love. Here, and in these circumstances, circumcision is likely to be a form of execution. But she insists, in spite of all the difficulties and refusals (after all, he is not Jewish), and so takes the critical step in initiating the child into this excruciating covenant. And the reason? Because her heart told her to, she says. In her new situation, she leaves the city, and once more sets out for the villages, to live a Jewish life, isolated, except for her child. There is murder all around, and she would like to insulate him, to create a cocoon of tranquillity. Yiddish will be his language.

But then the ultimate disaster occurs. Karel, an old acquaintance from her village, after plaguing her to abandon the child and go off with him, snatches Benjamin and crushes his head. In her anguish, she cuts Karel's throat with a knife, not letting go until she is sure that he is dead. Thus, as she says, she ends the first half of her life. We cannot say that there has been no build-up to the stark horror of the scene, but this, in its unfiltered brutality, surpasses anything that has gone before. She says of herself that it is she who has now been murdered, with only the stump remaining (p. 90). The prison regime to which she is submitted makes no impact on her. In prison, she is in an even better position to observe from afar and more objectively what is happening in normal, civil life. Rumours and stories abound about what is happening to the Jews. Their clothes and other property arrive at the prison to the unbridled joy of the recipients, spoils of the pogroms. The plunder and murder of the Jews did not await the Holocaust; it seems to have been continuing apace constantly, gaining momentum in the years leading up to the war.

For this reason too, then, Appelfeld cannot be defined as a Holocaust writer in the direct sense. Katerina is not in this novel a victim of it herself, and, since she is in prison, she is not even, literally, an observer. But she does dwell on the borders of Jewish identity, and is a victim of the horror as well as a witness to the ongoing hatred and murder that was to culminate in ultimate eradication. The testimony of the narrative is to a permanent situation of which the Holocaust is a part, albeit a part in its most extreme expression.

For Katerina, the martyred little Benjamin is the true Jesus. He has been Christianized, and Jesus has been Judaized. Her identity has been adulterated, and so her story is conveyed from an odd angle. Her evidence gains in authenticity from her status as outsider, whilst it is dependent for its reliability on her insider familiarity. She is one of the author's leading female characters; but unlike Tsili, Bertha and Kitty (leading female characters in other Appelfeld stories), she is non-Jewish, intelligent and dynamic (she takes the initiative). The model of this heroine type is adopted again in *Until the Dawn's Light*. The time span covered in this novel is extensive, and takes in the Holocaust period and beyond. During the 'terrible years of the 40s' (p. 114), Katerina could write almost nothing, and what she wrote she destroyed. For the other inmates, this is the occasion for much rejoicing, and so we see that the Holocaust was not a unique event for them, but rather the culmination of an historical process. Again, Katerina is a witness, but a witness at some remove, indirect. She bears testimony through the diseases that she receives on her own body, suffering in self-imposed isolation. The climax was a world without Jews. Then came the emptying of the prisons, and Katerina can wander off. She had been in prison for over 40 years by her own account, which conveys some notion of the time-scale of the novel, and of the huge span covered within some 30 pages. She is in the countryside in a strange Jew-free world. So she decides to live in the past, which she can achieve through her memoir, reliving her adopted family and the festivals, the rhythm of the year. And then she returns to the village of her birth to complete her own life cycle and to be reunited with those who have gone.

Witness to what?

It seems that there can be no simple answer to the question of whether Appelfeld is a Holocaust writer. In part, the reason is glaringly obvious; it depends what we mean by the term in question. But it is also because the narratives do lend themselves to be seen as an investigation into the Jewish condition, one of tribal fragility and exposure, that culminated in the full horror of virtual and calculated extinction. On the other hand, there is no direct portrayal of the process of mass murder itself, in fact, hardly even a direct mention, although the awareness is either assumed or filtered indirectly. Perhaps this is not surprising in the light of what is taken to be Appelfeld's *ars poetica* – his belief that all true spiritual concerns should be filtered through personal experience.[10] The personal experience of the survivor, the hunted, the involved observer, forms the content of the narrative, and also connects with the earlier and collective experience of the tribe. The narrative is most convincing and persuasive when the story holds sway, free of overt authorial intervention and comment. It is least successful when succumbing to static metaphorization and omniscient manipulation. The characters of the story can take over. It is their personal experience that creates the vital force of the narrative, and it is the linkage of that individual experience with the collective that can render a larger meaning and make the story worth conveying. In historical terms, the individual pieces of evidence belong to a pathetically small band of survivors, as against the vast numbers of those perished and rendered necessarily inarticulate. But, for the individual, it is his own experience that counts (recounts, tells).

In the story, 'bagovah haqar' ('On the Cold Heights'),[11] a few survivors of the war are gathered together, at the instigation of the well-meaning allies, at a beautiful but remote spot in Southern Italy, because 'they thought that this far off location, with the virtues of beauty and height, can serve as a creative gangway back into life' (p. 136). The collective story, it is decided too, has to be written up. A 'narrator' is appointed, but this narrator has difficulty in arriving at the necessary judgements. Generalizations, it seems, cannot be admitted; presumably, they are invalid. But further: 'What right has he to tell the story of this community?' The whole notion of the act of writing in this context becomes problematic and suspect. And, of course, this is precisely the activity that the author is engaged upon in this project and, for that matter, in his total opus. It is for this reason that Rattok regards this as a 'key story' in Appelfeld's opus; it opens up the question of the function and capacity of the Holocaust writer.[12] It becomes clear that it is not sufficient merely to describe the events, although that in itself may be extremely difficult, but one must strive for some sort of meaning. On the one hand, the 'narrator' fails in his appointed mission. But, on the other, his success is indicated by the existence of the text before us. So it looks as though the effort in itself constitutes the achievement. As Rattok says, the story tells us about a story that was not written.

As far as the narrator invoked in the story is concerned, the narratives must remain within him, where they will have their own life like fireworks (p. 143). 'The redemptive word did not appear' (p. 148). The narrator in fact comes to terms with his own incapacity, his inability to transform the experience into words, and recognizes the fact that other forces are operative here, and they will take over, imposing their own rule. That, in effect, is what happens. The remnants of the tribe move on, and so ends the story. The Italian episode has acted as an intermediary stage between the world of the camps and the life that awaits, whatever that may be. In parallel fashion, the narrator's function is to mediate between the experience of the survivors and the reality of the reader. Although he himself may negate the possibility of that function, the ambition to represent the situation faithfully remains in itself the achievement of that mediation. That is all that can be done at this stage, in view of the damage inflicted on the human capacity of characters involved. The implication is that any suggestion of immediately effective and adequate narrative would be facile, and thus do violence to the truth of what has taken place.

Do we know how long this intermediate stage is to endure? On the way from one situation to another, it may well be that, in terms of the ongoing Appelfeld narrative, we are still in the transition stage. The Israeli settings of the opus are nugatory, and, such as they are, they represent the figures from this European world in settings frozen in postures derived from the past. And his most recent work too does not enter more into the world of specifically current Israeli concerns, but more frequently goes further back, behind the Holocaust and to the sense of modern Jewry on the verge of disintegration following the stages of partial emancipation.

Appelfeld has rejected the label 'Holocaust writer', which is so often applied to him.[13] He argues that only about one-third of his work deals directly with the subject. This may indeed be the case in a literal sense. A great deal of his work, as we have indicated here, is set in earlier periods, before the rise of Hitler. And some of his narratives are placed in postwar Palestine and Israel. But the earlier settings cast the Jew in the role of failed assimilationist, inauthentic Christian, would-be European. They could have been written in the light of hindsight, with the prevision of ultimate disaster. The post-Holocaust stories, too, are preoccupied with the survivors, remnants of the tribe, a pathetic band of isolated and marginal individuals who gradually form something of a group in the shadow of a larger society. It is in this sense that we see Appelfeld as a 'Holocaust writer', a category that must be qualified, refined and individualized to take in his very specific narrative mould.

Notes

1 Aharon Appelfeld, *Ad sheyaaleh hashahar* (*Until the Dawn's Light*) (Jerusalem: Keter, 1995).
2 Aharon Appelfeld, *Katerina* (Jerusalem: Keter, 1990).
3 Everything here is based on the Hebrew editions of the author's work. Any quotations refer, in brackets following, to the Hebrew source in my own translation.
4 Yigal Schwartz, *Kinat hayahid venetsah hashevet* (*Individual Lament and Tribal Eternity*) (Jerusalem: Keter, 1996).
5 Aharon Appelfeld, *Masot beguf rishon* (*Essays in the First Person*) (Jerusalem: The Zionist Library, 1979), pp. 24, 25.
6 See, for example, Alan Yuter, *The Holocaust in Hebrew Literature: From Genocide to Rebirth* (Port Washington, NY: Associated Faculty Press, 1983), where he argues that the author examines '... the residual effect of the Holocaust on its survivors' (p. 61); in other words, he does not deal with the experience overtly, but rather with its later effect.
7 Gershon Shaked, *Gal hadash basiporet haivrit* (*New Wave in Hebrew Fiction*) (Tel Aviv: Sifriyat poalim, 1970), p. 79.
8 Published together with 'Badenheim, ir nofesh' in *Shanim veshaot* (*Years and Hours*) (Tel Aviv: Hakibbutz hameuhad, 1975).
9 See, for example, the novel by Isaac Bashevis Singer, *Enemies: A Love Story* (originally published in the Yiddish journal, *Forverts*, New York, 1966), where it is not only the central figure, Herman Broder, who feels that he is still inhabiting the hayloft which served as his home in Poland for three years during the war, but also the other major figures, the lustful Masha and her mother Shifra-Puah, who only manage to hold on to a residual life through their mutual dependence. Herman's original wife, Tamara, who he had thought dead, actually survived, but she is metaphorically and physically possessed by the bullet that had lodged in her.
10 See the author's statement in *Masot beguf rishon* and the development of the notion in the critical work by Lily Rattok, *Bayit al belimah: omanut hasipur shel a. apelfeld* (*A Precarious House: the Narrative Art of A. Appelfeld*) (Tel Aviv: Heqer, 1989).

11 Included in the volume *Bagay haporeh* (*In the Fruitful Valley*) (Tel Aviv: Schocken, 1963).
12 See Rattok, *Bayit al belimah*, p. 11ff.
13 See the reference to the interview in the *New York Times Book Review*, 15 November 1986, in Gila Ramras-Rauch, *Aharon Appelfeld: the Holocaust and Beyond* (Bloomington and Indianapolis: Indiana University Press, 1994), p. 18.

10

The Mirror of Memory: Patrick Modiano's *La place de l'étoile* and *Dora Bruder*

Samuel Khalifa

L'histoire est notre imaginaire de remplacement.

Pierre Nora

The revision of the history of Vichy France came to prominence at the beginning of the 1970s.[1] The events of May '68 and then the death of De Gaulle sparked off a questioning of 25 years of official history. The need for truth and the will to understand brought an end to the myth of the French *Résistance*. The hypocrisy of what François Nourrissier[2] has called the *'honneur inventé'* was confirmed. The crimes of the Occupation were denounced and, in particular, the moral and political responsibility of the Vichyists and of those who had actively collaborated, the *collaborationnistes*.[3] The taboo was first broken by artists. Through its chronicle of one provincial city, Clermont Ferrand, the film *Le Chagrin et la pitié* (1971), directed by Marcel Ophüls, André Harris and Alain de Sédouy, traces the doubts of a whole country faced with its deeds in the Second World War. The film radically upsets the perspective of the 1940s by dismantling the chimera of the *Résistance*. Two years later, the question of Vichy re-emerged on to the intellectual scene, with the translation of the book *Vichy France* by the American historian Robert Paxton.[4] Insisting on the specificity of Vichy, Paxton draws attention to its responsibilities, in particular for the deportation of Jews. The work provoked a heated controversy, stirred up old hatreds and opened old wounds.

And yet, several years earlier, Patrick Modiano was already exploring this terrain.[5] Anticipating the evolution of the collective conscience, *La place de l'étoile*, published in 1968, offered a rereading of the Occupation, and began not only to articulate the reawakening of a Jewish identity but also the resurgence of the Vichy past. Amongst the writers of the second generation, Modiano was the first in France to confront an alienating memory and, in doing so, to break the mould of traditional historiography.

An orphan of memory, Modiano is haunted by his own prehistory: 'I was only twenty years old, but my memory preceded my birth. I was sure, for example, that I had lived through the Occupation of Paris since I remembered some characters from that time and some remote and disturbing details, of the kind never mentioned in history books'.[6] This obsession has given rise to two major motifs: the author was born in 1945 and thus considers himself 'a product of the Occupation'; then there is the mystery of his father: of Jewish origin, Albert Modiano lived in Paris under the Occupation and avoided deportation for reasons never made clear.

The enigma of his origins provokes in the author a response which is difficult to define, mixing as it does a sense of absence – being cut off from his roots, shame – because of his father's past – and guilt – for having survived. To a certain extent, this state of confusion is shared by a whole generation of Jewish writers: Georges Perec, Pierre Goldmann, Alain Finkielkraut or Guy Konopnicki convey the same sense of mutilated origins. This comes across in the titles of their novels: *Obscure memories of a Polish Jew born in France*,[7] *A Void*,[8] *The Imaginary Jew*.[9] Inextricably linked, Memory and Identity are marked by absence, open wounds which the recourse to writing helps to heal.

As it appears in the novelist's concept of writing, the duty to remember seems, on the one hand, to be part of the quest for identity: the genocide becomes part of what it is to be Jewish; and, on the other, it is inscribed within the act of narration itself: the deconstruction of the narrative mirrors both the bewildering nature of what is evoked as well as the aesthetics of a voice recovered. Written thirty years apart and in completely different styles, *La place de l'étoile* (1968) and *Dora Bruder* (1997) make the same observation.[10] If memory is to be kept alive, it must not be rigidified, but rather recognized as a space traversed by forgetting. *La place de l'étoile* evokes the hallucinated, farcical journey of Raphaël Schlemilovitch, who epitomizes the archetypal Jew, from the genocide back to the remotest age of western antisemitic consciousness; whilst *Dora Bruder* recalls the rambling and anxious investigation of a young girl's last moments before being arrested, interned at Drancy and deported to Auschwitz. Published nearly thirty years after Modiano's first novel, *Dora Bruder* marks a notable return to the first sources of his inspiration: the Occupation and the role of the Vichy government in the 'Final Solution'. I use the word 'return' with some caution for this theme never really left his writing. The obsession – for it is this word which best describes his relationship to the theme – moved into the background during the 1980s, but remained latent and therefore all the more haunting and persistent. Fiction is no more capable of resisting the memory of the unspeakable than history. However, I hope to show that through shattering these previously legitimate forms of memory, History and Literature, two texts by Modiano succeed in reaching a partial, intermediate truth, perhaps the only kind which can be envisaged. This essay will first examine the ways in which the conventions of historiography and fiction are disrupted; it will then look at how this disruption is put to use in the author's pursuit of memory. Finally, it will focus on the specific case of *Dora Bruder* and argue that it is a book of commemoration which transcends personal memories.

'History, Stephen said, is a nightmare from which I am trying to awake' (James Joyce)

In Modiano's work, representation of the Occupation responds to an aesthetic imperative rather than a concern for historical factuality. When questioned by Victor Malka about his treatment of the period, he replied that:

> Of course, the Occupation I deal with is a mythical one. I didn't want to paint a realistic picture of the Occupation but instead to evoke a certain moral climate of cowardice and confusion. Nothing at all to do with the real Occupation. No historical accuracy, but, instead, an atmosphere, a dream, a fantasy.[11]

Neither a first-hand account nor a confession – how could it be when the author was born in 1945? – but an invented evocation constantly disrupted and chronologically dislocated. Raphaël Schlemilovitch and Dora Bruder are themselves the agents of this dislocation. Raphaël Schlemilovitch, whose vision of the world and of his own life is made up of disparate experiences or, in the words of Colin Nettelbeck and Penelope Hueston,[12] the '*entre-choc d'expériences/clash of experiences*', is the son of a kaleidoscope maker. Moreover, his name carries the stigmata of wandering and alienation. The prefix *Schlemil* is a Yiddish word which describes 'a poor fool' whilst the suffix *ovitch* means 'son of'.[13] The metaphor of disruption changes with *Dora Bruder*. Dora

Bruder runs away from the austere atmosphere of a Catholic institution where she is a boarder. This first disappearance is the prelude to a definitive one: Auschwitz. This motif of absence relates to a loss of meaning; the extinction of the *logos* which is such a central theme in Modiano's work.

The representation of the Occupation needs to be carefully examined first of all in *La place de l'étoile*. This novel, which constantly plays on doubt and ambiguity, poses a fundamental problem: how can one be both Jewish and French after the tragedy of the Occupation?[14] How is one to reconcile the two terms of this equation of identity? How is it possible to claim a double allegiance without denying the past? In the French imagination, the Place de l'Étoile symbolizes not only the capital of France but also the greatness of France's political and military past as enshrined in the Arc de Triomphe. As Maurice Agulhon notes, this monument, the result of one of Napoleon Bonaparte's projects, was primarily intended 'as a monument to the glory of the armies of the Republic and the Empire'.[15] This, at least, is how it is represented within the national memory. Maurice Barrès observes: 'The Arc de Triomphe is the image of our righteous pride; the Panthéon is the laboratory of our charity'.[16] However, Modiano interprets this national symbol in a different way, as becomes clear in the epigraph to the novel which is ironically signalled as a Jewish joke:

> In the month of June 1945, a German officer comes up to a young man and says to him:
> 'Excuse me, could you tell me where the Place de l'Étoile is?'
> The young man points to the left side of his chest. (*La place de l'étoile*, epigraph to the novel; my translation)[17]

The play on the word *étoile*/star distorts the reality evoked. It is not the glory of France's past that is recalled by the Place de l'Étoile but rather the repressed guilt of the State's collaboration with the Nazis. On 7 June 1942, the Vichy government passed a decree making it obligatory for all Jews in the northern zone to wear the Yellow Star which was, at first, an outward sign of their degradation and then a mark of their death sentence. Furthermore, it was in June 1942, following a speech made by Laval in the course of which he expressed the hope of a German victory, that France openly adopted a policy which was clearly in favour of collaboration. Moreover, Modiano's play on the meanings attached to the Place de l'Étoile allows him to highlight a further unpalatable truth of this period of French history. During the

Occupation, the Place de l'Étoile, which was and is the very incarnation of bourgeois respectability, became a centre for the most horrific deeds of the collaboration: torture, murder, frenetic debauchery, as well as for the black market. It is the dark underbelly of Paris that the author chooses in order to represent the Occupation. He introduces it to the reader through the sinister microcosm of a building used by the French Gestapo at 93 rue Lauriston, in the 16th *arrondissement*. This place, with its troubling atmosphere, was where the songs of Charles Trenet could be heard mixed with the screams of the tortured and the groanings of perversion.[18] It should be noted that it was in the Autumn of 1941, under the aegis of Lafont-Chamberlain,[19] that the 'Gestapo of the rue Lauriston' – a heterogeneous mix of real criminals, poor employees and opportunists of all sorts – decided to dismantle the *Résistance*. Buried within the archives of a guilty French conscience, this shady headquarters of the French Gestapo has been dredged up from oblivion most notably by Jacques Delarue, who presents a disturbing vision of a forgotten reality:

At no. 93 rue Lauriston, they tortured in the cellar, had parties on the ground floor, and undressed some of the most beautiful women in Paris on the third floor. But on all floors they played a double game: a double game in which the Occupier stood to gain most, and that was what mattered.

There was an extraordinary mix of characters who in normal times would never have met. Politicians rubbed shoulders with thugs, gangsters kissed the hands of Marquesses and cinema stars, and it is this cocktail of base criminality, bloody betrayal and entirely gratuitous and unpredictable acts of humanity or of generosity which sums up the unique atmosphere of the Occupation.[20]

Raphaël Schlemilovitch, the hero of the novel, tries hard to escape this world of anguish and moral decay. He travels in time and space in an illusory attempt to reconcile his Jewish and French identities and to put an end to his nightmare. His failure to do so, in any time or any place, leads him back to the dark years of Occupied Paris (*La place de l'étoile*, hereafter *PE*, p. 177). Mixed into this fantastical representation of the Occupation, Modiano includes a veritable catalogue of clichés inflicted upon the Jewish people from the days of anti-Judaism to its modern expression in the form of antisemitism. Once more, the evocations are both allusive and selective: the condemnation of a people for deicide (*PE*, pp. 108, 110–11), the impure race (*PE*, pp. 13–14, 48, 107), the myth of the Jewish Plot (*PE*, p. 49), the Jew as depraved, a swindler and pimp (*PE*, pp. 28, 95, 151), the Jew as a monied and frivolous reveller (*PE*, pp. 14, 47–8), the Jew Süss idolizing his money (*PE*, pp. 50, 142, 161–2), the vulgar individual incapable of sophistication (*PE*, pp. 17, 55, 68), the Israelite who is spineless and cerebral since his exile from the promised land (*PE*, pp. 73–4) ...

In the novel *Dora Bruder* the perspective is different. Situated in the years 1941–2, this novel gives a chronological account of the events of this period through fragments and shards of memories. Sometimes the author makes use of the anecdotal. The author recalls 'those women whom the Germans called "friends of the Jews": a handful of French "Aryans" who, in June, on the first day the Jews had to wear the yellow star, had the courage to wear the star themselves as a mark of solidarity' (*Dora Bruder*, hereafter *DB*, p. 142; my translation).[21] Taken as a whole, the novel's portrayal is impressionistic and suggests more than it says. As Henri Rousso rightly observes: 'For him [Patrick Modiano], the Occupation has lost all historical status. It is a puzzle which shouldn't be put together; truth filtering through the emptiness'.[22]

Narrating memory: the art of the 'Fugue'

A direct consequence of this dislocation of history is the rupturing of literary conventions. *La place de l'étoile* abandons the unities of place, time and action. The periods related and the places mentioned are the product of Raphaël Schlemilovitch's delirium as he vainly tries to reconcile himself to the realities of Occupied France. Moreover, the hero appears to be a phantasmagoria crossing time and space like a comet. He has more than one life. Thrice killed, he is thrice brought back to life. Furthermore, Raphaël, is a writer who specializes in the art of caricature and pastiche, and who ridicules many antisemitic authors of the 1930s and 1940s, such as Céline (*PE*, pp. 14–15, 134), Brasillach (*PE*, pp. 33–4), Rebatet (*PE*, pp. 13, 48–9) or Drieu la Rochelle (*PE*, pp. 36–8). This powerful use of parody and farce breaks the traditional form of narrative, which is systematically tagged as a fiction, a lie.

With the exception of the unity of place – Paris – *Dora Bruder* presents a polymorphous plot which covers several periods. The novel, written in 1997, narrates the result of research begun eight years earlier – in 1989 – into the life of a young girl deported to

Auschwitz in 1942. Finally, this gap of 40 years is filled in with the personal memories of the author dating back to the 1960s and 1970s. This stratification, this layering of events disrupts the flow of time and undermines its linearity. Following the pattern established by *La place de l'étoile*, we pass from one period of time to another without any logical link or artificial association of ideas. By following a musical structure – a fugue for two voices – the narrative alternates between the real memories of the author and the invented ones of Dora and in this way avoids a linear chronological development. Does this imply that these two texts formulate an incapacity to articulate the experience of absence or silence? Does the author balk at a past he has not lived and of which he knows nearly nothing? Quite the opposite, his aesthetic choices reflect an ontological obsession. As Norbert Czarny notes: 'The Occupation is primarily the metaphor of a deeper and more distant sadness ... To use René Char's aphorism, writing, like living, is to persist in completing a memory'.[23] Writing thus becomes a way of exorcizing the author's pre-history. It becomes a means of deliverance from his sense of guilt about the past: the dark years of the Occupation and, more especially, the uncertainty surrounding his parents, in particular his father.[24] By a recourse to fiction, which allows Modiano to forge his own language, writing becomes a means of compensating for emptiness and, in doing so, of creating an identity. Looking for himself, and progressively revealing himself to himself, in the practice of writing, Modiano overcomes the question of *how to speak* differently in both novels. *La place de l'étoile* provides the author with a necessary outlet to exorcize the uncertainty of his origins. Several clues indicate the autobiographical import of the novel. Like the author, Raphaël Schlemilovitch is a writer and, like him, uses pastiche and irony. In addition, he has the same place of birth as Modiano: Boulogne-Billancourt.

Finally, Schlémilovitch Senior, the cowardly and farcical father who has dubious connections with the Gestapo, resonates with autobiographical echoes. Living in Paris during the Occupation, Albert Modiano escaped two *rafles*: the first, it would seem, by his own means, the second with the help of some suspect contacts, people who were associated with the Gestapo. [25] In *La place de l'étoile* Patrick Modiano describes his father's arrest without making clear the cause of his release:

On 16 July 1942, Gérard had forced Schlemilovitch senior into a Gestapo car: 'What would you say to an ID check in the rue

Lauriston and a little spin around the Vel' d'Hiv?' Schlemilovitch junior had forgotten by what miracle Schlemilovitch senior managed to decline the gentleman's invitation' (*PE*, p. 136; my translation).[26]

The scenes of the round-ups haunt the author and are repeated over and over again in his work.[27] In *Dora Bruder*, the author, recalling the first time his father was rounded up, admits to the influence of these events in his first novel, *La place de l'étoile*:

> I had begun a book – my first book – in which I tried to experience for myself the malaise that he had experienced during the Occupation. I had discovered in his library, several years earlier, antisemitic books of the forties which he had bought at the time, no doubt to try and understand what these people had against him. ... What I wanted to do in my first novel was to reply to all those people whose insults had wounded me through my father. (*DB*, pp. 72–3; my translation)[28]

The autobiographical 'grafting' is most explicit in *Dora Bruder*, as is clear from the identification between the narrator and the author. Modiano provides the narrator with his own neutral, personal memories, more often than not insignificant, which reveal an identity emptied of substance: there is an adolescent who runs away (*DB*, p. 59), a visit to a flea-market with his mother (*DB*, p. 9), a trip to Vienna at the age of twenty (*DB*, p. 23), the handling of stolen goods (*DB*, pp. 134–5) walks in Paris ... The contrast with Dora's fate is striking. But if the tragic evocation of Dora creates a gap, reveals the empty memory of the author, it also allows this same memory to express itself, to emerge. The evocation of Dora helps to engender the author's memory. The intertwining of the two narrative threads leads, at one point, to a meeting of the two when the author imagines his father and Dora arrested in the same round-up: 'The presence of that young girl in the police van with my father and other strangers ... I wondered if it wasn't Dora Bruder' (*DB*, p. 65; my translation).[29] This evocation has the effect of freeing the author from the guilt of the past and allows him to come to terms with a painful memory which he had tried to deny by claiming to have no childhood memories, like Georges Perec in *W or the Memory of Childhood*.[30]

In the working through, and gathering in, of this obliterated past, Modiano discovers that he can come to his identity only through his own writing which, paradoxically, is founded upon the use of artifice. It is precisely by means of these literary artifices that he can forge a memory and even a sense of commitment, and it is within the aesthetic dimension of his writing that his identity is united to a universal reality. If the first encounter with the past in *La place de l'étoile* describes a personal experience drawn from the limited perspectives of an œdipal father–son relationship, then *Dora Bruder* pays dignified homage to those whose lives were cancelled and whose memories were obliterated. It is, then, with this idea of a book of commemoration that I shall conclude this essay, concentrating solely on *Dora Bruder*.

Dora Bruder – a book of memory

It is the title, *Dora Bruder*, which signifies the work performed by the text. The eponym is a traditional device used to both dedicate a book and to pay homage. Nevertheless – with the exceptions of *Emmanuel Berl. Interrogatoire*[31] and *Lacombe Lucien*[32] – this was the first time that Modiano used such a device.[33] Moreover, Dora Bruder is not marked by the absence of a proper name, as are most of Modiano's characters whose surnames are rarely given and who sometimes do not even have a first name: even when revealed, the name is more often than not a false one. In contrast, it seems that this time by presenting a stable nominal identity, Modiano may have wished to restore a 'presence', to make public Dora's absence. Announcing the *'dawn of a certain intelligibility'* after the Shoah, Emmanuel Levinas asks: 'The names of people call forth a face … do they not resist the dissolution of meaning and help us to speak …?'[34]

This destiny which History has legally confiscated and which Time has officially dismissed is one which Dora Bruder shares with no other character among the 17 novels of Modiano's oeuvre. The memory of the Holocaust does not emerge through fleeting sketches (*Fleurs de ruine*, 1989) or incipient disorder (*Chien de printemps*, 1993) but weaves the central narrative thread. This is made clear by the explicit intention and resolute tone of the author: 'If I was not here to write it, there would be no trace of this unknown person's presence' (*DB*, p. 67; my translation).[35] Modiano's claim is to act as a guardian of the past. This working through of the inexpressible responds not only to a desire to return to his prehistory through the mediation of another's experience, but also to communicate effacement through writing.

Retracing Dora's past, moreover, required long and patient research, minute attention to every detail in order to resurrect her memory from the tomb of the forgotten. Who was Dora Bruder? What school did she go to? Why did she run away from home? How did she survive during her lengthy escapade? In what circumstances was she arrested and brought to Drancy? So many questions which the author, like a detective, tries to solve by returning to each scene, questioning the locals and living witnesses, consulting the administrative archives and looking for clues: 'It took me four years to find her exact date of birth.... And two more years to discover her place of birth.... But I am patient. I can spend hours waiting in the rain' (*DB*, p. 16; my translation).[36] This investigation, the outline of which is traced in the novel, had begun, moreover, nine years earlier with *Voyage de Noces*: 'It seemed as if I would never be able to retrace Dora Bruder's steps. Not being able to do so pushed me to the writing of a novel, *Voyage de Noces*, as another way of keeping Dora Bruder alive in my thoughts, perhaps another way, I told myself, to make things clearer, to gain some insight into her' (*DB*, pp. 54–5; my translation).[37]

With its oppressive atmosphere of death, *Dora Bruder* strongly evokes the reality of the Nazi extermination camps. Apart from Dora and her parents, Ernest and Cecile Bruder, the author draws from the forgotten past scores of other lost names, victims of the same fate: 'I found, by accident, two years ago ... the last letter of a man who left in the convoy of the 22nd of June, with Claude Bloch, Josette Delimal, Tarama Isserlis, Hena, Annette, the girlfriend of Jean Jaurison ...' (*DB*, p. 123; my translation).[38] In saving the names of those who died in the death camps from the amnesia of time, Modiano carefully avoids the pitfalls of explanation, indignation and lamentation. Confronted with the prospect of the ossification of the banal and the comfort of repression, the text responds by taking the reader into the gaping lacuna of memory and reveals the incandescent truth of absence. Out of this absence come a few shreds of existence but enough to supply that 'invisible thread ... which runs through life' (*Voyage de Noces*, pp. 118–19; my translation).[39] What's more, the narrator returns several times to the memory of those whose death has marked him: writers he has admired – many of whom were killed, persecuted or hunted down (*DB*, pp. 94–102), but also acquaintances from his youth (*DB*, pp. 98, 135–7), friends (*DB*, pp. 76, 102) and also his father. *Dora Bruder* is the first novel in which Modiano evokes his father's death (*DB*, pp. 19–20).

The symbolism of places serves to accentuate the climate of death which prevails: the hotel room where Dora's parents lived in hiding after the antisemitic curfew laws were passed (*DB*, pp. 35, 58), the Catholic institution from which Dora runs away (*DB*, pp. 39–40), the army barracks where the narrator is called to do his military service (*DB*, p. 74), the hospital where his father dies (*DB*, pp. 19–20), the police headquarters where Ernest Bruder registers as a Jew and receives in return the standard three yellow stars (*DB*, p. 78), the Tourelles prison where Dora is interned (*DB*, p. 63), the Drancy deportation camp (*DB*, p. 63) from where Dora, and so many others, are transported in train wagons to an unknown destination: Auschwitz. This claustrophobic atmosphere seems to be inscribed in the very topography of the capital, whether it be that part of the city where Dora's boarding school is: 'that peaceful area, which seems cut off from Paris, with its convents, its secret cemeteries and its silent avenues, is also the place of departures' (*DB*, p. 75; my translation);[40] or whether it be that of the hotel where the Bruders stayed: 'the darkest area of Paris' (*DB*, p. 30; my translation).[41]

From *La place de l'étoile* to *Dora Bruder*, then, there is a clear evolution. The provocation of the first narrative, which expressed the burning despair of an orphaned memory, becomes, in *Dora Bruder*, an appeal to collective remembrance. But this outcome is not simply a result of Modiano's maturing as a writer. He has put on record the extent to which Serge Klarsfeld's work, *Mémorial des enfants juifs déportés en France* (1994), had made him 'doubt literature': 'Since the driving force of literature is often memory', he said, 'it seemed that the only book to write was one of memories'.[42] I believe that this observation underlies the writing of *Dora Bruder*. Dora's 'poor and precious secret' which Modiano seeks to communicate to us draws the reader to return to that point of origin which is both intimate and alienating: the Shoah.

Notes

1 Recent historiographical studies on the memory of Vichy lie behind this summary opening. The evolution of the representation of Vichy, especially in the official memory, has been analysed by Henri Rousso, one of the first to undertake this work. Rousso locates four phases of repression and reactivation of what he calls the 'Vichy syndrome'. The work of the Institut d'Histoire du Temps Présent (*La Mémoire des Français. Quarante ans de commémoration de la Seconde Guerre Mondiale* (Paris: Éditions du CNRS, Centre régional de publication de Paris, 1986)) as well as studies by Jean-Pierre Azéma (*Le Régime de Vichy et les Français*, under the direction of Jean-Pierre Azéma (Paris: Fayard, 1992) and *Vichy, 1940–1944* (Paris:

Perrin, 1997)); François Bédarida (*La France des Années Noires*, under the direction of Jean-Pierre Azéma and François Bédarida, 2 vols. (Paris: Seuil, 1993) and Bédarida, *Touvier, Vichy et le crime contre l'humanité: le dossier d'accusation* (Paris: Seuil, 1996); and Pascal Ory (*Les Collaborateurs 1940–1945* (Paris: Seuil Points Histoire, no. 43, [1976] 1980) and 'Comme de l'an quarante. Dix ans de 'rétro satanas', *Le Débat*, 16 (1981), 109–17) have also informed this article.

2 François Nourissier, 'Le Cadavre dans le placard', *Le Point*, 11 March 1974, pp. 86–7.

3 The term is borrowed from Pascal Ory who distinguishes the word '*collaborateur*', meaning someone who remained in occupied territory and willingly submitted to the German army, from the word '*collaborationniste*' which he uses to denote those who actively subscribed to the cultural and economic phenomenon of ideological Collaboration.

4 Robert Paxton, *Vichy France: Old Guard and New Order 1940–1944* (New York: Columbia University Press, [1972] 1982).

5 *La place de l'étoile* appeared in 1968, *La Ronde de nuit* in 1969 and *Les Boulevards de ceinture* in 1972.

6 'Je n'avais que vingt ans, mais ma mémoire précédait ma naissance. J'étais sûr, par exemple, d'avoir vécu dans le Paris de l'Occupation puisque je me souvenais de certains personnages de cette époque et de détails infimes et troublants, de ceux qu'aucun livre d'histoire ne mentionne.' Patrick Modiano, *Livret de Famille* (Paris: Gallimard, 1977), p. 96.

7 Pierre Goldman, *Souvenirs obscurs d'un juif polonais né en France* (Paris: Seuil Points Actuels no. 14, 1977).

8 Georges Perec, *A Void*, translated by Gilbert Adair (London: Collins Harvill, 1994).

9 Alain Finkielkraut, *The Imaginary Jew*, translated by Kevin O'Neill and David Suchoff with an introduction by David Suchoff, 'Texts and Contexts' (Lincoln, Neb. and London: University of Nebraska Press, 1994).

10 Page references in this article refer to the Gallimard editions of Modiano's books. The following abbreviations are used: *La place de l'étoile* (Paris: Gallimard 'Folio' no. 698, 1968) [*PE*]; *Voyage de Noces* (Paris: Gallimard 'Folio' no. 2330, 1990) [*VN*]; *Dora Bruder* (Paris: Gallimard, 1997) [*DB*].

11 'Bien sûr, il s'agit d'une Occupation mythique. Je n'ai pas voulu faire un tableau réaliste de l'Occupation mais rendre sensible un certain climat moral de l'âcheté et de désarroi. Rien à voir avec l'Occupation réelle. Aucune vérité historique, mais une atmosphère, un rêve, un fantasme'; interview with Victor Malka, 'Patrick Modiano: un homme sur du sable mouvant', *Les Nouvelles Littéraires*, 30 October 1972, p. 2.

12 Colin W. Nettelbeck and Penelope Hueston, *Patrick Modiano, pièces d'identité: écrire l'entretemps* (Paris: Minard 'Archives des lettres modernes' no. 220, 1986), p. 13. It should be noted that this work was for long the only study done on Patrick Modiano.

13 The character of the *Schlemil* has largely inspired Yiddish and then German literature, following the example of the well-known story by Adelbert von Chamisso, *Peter Schlemil, the man with no shadow* (Aldelbert von Chamisso, *L'Étrange histoire de Peter Schlemil* (Paris: Librairie Générale Française, 1995).

14 As well as the perceptive analysis of this theme by Nettlebeck and Hueston,

the following are worthy of note: the preface by Jean Cau to the original edition of *La place de l'étoile* (Paris: Gallimard, 1968), pp. 3–4 as well as the studies by Janine Chasseguet-Schmirgel: *'La place de l'étoile* de Patrick Modiano. Pour une définition psychanalytique de l'authenticité', in *Pour une psychanalyse de l'art et de la créativité* (Paris: Payot, 1968), pp. 217–55; and by Charlotte Wardi, 'Mémoire et écriture dans l'œuvre de Patrick Modiano', *Nouveaux Cahiers*, 80, (1985), 40–8.

15 'L'Arc de triomphe, rendu à sa vocation initiale – la gloire des armées de la République et de l'Empire – est vite achevé.' Maurice Agulhon, 'Paris', in *Les Frances, Les lieux de mémoire*, edited by Pierre Nora, Quarto, 3 vols (Paris: Gallimard, [1984–92] 1997), III, ([1992], 1997), p. 4600.

16 'L'Arc de triomphe, c'est le signe de notre juste orgueil; le Panthéon, le laboratoire de notre bienfaisance', Maurice Barrès, *Les Déracinés* (Paris: Émile-Paul éditeurs, 1922), p. 462.

17 Modiano plays on the meaning of the word 'Histoire' which means both 'History' and 'joke' in French: 'Au mois de juin 1942, un officier allemand s'avance vers un jeune homme et lui dit: "Pardon, monsieur, où se trouve la place de l'Étoile?" Le jeune homme désigne le côté gauche de sa poitrine. (Histoire juive)'.

18 *PE*, pp. 180–5, 211–12.

19 Known variously under the names 'Capitaine Henri' or 'Monsieur Henri' under the Occupation, Henri Normand used several pseudonyms (Rigaud, Chaise, Chamberlain) but during the rue Lauriston period he adopted the name Lafont which he kept until his execution on 27 December 1944 at the Fort de Montrouge. Taking advantage of confusion surrounding the Armistice, Lafont, who already had a criminal record, showed cunning in making himself as useful as possible to the occupying forces. His talents were quickly recognized by the Gestapo which obtained from Berlin his naturalization as a German citizen. As such he was beyond the reach of the French police and justice system and pursued his ambitions without hindrance.

20 'Au 93 de la rue Lauriston, on torture au sous-sol, on festoie au rez-de-chaussée, on déshabille au troisième quelques-unes des plus belles femmes de Paris mais on joue double jeu à tous les étages. Un double jeu où l'Occupant est très largement gagnant, et c'est ce qui lui importe.

Ce mélange extraordinaire de personnages dont la rencontre en temps normal était inconcevable, ces hommes d'État côtoyant des voyous, ces gangsters baisant la main de marquises et de vedettes de cinéma, ce cocktail de basses crapuleries, de trahisons sanglantes et de gestes d'humanité ou de générosité totalement gratuits et imprévisibles, font un saisissant raccourci de l'atmosphère unique de l'Occupation': Jacques Delarue, *Histoire de la Gestapo* (Neuilly-sur-Seine: Saint Clair, 1975), p. 67.

21 'Parmi les femmes que Dora a pu connaître aux Tourelles se trouvaient celles que les Allemands appelaient "amies des juifs": une dizaine de Françaises "aryennes" qui eurent le courage, en juin, le premier jour où les juifs devaient porter l'étoile jaune, de la porter elles aussi en signe de solidarité'.

22 'Chez lui [Patrick Modiano], l'Occupation a perdu tout statut historique. C'est un puzzle qu'il ne faut surtout pas reconstituer, la vérité filtrant des

vides'; Henri Rousso, *Le syndrome de Vichy de 1944 à nos jours* (Paris: Seuil 'Points Histoire' no. 135, [1987] 1990), p. 152.

23 'L'Occupation est d'abord la métaphore d'une douleur plus lointaine et plus profonde ... écrire comme vivre, c'est, pour reprendre l'aphorisme de René Char, s'obstiner à achever un souvenir'; Norbert Czerny, 'La trace douloureuse. L'Occupation dans *Les Boulevards de ceinture, Livret de famille* et *Remise de peine* de Patrick Modiano', *L'école des lettres II*, LXXXII, 14 (1991), pp. 171–8.

24 The figure of the mother remains in the background if one compares it to that of the father which is omnipresent in Modiano's works. Does this obvious imbalance signal indifference or scorn? The author himself has stated that: 'My mother is absent from my work because I wish to protect her from the impurity' (in an interview with Jean-Claude Texier, 'Rencontre avec un jeune romancier', *La Croix*, 9–10 November 1969, p. 8). One interpretation of 'impurity' would be the shadow of those dark years which is indissolubly linked to the father.

25 The careful research done by Pierre Assouline provides an excellent source of biographical detail on the complex life of Albert Modiano: 'Modiano: lieu de mémoire', *Lire*, May 1990, pp. 34–46.

26 'Le 16 juillet 1942, Gérard avait fait monter Schlémilovitch père dans une traction noire: "Que dirais-tu d'une vérification d'identité rue Lauriston et d'un petit tour au Vél' d'Hiv?" Schlémilovitch fils avait oublié par quel miracle Schlémilovitch père s'arracha des mains de ce brave homme'.

27 These occurrences are worth noting even if the versions reveal differences too complex to untangle here: *Les Boulevards de ceinture*, Folio, no. 1033 (Paris: Gallimard, 1972), pp. 180–1; *Livret de famille* (Paris: Gallimard, 1977), pp. 105–6; *Remise de peine* (Paris: Seuil, 1988), pp. 116–17; *Fleurs de ruine* (Paris: Seuil 'Points Roman' no. 546, 1991), p. 103.

28 'J'avais commencé un livre – mon premier livre – où je prenais à mon compte le malaise qu'il avait éprouvé pendant l'Occupation. J'avais découvert dans sa bibliothèque, quelques années auparavant, certains ouvrages d'auteurs antisémites parus dans les années quarante qu'il avait achetés à l'époque, sans doute pour essayer de comprendre ce que ces gens-là lui reprochaient.... Moi, je voulais dans mon premier livre répondre à tous ces gens dont les insultes m'avaient blessé à cause de mon père'.

29 'La présence de cette jeune fille dans le panier à salade avec mon père et d'autres inconnus ... je me suis demandé si elle n'était pas Dora Bruder'.

30 Georges Perec, *W or the Memory of Childhood*, translated by David Bellos (London: Collins Harvill, 1988).

31 Patrick Modiano, *Emmanuel Berl. Interrogatoire* (Paris: Gallimard 'Témoins', 1976).

32 Louis Malle and Patrick Modiano, *Lacombe Lucien* (Paris: Gallimard, 1974).

33 In Modiano's work titles usually refer to places which may be real (*La Place de l'Étoile, Les Boulevards de ceinture, Rue des Boutiques obscures*) or imaginary (*Villa Triste, Quartier perdu*) as well as referring to stages in life which he couches in either dry administrative terms (*Livret de famille*) or lyrically (*Vestiaire de l'enfance*) and even symbolically (*Fleurs de ruine*). He also borrows from the language of everyday expressions or worn idiom (*De si braves garçons, Un cirque passe, Chien de printemps*). He draws upon cultural

history such as a song title (*Memory Lane*) a famous picture (*La Ronde de nuit*) or even a *quotation* (*Du plus loin de l'oubli*). He has also taken a title from the cyclical nature of the seasons (*Dimanches d'août*).

34 'Les noms de personnes dont le dire signifie un visage ... ne résistent-ils pas à la dissolution du sens et ne nous aident-ils pas à parler ...?', Emmanuel Levinas, 'Sans nom', *Noms propres* (Paris: Le livre de poche 'Biblio essais' no. 4059, 1987), p. 9.

35 'Si je n'étais pas là pour l'écrire, il n'y aurait plus aucune trace de la présence de cette inconnue'.

36 'J'ai mis quatre ans avant de retrouver la date exacte de sa naissance.... Et deux ans ont encore été nécessaires pour connaître le lieu de cette naissance.... Mais je suis patient. Je peux attendre des heures sous la pluie'.

37 'Il me semblait que je ne parviendrais jamais à retrouver la trace de Dora Bruder. Alors le manque que j'éprouvais m'a poussé à l'écriture d'un roman, Voyage de noces, un moyen comme un autre pour continuer de concentrer mon attention sur Dora Bruder, et peut-être, me disais-je, pour élucider ou deviner quelque chose d'elle'.

38 'J'ai trouvé, par hasard, il y a deux ans ... la dernière lettre d'un homme qui est parti dans le convoi du 22 juin, avec Claude Bloch, Josette Delimal, Tarama Isserlis, Hena, Annette, l'amie de Jean Jaurison ...'.

39 'Il arrive aussi qu'un soir, à cause du regard attentif de quelqu'un, on éprouve le besoin de lui transmettre, non pas son expérience, mais tout simplement quelques-uns de ces détails disparates, reliés par un fil invisible qui menace de se rompre et que l'on appelle le cours de la vie'.

40 'Ce quartier paisible, qui semble à l'écart de Paris, avec ses couvents, ses cimetières secrets et ses avenues silencieuses, est aussi le quartier des départs'.

41 'Je ne savais encore rien de Dora Bruder et de ses parents. Je me souviens que j'éprouvais une drôle de sensation en longeant le mur de l'hôpital Lariboisière, puis en passant au-dessus des voies ferrées, comme si j'avais pénétré dans la zone la plus obscure de Paris'.

42 'Puisque le principal moteur de celle-ci [la littérature] est souvent la mémoire, il me semblait que le seul livre qu'il fallait écrire, c'était ce mémorial'; Antoine de Gaudemar, 'La dernière fugue de Dora Bruder', *Libération, The Libération Literary Supplement*, 3 April 1997, p. iv.

11

'Il n'y a qu'une espèce humaine': Between Duras and Antelme

Martin Crowley

In 1947, Les Éditions de la Cité universelle, a publishing house established by Marguerite Duras and Robert Antelme, published (under the auspices of Robert Marin) *L'espèce humaine*, Antelme's account of his experiences in the concentration camps. Duras and Antelme had married in 1939, and were divorced in 1946. Arrested as a member of the *Résistance* in June 1944, Antelme was initially interned at Fresnes, then transferred to Compiègne, from where he was transported to Buchenwald. Having spent three months in Buchenwald, he was then moved to a related work camp at Gandersheim, which was evacuated under Allied pressure on 4 April 1945. Its surviving prisoners were then forcibly marched as far as Bitterfeld, from where, on 14 April, they were taken by train to Dachau. Following the liberation of Dachau, François Mitterrand (then 'sous-secrétaire d'État aux Refugiés, Prisonniers, et Déportés') happened to recognize the voice of Antelme (with whom he had worked in Paris in 1943) from among the emaciated survivors, and arranged for his clandestine repatriation by Georges Beauchamp and Dionys Mascolo.[1] Some 40 years later, in 1985, P.O.L. published Duras's *La douleur*, of which the eponymous 'Journal', echoing the testimonial status of *L'espèce humaine*, recounts the wait of 'Marguerite' in occupied Paris for her husband, 'Robert L.', held prisoner in the camps, his return, and his subsequent, fragile return to health. *La douleur* (both in the 'Journal' and in the volume's other texts) refers to and engages with *L'espèce humaine* in various ways, primarily by suggesting a series of reciprocities between the two texts and by offering a version of the main argument of Antelme's work which extends its ethical significance to a point of considerable difficulty. Antelme's response to the suffering he experienced was to insist that victim and torturer are bound by an ineradicable mutual humanity which will always frustrate the torturer's desire to remove his victim from the ranks of the human. In *La douleur* and elsewhere, Duras takes up this argument and explores it in ways which have uncomfortable implications. My aim here will be to examine the relationship between the work of these two writers by means first of an analysis of the reciprocity that binds their texts, with reference to the question of the representation of trauma; this will then allow an account of the ethical importance of their differing treatments of the central thesis of Antelme's book, namely that of the ultimate, irreducible unity of the human race.[2]

Such reciprocity as exists between *L'espèce humaine* and *La douleur* is, then, initially of significance for the argument it implies about the question of representing trauma. In Antelme's work, the horrors he does describe are already set against the background of a specific scale of suffering he acknowledges as absent from his account:

I relate here what I lived through. The horror in it is not gigantic. At Gandersheim there was no gas chamber, no crematorium. The horror there was darkness, absolute lack of any kind of landmark, solitude, unending oppression, slow annihilation. (p. 5)

Magnifying Antelme's careful declaration, in the bulk of Duras's text, the concentrationary universe is present *in absentia,* as the texts mostly describe an *elsewhere* of the suffering of the camps, namely Paris during the last days of the war. The concentration camps form the backdrop against which the texts unfurl; in the case of the diary which constitutes the volume's eponymous lead text, and which narrates the wait for and subsequent treatment of Antelme's semi-fictional *alter ego,* Robert L., they represent the condition of possibility of the text's existence. But they are never addressed directly; rather, the text figures them obliquely, as the shadowy other scene of a location which has somehow taken their place, crowded them out: 'We sit down to eat. But at once I want to throw up again. The bread is bread he hasn't eaten, the bread for lack of which he died.'[3] The suffering of the camps (which Antelme himself, in his Foreword, calls 'unimaginable' (p. 3)) is preserved from what has been seen as the danger of reduction entailed in the representation of its trauma by the doubling of its singularity, the displacement of this suffering into a location in which its absence roars. Thus, the anguish of the waiting narrator is presented as the doubling of Robert L.'s suffering, as she begins to mimic physically his agony. In the second text of the volume,

'Monsieur X, Here Called Pierre Rabier', we are told: 'I get very thin, until I weigh the same as a deportee' (Duras, *The War*, p. 80). As Robert L. is being starved in a concentration camp, so those who wait for him are also hollowed out by the wait: 'You don't exist any more in comparison with his waiting.' (p. 34) For the narrator, this erosion of the waiting self appears particularly extreme, earning her the criticism of D., who protests that 'No one has the right to destroy himself like that, ever' (p. 22). Separated both from Robert L. and from her immediate surroundings, she as it were mimes the experience of her absent loved one, dragging them somehow closer together. This apparent mimicry is clearly also marked by the possible reductionism of representation: the narrator's implication that her experience shares a point of comparison with that of those in the camps, which would make this physical simile possible, suggests in part a self-dramatization rather lacking in perspective. On the other hand, however (and the question of the relationship between the work of Duras and Antelme repeatedly necessitates this kind of turn, as will be seen), such statements also suggest a moment of generous doubling, a refusal to let the suffering of her husband go unaccompanied.

Both poles of this doubling are, moreover, themselves split in its writing: the narrator into both 'I' and 'she' (p. 38), and Robert L. by the punning erosion of his full name, Antelme. (That Robert L. refers to Antelme is confirmed in the text by the narrator's apparently dismissive comment that 'He wrote a book on what he thought he had experienced in Germany. It was called *The Human Race*' (p. 65).) This reciprocal doubling may, in turn, be read across the gap between the two texts, which present the twin ends of a common experience (Antelme's captivity, Duras's wait), and so begin to open this experience out into a space of fragile communicability. The unique knowledge of Robert L. possessed in love by Duras's diary narrator (see *The War*, p. 10), has its painful, threatened counterpart in Antelme's testimony:

Back there, I always see myself from behind, always from behind. M...'s face smiles at the person I see only from behind. And she laughs. She laughs, but no, not like that: I don't think she laughs like that. What is this new laugh of M...'s? ... Knowing is all I have left. Knowing that M... has a voice, the voice I know she has. Knowing that her face opens up, and that she laughs the laugh I know she has. (*The Human Race*, p. 108)

Similarly, in Paris, Marguerite is pathetically sure of one fact in the imagined scene of Robert L.'s death: 'He died speaking my name. What other name could he have spoken?' (*The War*, p. 8). In Gandersheim, her name does indeed figure; but it represents an element of the outside world to be resisted, as too painful: 'Language acted like a sorcery. When your body was rotting, *the sea, water, sunshine* could make you suffocate. With these words, as with M...'s name, you were in danger of not wanting to take another step, not wanting to get up again' (*The Human Race*, p. 162; original emphasis). Such moments of reciprocity (which, founded on mutual absence, we might perhaps see as a kind of *negative* reciprocity) establish an *elsewhere* for each text, in which the figures of Marguerite and Robert L. are shadowed by those of M... and Robert Antelme respectively. (Davis, accordingly, states that Antelme is a 'spectral presence' in Duras's text and Duras is 'present-in-absence' in Antelme's (Davis, p. 2).) This chiasmus allows the suffering of both to avoid (as far as possible) the potential problems of reduction created by what may be seen as the recuperative moment of comparison involved in any positive representation; its intertextual diptych presents a technique employed by Duras in her writing throughout the 1980s and 1990s, namely the sympathetic doubling of the sites of trauma, the better (paradoxically) to preserve their singularity. For Duras, as for others, the uniqueness of trauma cannot be represented as such. So, it is never allowed to live alone in its singularity, its pain is multiplied in restless substitutions and displacements, this constant accompaniment and transposition figuring the impossibility of isolating a part which could adequately represent such a whole. Nothing can stand for the traumatic event, which stands alone – and must therefore be doubled.

The key debate about reciprocity between Duras's work and *L'espèce humaine* concerns not this chiastic accompaniment, however, but their respective treatments of Antelme's central thesis, that of the ultimate (if fragile, residual, and vulnerable) unity of the human race. This thesis is the conclusion drawn by Antelme from his experience of the camps, which he presents as the revelation of a particular human truth:

> I went out of the office and put my cap back on. On the stairway I passed a civilian a bit too closely. He was wearing boots, a gray smock, and a little green hat.
> '*Weg!*' – Get the hell out of the way! – he said to me in a rasping voice.
> I shrugged it off. Here, perhaps, it did not have overmuch

importance. But there in its purest form was that disdain which is the world's affliction, such as, more or less camouflaged, it still reigns in human relations everywhere – such as it reigns yet in the society we were removed from. It was clearer here, however. We provided a disdainful humanity with the means of revealing itself completely. (*The Human Race*, p. 51)

The extremity of the camps is, according to Antelme, unique inasmuch as it affords a unique insight into certain human tendencies: 'Here is where we'll have known both the greatest esteem and the most definitive contempt, both love for mankind and loathing for it, with a more total certainty than anywhere else, ever' (p. 88). The particular truth revealed in this extremity is precisely what those orchestrating it are attempting to deny: that humanity is, ultimately, indivisible. At the limit of the 'slow annihilation' to which the prisoners are being subjected by their torturers, there appears a truth which constitutes the denial of this very project:

Next, that the variety of relationships between men, their color, their customs, the classes they are formed into mask a truth that here, at the boundary of nature, at the point where we approach our limits, appears with absolute clarity: namely, that there are not several human races, there is only one human race. It's because we are men like them that the SS will finally prove powerless before us.

And so, seen from here, luxuriousness is the property of the animal, and divineness is the property of trees, and we are unable to become either animals or trees. We are not able to, and the SS cannot make us succeed in it. (p. 219)

Antelme's reasoning is explicit: it is the fact that this truth is revealed *in extremis* that forces it to be received as indisputable:

And if, at that moment, we believe what, here, is certainly that which requires the most considerable effort to believe, that 'The SS are only men like ourselves'; if, at the moment when the distance between beings is at its greatest, at the moment when the subjugation of some and the power of others have attained such limits as to seem frozen into some supernatural distinction; if, facing nature, or facing death, we can perceive no substantial difference between the SS and ourselves, then we have to say that there is only one human race. (pp. 219–20)

Those subject to the violence of the camps thus have their suffering presented defiantly by Antelme (who has also shared this suffering) as the ultimate refutation of the logic of those at whose hands they are suffering, the attempt to exclude them for good from the ranks of the human:

> The worst of victims cannot do otherwise than establish that, in its worst exercise, the executioner's power cannot be other than one of the powers that men have, the power of murder. He can kill a man, but he can't change him into something else. (p. 220)[4]

This defines humanity as an irreducible residue, what remains, weak but stubborn, in the face of its attempted abolition: 'The motivation underlying our struggle could only have been a furious desire, itself almost always experienced in solitude; a furious desire to remain men, down to the very end' (p. 5). And the testimonial expression of this truth comes to refute the efforts of those who had attempted to deny it: as a survivor, Antelme aligns his written testimony with the remains of those who did not survive, this solidarity constituting a trace which, as it records their suffering as *human*, reveals the futility of the torturer's would-be commandment:

> The SS cannot alter our species. They are themselves enclosed within the same humankind and the same history. *Thou shalt not be*: upon that ludicrous wish an enormous machine has been built. They have burned men, and tons of ashes exist, they can weigh out that neutral substance by the ton. *Thou shalt not be*: but, in the man's stead who shall soon be ashes, they cannot decide that he not be.... Nor can they check the history that will make those dry ashes more fruitful than the *Lagerführer's* meaty remains. (p. 74; original emphasis)

We have already met one resonance of this vision of a residual humanity in the virtual self-abolition of the narrator of Duras's diary, which mimes her anguished vision of the suffering of her husband. And when he returns, his body is described in terms which convey precisely the importance of this understanding of residuality in the thesis which he will later articulate, as his identity is most strongly declared at the very limit of its abolition:

> There's a supernatural weariness in his smile, weariness from

having managed to live till this moment. It's from this smile that I suddenly recognize him, but from a great distance, as if I were seeing him at the other end of a tunnel. It's a smile of embarrassment. He's apologizing for being here, reduced to such a wreck. And then the smile fades, and he becomes a stranger again. But the knowledge is still there, that this stranger is he, Robert L., totally. (Duras, *The War*, p. 54)

And later, the narrator states simply: 'That it was then, by his deathbed, that I knew him, Robert L., best, that I understood forever what made him himself, himself alone and nothing and no one else in the world' (pp. 67–8). More generally, however, Duras's treatment of Antelme's thesis is the source of some difficulty, and has led to very different accounts of the relationship between their work. I will now attempt to describe this treatment, and then to assess this relationship; first, it might perhaps be helpful to situate Duras's position in some sort of context.

Throughout her writing on historical trauma, Duras consistently refuses any easy separation of antagonistic positions. An especially significant version of this argument is the claim made in a key passage that, if the Holocaust is not to be reduced to a mere local aberration, responsibility for its horrors must be borne by all:

If you give a German and not a collective interpretation to the Nazi horror, you reduce the man in Belsen to regional dimensions. The only possible answer to this crime is to turn it into a crime committed by everyone. To share it. Just like the idea of equality and fraternity. In order to bear it, to tolerate the idea of it, we must share the crime. (Duras, *The War*, p. 50)[5]

Just as the traumatic event is habitually doubled by Duras so that its singularity may not be reduced, so those who did not orchestrate the Holocaust – but who may, as Duras says was her case, have somehow allowed it to happen, and who may do so again and again – must accept its burden, in a principled universalization of mourning ('just like the idea of equality, of fraternity') which surpasses national boundaries. It should be stressed that, in its context, this is *not* an attempt to make victims as responsible for their suffering as their torturers; it is addressed, retrospectively and polemically, to the supposedly innocent bystanders in the celebratory atmosphere of post-Liberation France.[6] None the less, the consequences of this broad responsibility for thinking about what it is to be human (and thus for Antelme's thesis) are profound and disconcerting, and Duras develops them both in *La douleur* and elsewhere.

In texts published throughout the 1980s, Duras consistently argues that Nazism should be understood as embodying qualities which we need to integrate into our fundamental notion of humanity. In *Les yeux verts*, she claims that Nazism represents not an aberration from the human, but rather a failure to acknowledge a tendency to violence as part of a common humanity: 'It's because the Nazis did not *recognize* this horror in them that they committed it.'[7] And crucially, in a text entitled 'The Happy Dream of Crime' ('Le Rêve heureux du crime'), which immediately precedes an early version of part of *La douleur* in the 1981 collection *Outside*, it is made plain that the recognition of this shared tendency is an essential move in its prevention. In this piece, Duras declares that, during the war, she often dreamed of what she terms 'the extermination of Germany'.[8] This dream – 'a violent, terrifying, and intoxicating dream', and yet, supposedly, 'a creative dream' – plays out what Duras calls a God-like ability to punish 'without discrimination both the innocent and the guilty, the German land along with its natives, trees along with men' (Duras, *Outside*, p. 283). Alleging that this represents in fact a universal dream, Duras claims that only those who acknowledge both this dream and its universality understand their non-negotiable link to a common humanity: 'The difference is not in having the dream or not, it's between those who see and those who do not see that the whole world is in each one of the men who make it up and that each one of these men who make it up is a potential criminal' (p. 284). Duras's language in this piece is exaggerated, vengeful, and occasionally distasteful, and the implications of this will be discussed shortly; for all this, however, Duras is not claiming that there is no difference between victims and torturers. Rather, she is claiming that the crucial difference is between those who acknowledge the violence of their desires and those who, because of a failure to understand this violence as part of a common humanity, allow this violence expression. 'As I dream, they acted', she declares of the Nazis (p. 284). The argument, then, is that only a recognition of our shared propensity for violence can prevent what Duras describes as the naïve attempt to separate oneself from the rest of humanity, to 'take sides against the human race' ('prendre partie contre l'espèce humaine') (p. 284).

Duras's use here of the term 'l'espèce humaine' indicates a difficult espousal of the principal thesis of Antelme's book. Indeed, she seems here deliberately to be refusing the terms of Antelme's argument, stressing that her dream annihilates 'trees along with men': Antelme, we may recall, uses precisely the image of the irreducible difference between a tree and a human being to emphasize his claim of an indivisible humanity. As we have seen, Antelme's impassioned argument is that the SS can never remove those they torture from the humanity which insistently binds torturer and victim together. Duras's version of a shared humanity in a sense turns this argument on its head: rather than insisting on the unity of 'l'espèce humaine' by denying the torturer the ability to remove the humanity of his victim, she claims paradoxically that it is precisely the urge to deny a common humanity that is shared by all – and that the torturer, as torturer, is therefore already affirming the common humanity he attempts to deny. Rather than the victim, it is here the torturer who – contrary to his violent intentions – represents an irreducibly mutual humanity.

While this may seem a perversion of Antelme's thesis, it also constitutes, importantly, its necessary extension.[9] Antelme sees that the attempt to create distinctions within 'l'espèce humaine' leads to the dreadful cruelty and suffering he records; and so he refuses the force of this cruelty, by refusing the supposed distinctions from which it proceeds. The victim asserts the humanity he shares with his torturer, and so deprives the torturer of his supposed justification. But the further implications of this assertion are genuinely disturbing; and it is these implications that Duras – albeit provocatively – draws out.[10] For if the victim and the torturer may not be distinguished in their common humanity, this suggests that to torture is as much a part of this shared condition as to suffer. The torturer does not participate in a shared humanity only when he is not torturing, or on the understanding that he may one day stop, or himself be tortured; on the contrary, Antelme argues that it is 'at the moment when the distance between beings is at its greatest' (*The Human Race*, p. 220) that the unity of the human race is affirmed. If the reasoning of the torturer is not to be repeated, his violence must be integrated into an understanding of the humanity in which he is caught. Duras is neither repeating nor quite betraying Antelme's argument: she is inverting it in order to draw out its ultimate implications.

Duras presents a particularly significant illustration of these implications in her piece 'Albert des Capitales', also in *La douleur*. A collaborationist informer is tortured by members of the *Résistance*, led by 'Thérèse', who is identified with the author ('Thérèse is me' (Duras, *The War*, p. 115)). Throughout this piece, Thérèse is distinguished by the violence of her desire for revenge, demanding, for example, the execution of German prisoners, to the ridicule of her fellow *résistants* (*The War*, p. 121). And her behaviour during the cruel, bloody torture that she orchestrates is both determined and, moreover, sustained by her ability to separate the informer from his humanity: 'He's become someone without anything in common with other men' (p. 132). Thérèse (*Résistance* member and torturer) and not the informer (and victim) thus incarnates the essence of criminality, the ability to impose divisions upon 'l'espèce humaine'. At no point in this piece is this violence criticized; and its use of free indirect discourse may even, it has been argued, imply a certain collusion in Thérèse's removal of her victim's humanity.[11] The concern provoked by this aspect of the text does not quite, however, represent a response to the text as a whole: for this collusion is only one half of the tension which makes up its dynamic. At this point in her career, Duras's writing is constantly marked by a line of uncertainty between two antagonistic interpretations, both of which are maintained as valid by the same textual material. And 'Albert des Capitales' is a case in point. While its free indirect discourse *may* be espousing Thérèse's position, this collu-sion must, by virtue of the nature of this technique, remain only one of two possibilities. It is also the case that this text can be interpreted as a dramatization of precisely what happens when the tendency to impose essential divisions upon 'l'espèce humaine' is given expres-sion. There is, in fact, some evidence of critical distance between the narrative of 'Albert des Capitales' and Thérèse's position: crucially, in the description of her as alienated, 'invaded, spellbound by images' (p. 133). This perspective – briefly suggested in the narrative – provides some evidence for a reading of the text as *in part* a critical presentation of the consequences of the attempt to divide 'l'espèce humaine'. The text cannot simply be safely recuperated within this interpretation – which remains one half of its dynamic – but nor can this half (which is also the inevitable implication of the technique of free indirect discourse) be ignored, for all that it is less explicit than the possible collusion between the narrative and Thérèse. The lack of stability of this possible critical ethical dimension to the text need not simply be collapsed into its supposed absence.

In 'Albert des Capitales', Duras is certainly exploiting the aestheti-cization of violence presented as intoxicatingly amoral, and in a way which does open shamefully onto the supposed transcendence of the ethical by such violence on the grounds of this intoxication. But there is more to 'Albert des Capitales' than this. For free indirect discourse

implies not only the collapse of narrative distance and ethical discrimination, but also a remaining, virtual, external vantage point on this
collapse. The ultimate ethical implication of this technique as Duras
uses it here is the recognition (which, in the face of the historical
evidence, is surely inevitable) that violence represents a human potential which both fascinates and intoxicates; that this fascination can
appear to provide an excuse for violence; but that despite this apparent amorality, the possibility of an ethical response remains – figured
here in the remaining possible narrative perspective (which is marked
in the text) on Thérèse's actions.

Thérèse's actions, as the denial of a common humanity, demonstrate the consequences of the assumption of an ontological difference
between members of 'l'espèce humaine'. The text's narrative techniques do indeed work to bind reader, torturers, and victim together;
but this is also evidence of a refusal on the part of the text of just the
kind of essential separation practised by Thérèse, and by means of
which she seeks to justify her torture. The narrative technique of
'Albert des Capitales' in fact works extremely well as a representation
of the ethical dialectic implied by Antelme's thesis: reader, torturer,
and victim are bound together; this unity includes an identification
with its criminal component; but this component is also contested by
this very unity. Thérèse tortures because she thinks she can remove
her victim from a shared humanity. If we are to deny the grounds for
her actions, then, we must assert once again the indivisibility of this
humanity – which means that, while we can, and must, continue to
abhor her actions ethically, we must at the same time integrate them
and the tendencies of which they are the expression into our understanding of what it means to be human. This does not, I think,
necessarily represent a contradiction.

That the unity of 'l'espèce humaine' implies a shared violence as
part of an irreducible humanity is suggested by Antelme in the following scene:

> Fritz was striding importantly around the room, a riding crop in his
> hand. The naked guys kept their eyes on him. They would have
> liked to hang him up by the heels, bare-assed, with his balaclava
> helmet on his head; they would have liked to slap his plump ass
> and listen to him sob. To make Fritz cry ... It would have made us
> swoon with delight ... (*The Human Race*, p. 123)

It is by no means clear that the violence of this image is definitively redeemed by its status as revenge fantasy. Antelme does not dwell on the consequences of this for his central thesis. Duras, however, does. She introduces explicitly the notion that the irreducibly human is also marked by a shared tendency to violence; but this introduction in fact represents the necessary extension of Antelme's thesis, an important attempt to think through what it may, ultimately, imply. On this point, the reciprocity between Duras and Antelme is a matter less of symmetry than of an uneasy, if vital, extension. Nor is it quite possible, however, to argue that this treatment of Antelme's thesis forces writing away from his relatively straightforward humanist ethics, to a point where any ethical dimension in fact collapses.[12] While we are not dealing with symmetry, neither are we, I believe, definitely dealing with distortion.

For it should be acknowledged that the behaviour of his torturers *is* presented by Antelme as in some sense essentially human, as part of his argument that the world of the camps represents the condensation of a general human truth, however difficult this may be to accept:

> Yet their behaviour, and our situation, are only a magnification, an extreme caricature – in which nobody wants or is perhaps able to recognize himself – of forms of behaviour and of situations that exist in the world, that even make up the existence of that older 'real world' we dream about. (p. 219)

This presentation is, certainly, less to the fore in *L'espèce humaine* than it is in Duras's work; but this does not mean that it either can or should be minimized – especially given its important implications for the text's central thesis. Antelme, in fact, demonstrates elsewhere – in a text from November 1945 – that the refusal of violence and its recognition as essentially human are linked in his thinking. In a short piece entitled 'Vengeance?', written for *Les Vivants (Cahiers publiés par les prisonniers et déportés)*, Antelme is concerned – speaking as a survivor, and on behalf of all survivors – to expose the mistreatment of German prisoners of war as the manifestation of precisely that violence which those opposed to the Nazis had been fighting. With reference to acts of random vengeance carried out on German prisoners, he states that the experience of captivity through which he and his comrades have lived imposes a definite ethical position: 'a true awareness of the condition of captivity must entail a total refusal to allow these acts'.[13] This means that condemnation of the violence inflicted by the Nazis on their prisoners leads necessarily to a similar condemnation of such violence when practised by those who had been opposing the Nazis:

> More generally, the same indignation, whether expressed or kept secret, which impelled the French to oppose Nazi barbarity, must now be expressed just as clearly, just as secretly, in opposition to the attitude of certain Frenchmen. (Antelme, 'Vengeance?', p. 18)

Far from avenging the victims of the Nazis, those who repeat their violence against German prisoners are in fact insulting them, Antelme claims: for this thinking implies that the surviving deportees have somehow embraced the logic of their torturers, 'in an infernal form of mimicry' (p. 21). The only true vengeance for those who have died, he argues, would consist in 'a victory of the ideas and the behaviour for which they died' (p. 19):

> Hundreds of thousands of comrades died in the German camps for the sake of the victory of the simple notions of justice, freedom, respect for one's fellow man. Perhaps we may still hope that it is not already too late to believe in this victory. By mistreating prisoners of war, or by quietly letting them die of hunger, we betray these notions, which represent the most valuable content of the victory; we hold those who have died and ourselves up to ridicule. How could we accept this? Why, on returning to France, would we have changed our ideas? (pp. 21–2)

The first stage in Antelme's argument, then, is the insistence that German prisoners are human beings; and that, since those opposing the Nazis were fighting for the universal respect for an irreducible humanity, these prisoners must be treated humanely.

Antelme does not stop here, however: as Duras will later do with *L'espèce humaine*, he draws out the more uncomfortable side of this case. For the fact that captured German soldiers belong to the human race also implies that the violence of the Nazis is to be understood as a human phenomenon. Indeed, the fact that his argument is necessary in the first place clearly shows that the tendency to such violence is not simply confined to Nazi soldiers. Thus, Antelme builds a steady progression into his piece: beginning with the world of the camp, he presents the sense of the prisoners that responsibility for their situation is not limited to their immediate torturers, but rather that it extends also to the German civilians who also take the opportunity to humiliate them: 'We did not feel that a punishment was being imposed on us for which its instigators and its perpetrators were solely responsible' (p. 20). Responsibility for the crimes of the camps is, in fact, for Antelme, a 'diffuse responsibility' (p. 20): first spreading from the camp guards to the surrounding civilians, and then, potentially, to the France to which he and his comrades have returned: 'This German attitude seemed overwhelming to us, and now, in France, in infinitely easier circumstances, whose nature is essentially different, we would not wish to meet its shadow again' (pp. 20–1). The attempts of some French people 'to play at a miserable barbarity' (p. 23) are, for Antelme, the manifestation of this terrible attitude, the arrival of its shadow in the France to which he has returned. While he refuses the violence of his torturers, then, Antelme nevertheless crucially insists that 'The crimes of Nazism cannot be qualified, but they belong to a possible human genre' (p. 19). Even as he opposes the tendency to the violent division of humanity, he declares this tendency to be part of a common humanity. Following this gesture in the details of its elaboration by Antelme, we may see just how close its structure in fact is to Duras's controversial re-working of Antelme's central thesis in the 1980s: quite clearly, here, Antelme is arguing that the universal humanity which is 'the most valuable content' of what he has brought back from his experiences entails the tendency – which must be resisted – to deny precisely this humanity. 'Vengeance?' suggests that this move may be less marginal in Antelme's thinking than one might otherwise have suspected – and its appearance both in *L'espèce humaine* and in a text written only months after his return from Dachau indicates that its importance demands to be thought through.

And such a thinking through is, I would argue, what we find in Duras. Her tone and general approach certainly tend more towards an aesthetic love of provocation than towards a patient examination of the demands of this question, and this tendency may at times be extremely distasteful; it is none the less the case that aspects of her work – such as the use of free indirect discourse in 'Albert des Capitales' – which are touched by this tendency may also represent accurate condensations of the ethical complexities with which we are here confronted. (And this is occasionally true of Antelme, as well; the reverence his work deserves should not blind us to its own moments of provocation, such as the description quoted above of the fantasy of Fritz's torture.) Duras's work in this area, I believe, ultimately demonstrates that the assertion of the essential indivisibility of humanity takes us to a point where, while it may be difficult, it none the less remains both possible and necessary to insist on ethical distinctions among human actions – the very double move performed by Antelme in 'Vengeance?' It may indeed be the case that declarations of a shared tendency to violence, or of a universal responsibility for the Holocaust, appear to lead to a point of ultimate ethical breakdown.[14] But if it is also the case – as is indicated, but not stressed, by Antelme in *L'espèce humaine* – that such a tendency, or such a responsibility, is part of what is implied by the indivisibility of humanity, then this implication surely must be confronted.

This confrontation entails some extremely difficult arguments; they may, perhaps, be presented schematically, as follows:

1. We must accept Antelme's thesis; otherwise, we repeat the divisive logic of his torturers.
2. Therefore, we must accept that the torturer and his victim are bound by an essential humanity – that, at the level of their humanity, there can be no essential difference between them.
3. Therefore, we must accept that to torture is, in some sense, also part of what it means to be human.

At this point, it seems to me that we have two alternatives. Either we feel compelled to reject the third of these steps, on the grounds that it ultimately abolishes any essential difference between torturer and victim, and turns the question of whether one becomes torturer or victim into a mere historical accident.[15] This fear seems largely justified. Or we may, on the other hand, feel that this third step, while ethically difficult, may yet be ethically necessary: for to refuse it surely implies that there *can* be established some essential difference between torturer and victim – which rejects Antelme's argument. I believe, accordingly, that only the second of these alternatives is consistent with Antelme's conclusions. Does this mean, therefore, that any *ethical* distinction between victim and torturer is indeed reduced to historical contingency? Surely not. That torturer and victim are essentially indivisible at the level of their humanity does not mean that they are ethically equivalent. This argument may even imply that there is no essential moral distinction between a member of the *Résistance* and a member of the Gestapo, inasmuch as both are human; but the absence of any essential, watertight moral barrier between the two at the level of their shared humanity does not mean that they cannot be distinguished ethically at the level of their actions. The complication of moral distinctions implied in this argument means just that: the complication of ethical judgements, not their abandonment. It does not mean that it is either impossible or unnecessary to criticize ethically torture when it is practised by either *résistant* or Gestapo agent. The two may not essentially be distinguished at the level of their humanity; and this humanity must, therefore, be understood as incorporating the violence of the torturer – in order, however, as both Antelme and Duras indicate, for this violence to be prevented. For, as seen above, Duras's insistence is that this material must be confronted *in order that it not reproduce itself.* She emphasizes that a recognition of the violent tendencies she identifies as essentially human must take place so that these tendencies should not again be allowed – by what she calls a kind of naïveté, incarnated in Thérèse, 'spellbound by images' (Duras, *The War*, p. 133) – to prosper. It seems to me that only such an understanding can avoid the assumption of an essential difference – an assumption which, as Antelme argues in 'Vengeance?', is a necessary condition for the perpetration of just this kind of violence. It is thus, I believe, necessary, in order ethically to oppose the imposition of divisions upon 'l'espèce humaine', to recognize that this very indivisibility implies the integration – but not the acceptance – of an essential violence before which this ethical moment certainly trembles – but does not, for all that, collapse.

So how, then, might we best describe the relationship between the work of Antelme and that of Duras? There exists a certain reciprocity between them; and Duras develops Antelme's thesis in ways that are both disturbing and, ultimately, ethically important. But the two are neither simply symmetrical, nor in an easy relationship of cohabitation, as the difficulty of the above arguments indicates. For a concluding image to express the nature of this relationship, perhaps we might look to the relationship beween 'Marguerite' and 'Robert L.' in the diary of *La douleur*. Marguerite, the narrator, displays behaviour towards her returning husband which ranges from the extreme but perhaps understandable (her terror, and flight, on seeing him for the first time on his return) to the arguably more problematic declaration of her intention to divorce him soon after his return.[16] And yet this does not represent the entirety of her behaviour: she also nurses him back to some kind of health. Indeed, just as Duras's divorce from Antelme in order to have a son by Mascolo is a matter of biographical fact, so did this assistance apparently, according to Edgar Morin, save Antelme's life. In his 'Homage to Robert Antelme', Morin states that the doctors thought Antelme was lost, until 'Marguerite Duras's determination enabled her to find a doctor who, having lived in India, was familiar with the deficiencies that result from famine, until then unknown in the West of modern times; and after a period of uncertainty Robert Antelme was saved'.[17] In Duras's diary text, this care is itself ambiguous, punctuated as it is by suggestions that Robert L.'s state is verging on the 'inhuman' (see Duras, *The War*, p. 58); and yet care she does, until the fever is beaten, some sort of diet established, and even a holiday with friends in Italy becomes possible. Given the ambiguities of this relationship, it would be perverse to redeem the entirety of the behaviour of Duras/the narrator under the heading of some sort of patient bedside manner. And yet she does accompany Antelme/Robert L. in his suffering. Equally, given this accompaniment, it seems hardly appropriate to interpret the narrator's behaviour principally as a betrayal. While her declaration that she intends to divorce Robert L. to have a child by D. may indeed be difficult to accept, it does not exhaust the quality of their relationship; and neither is the relationship between the work of Antelme and that of Duras definable solely in terms of betrayal. Perhaps we might characterize this relationship as marked by a similarly uncertain accompaniment to that shown by the narrator in her care for Robert L.: verging on betrayal, certainly, but also, importantly, an attempt at some kind of fragile solidarity. For all their exorbitance and scandal-hungry rhetoric, at no point do the implications of Duras's texts in fact exceed what is already implied – and occasionally highlighted – both in *L'espèce humaine* and elsewhere in Antelme's writings. Duras's contributions to our appreciation of Antelme's thinking bring to the fore elements which Antelme does not always emphasize, but which cannot be overlooked in an attempt to come to terms with the overall ethical importance of this thinking. While it is itself often at least on the very verge of an amoral aestheticization of the potential for fascinating violence, her writing also forms an active part of a positive ethical intervention arguing for a conception of the nature of humanity that aims, ultimately, to prevent the realization of this potential. While they are undoubtedly difficult to accept, Duras's arguments – which are also, as I have argued, Antelme's – nevertheless represent an accompaniment to *L'espèce humaine* which helps us, I believe, to embrace the full ethical challenge of its vital thesis.

Notes

1 For details of the Éditions de la Cité universelle, and Antelme's itinerary, see Dionys Mascolo, *Autour d'un effort de mémoire* (Paris: Maurice Nadeau, 1987), pp. 45–50. Some confusion appears to exist between the two available detailed versions of this itinerary: Mascolo states that Antelme was transferred from Fresnes to Compiègne on 17 or 18 August, from where he was deported to Buchenwald; Antelme, however, says that, having spent three months in Buchenwald, he was transported to Gandersheim on 1 October 1944 – which would have to place his arrival in Buchenwald at the latest in July. See Robert Antelme, *The Human Race*, translated by Jeffrey Haight and Annie Mahler (Marlboro, Vermont: The Marlboro Press, 1992), pp. 11, 28. (Published in French as *L'espèce humaine* (Paris: Gallimard, 1957; coll. "Tel", 1978).) Henceforth referred to in parentheses in the body of the text. When referring to Antelme's text in general terms, I will refer to it as *L'espèce humaine*; when citing specific passages, references will be to *The Human Race*.

2 These two aspects of the texts are also discussed in Colin Davis's article, 'Duras, Antelme and the Ethics of Writing', *Comparative Literature Studies*, vol. 34, no. 2 (1997), 170–83. The significant differences between Davis's position and the argument in this chapter will be apparent below. For the moment, it should be noted that Davis mentions the following examples of 'echoes and cross-references' between the texts: the incident of Antelme's 'escape'; the concentration on bodily functions; the use of diary format; and the closeness between the dates of parts of the texts (p. 171). Davis observes that, while *La douleur* and *L'espèce humaine* are 'closely related texts', 'little has been done to specify the nature of their relationship to one another' (p. 172). Perhaps this chapter – not least in its dialogue with Davis's article – can help to remedy this situation. (I am, incidentally, extremely grateful to Colin Davis for the opportunity to read his article prior to its publication.) Work in English on Antelme is scarce, but the field is now growing rapidly. See, in addition to the works by Davis and Leslie Hill which will be discussed here, Claire Gorrara, 'Bearing Witness in Robert Antelme's *L'espèce humaine* and Marguerite Duras's *La douleur*', in *Women in French Studies*, 5 (October–November 1997), and references to Antelme in Anthony Rudolf, *Engraved in Flesh* (London: The Menard Press, 1996). I would like to thank both Claire Gorrara and Anthony Rudolf for their help and advice during the preparation of this chapter.

3 Marguerite Duras, *The War*, translated by Barbara Bray (New York: The New Press, 1994), p. 10. (Published in French as *La douleur* (Paris: P.O.L., 1985).) Henceforth referred to in parentheses in the body of the text. As with *L'espèce humaine*, in general references Duras's text will be referred to as *La douleur*, while specific textual references will be to *The War*. Claire Gorrara reads these lines, in terms established by Dori Laub, as evidence of the narrator's becoming 'a co-owner of the traumatic events she hears about and as such a participant by proxy' (Gorrara, 'Bearing Witness', author's typescript, p. 9).

4 Cf. Albert Camus (who was, according to Mascolo, responsible for the

original Gallimard publication of *L'Espèce Humaine* (see Mascolo, p. 45)), *L'Homme révolté* (Paris: Gallimard, 1951; coll. Folio, 1985): 'La communauté des victimes est la même que celle qui unit la victime au bourreau. Mais le bourreau ne le sait pas' ('The community of victims is the same as the one that links the victim to the torturer. But the torturer does not know it.') (p. 30, n. 1).

5   This passage is also quoted by Davis, 'Duras, Antelme and the Ethics of Writing', p. 176 and Leslie Hill, *Marguerite Duras: Apocalyptic Desires* (London: Routledge, 1993), p. 129.

6   For a full treatment of this aspect of the diary, see Gorrara, 'Bearing Witness'.

7   Marguerite Duras, *Green Eyes* (New York: Columbia University Press, 1990), p. 138; original emphasis. (Published in French as *Les yeux verts* (Paris: Cahiers du cinéma, 1980; nouvelle édition augmentée, 1987).)

8   Marguerite Duras, *Outside* (Paris: Albin Michel, 1981; P.O.L., 1984), p. 283. All translations from this text are mine. References henceforth given in parentheses in the body of the text.

9   These arguments should be read in conjunction with those presented by Colin Davis in his 'Duras, Antelme and the Ethics of Writing'. Davis, too, demonstrates that Duras's position 'develops a possibility inherent in Antelme's position, but one which remains in the background of *L'espèce humaine*' (p. 176); his argument, however, is that the ethical implications of this development in fact ultimately undermine Antelme's thesis. As will be seen, it is at this point that our arguments part company.

10   As Davis states, 'the boldness of *La douleur* resides in its readiness to explore the bleakest side of [Antelme's] insight' (p. 181).

11   This interpretation of 'Albert des Capitales' is offered by Davis: see pp. 179–81.

12   This argument is put forward by Davis: see Davis, *passim*, esp. p. 179. A view of the relationship between Duras and Antelme as symmetrical – which Davis explicitly opposes – is implied by Leslie Hill, who argues that 'Duras's response to the discovery of the camps accords perhaps most clearly with the view expressed by Antelme himself' (Hill, pp. 129–30).

13   Robert Antelme, 'Vengeance?', in *Textes inédits/Sur L'espèce humaine/ Essais et témoignages* (Paris: Gallimard, 1996), p. 18. All translations mine; henceforth referred to in parentheses in the body of the text.

14   See Davis, who describes Duras's extension of Antelme's thesis as leading to an 'erasure of ethics' (p. 181), and to 'a literature which holds open no prospect for the recovery of moral value' (p. 182).

15   See Davis, p. 181.

16   Focusing on the notion of rejection, these particular aspects of the narrator's behaviour are used by Davis as an image of the relationship between the two texts: see Davis, pp.170, 172.

17   Edgar Morin, 'Homage to Robert Antelme', preface to *The Human Race*, pp. ix–xi (p. xi). (Originally in *Le Monde*, 2 November 1990.)

Index